Classical Ballet Terminology

Rhonda Ryman
Associate Professor
University of Waterloo
Waterloo, Canada

Royal Academy of Dance Enterprises Ltd 2007

3rd Edition

Substantial portions of this book were first published in 1993 under the title *Dictionary of Classical Ballet Terminology as Used in The Royal Academy of Dancing.*
First published 1995
Second edition published 1997
Third edition published 2007

Published by:

Royal Academy of Dance Enterprises Ltd for
Royal Academy of Dance
36, Battersea Square
London SW11 3RA
www.rad.org.uk
www.radenterprises.co.uk

in co-operation with
Rhonda Ryman University of Waterloo
Waterloo, Ontario N2L 3G1 Canada

ISBN 1-904386-87-3

FOREWORD

In 1920 the Association of Teachers of Operatic Dancing was formed by a group of famous dance professionals who represented the principal teaching methods of the day. They were Adeline Genée, Tamara Karsavina, Lucia Cormani, Phyllis Bedells and Edouard Espinosa. Brought together by Philip Richardson, who was then Editor of the British magazine, *The Dancing Times,* their aim was to improve the standard of ballet tuition and thus the standard of ballet.

In 1936, in recognition of its role, the Association was granted a Royal Charter and became the Royal Academy of Dancing. In 2000 the organisation was renamed the Royal Academy of Dance to reflect more accurately the Academy's mission – *to promote knowledge, understanding and practice of dance internationally.*

The Academy has always had a policy of creating new ways in which to assist teachers and students in their studies. With the publication of the *Dictionary of Classical Ballet Terminology, The Foundations of Classical Ballet Technique* and *The Progressions of Classical Ballet Technique,* we offer another way in which they can further their knowledge of the art form through a deeper understanding of the syllabi. This reference book, unique in the history of the Academy, has taken years of dedicated preparation and research by its author, Rhonda Ryman. We are sincerely grateful for her enormous contribution to the Academy's work over the last thirteen years, which has made possible three editions of this *Dictionary.*

Lynn Wallis
Artistic Director
Royal Academy of Dance
London, 2007

AUTHOR'S PREFACE

An early word of caution: "Do not read this dictionary!". Its content surely reads like a telephone book. Rather use it as a reference. It is intended for students and teachers of classical ballet, who must often navigate through the maze of terminology used to describe an art form passed on by physical demonstration more than by words.

One often hears that the language of Dance is universal. The language of Classical Ballet, despite claims to the contrary, is not. It is a highly refined system that has evolved over several centuries, adapting to changing styles and varying geographic locales throughout the world. Stemming from the social dance and court entertainment of Renaissance Europe, particularly Italy and France, today there exist numerous academic "schools" or types of "danse d'école". These include Bournonville (Danish, from the French school of Vestris), Cecchetti (from the Italian school), Royal Academy of Dance (English) and Russian (including the Vaganova school).

Inevitably, different "dialects" have emerged, leading at times to confusion. Different terms may be used to describe the same movement, as for example the beaten jump known as *entrechat royal* in the Cecchetti method and *changement battu* in the Royal Academy of Dance. Or the same term may refer to movements performed differently in the various schools as, for example, the term *promenade*.

Now, more than a century after the creation of *The Sleeping Beauty,* considered the epitome of classical ballet technique, this dictionary is offered as a record of current usage, in particular that of the Royal Academy of Dance for which no dictionary has been available. It may also serve to document the sophistication and breadth of knowledge gained in the study of an art form so often described as non-literate.

Compiling this *Dictionary* has been a labour of love – almost every term has brought back memories of years spent in the classroom. I remember with gratitude my teachers and mentors: (Russian) Diana Francy, Diana Jablokova-Vorps, Hilda Strombergs; (Cecchetti) Alexandra Caverly-Lowery, Grant Strate, Angela Leigh, Yves Cousineau, Margaret Saul; (RAD) Sheila Finstein Katz, Tina Collett, Sonia Chamberlain, Jillian Officer, Anuschka Roes; (Bournonville) Dinna Bjørn.

I would also like to make special mention of my Labanotation colleagues, particularly Dr. Ann Hutchinson Guest and Muriel Topaz. It was their intriguing dialogue at the 1989 conference of the International Council of Kinetography Laban which piqued my interest in developing ballet glossaries to reflect nuances of the various "schools" of ballet. This exploration was encouraged by my Benesh notation colleagues, Adrian Grater, Linda Pilkington, and Robyn Hughes Ryman. The specialized knowledge and insight gained through the study of dance notation have, I hope, added a dimension to the descriptions which follow.

Rhonda Ryman
Waterloo 1994.

PREFACE TO THE SECOND EDITION

Since the publication of this *Dictionary* in 1995, the Royal Academy of Dance has produced *The Foundations of Classical Ballet Technique,* a text explaining the fundamental concepts, positions, and actions of ballet training according to its method of instruction.

In the *Foundations* book, the Academy introduced a new system for direction numbering which has been incorporated into the definitions in this edition.

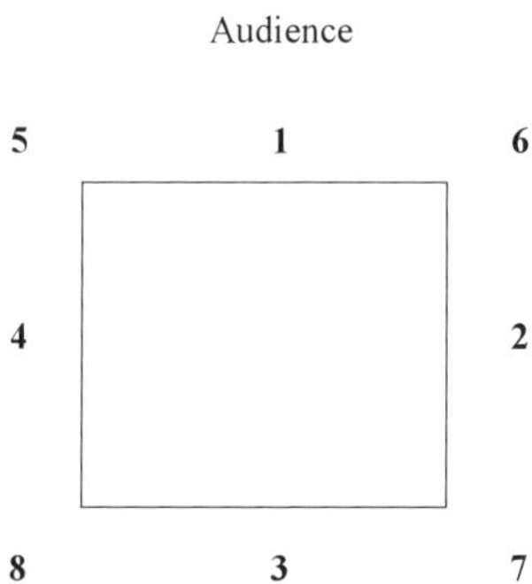

As a panel member and editor of that volume, I was privileged to work with a distinguished group of artists and teachers whose experience on the stage and in the studio spans most of this century and much of the globe. Many refinements formulated by the panel have been incorporated into this second edition of the dictionary.

Rhonda Ryman
Waterloo, 1997

PREFACE TO THE THIRD EDITION

A decade has passed since the publication of the second edition. In this volume we have taken the opportunity to update a few terms and make corrections to that edition.

Rhonda Ryman
Waterloo, 2007

ACKNOWLEDGEMENTS

I am indebted to my colleagues on the Artistic Panel of *The Foundations of Classical Ballet Technique,* chaired by Lynn Wallis, FISTD, Artistic Director of the Royal Academy of Dance*, for the clarity of their insights on fundamental ballet concepts and vocabulary. Sincere appreciation to Morwenna Bowen, FRAD; Julia Farron, FRAD; Jacqueline Ferguson, ARAD, FISTD; Frank Freeman, ARAD (Dip) PDTC; Pamela May, FRAD; Moira McCormack, MCSP ARAD (Dip) PDTC; and Eileen Ward, FRAD.

Sincere thanks are extended to Anuschka Roes, Head of Teacher Training, The National Ballet School, Toronto, Canada, ARAD (ATC), FISTD (National), LISTD (Modern Theatre), Grade Examiner, RAD, Member of Canadian Dance Teachers Association, National Examiner for the Imperial Society of Teachers of Dancing, for her extensive advice and input. I am also grateful for comments from Jean Bedells, FRAD; Audrey Looker, ARAD, Grade Examiner, RAD and on the faculty of the Dance Program, Ryerson Polytechnic University; and Nadia Potts, Professor and Director of the Dance Program, Ryerson Polytechnic University, and former principal dancer with the National Ballet of Canada.

Louise Chaput, Department of French Studies, University of Waterloo, provided advice regarding French pronunciation; Sonia Kadela compiled French word derivations; Cairine McKillop entered phonetic transcriptions; Sharon Lee worked on definitions; and Gayle Shellard provided proofreading assistance.

Dr. John Beatty, Associate Professor, Computer Science, University of Waterloo, designed and implemented the database software used to manage the information from which this dictionary was produced. He also provided a means of transferring text from the database into the layout program which typeset the final manuscript. Anil Goel, Mathematics Faculty Computing Facility, University of Waterloo, very kindly provided crucial assistance in obtaining the desired layout.

This project was funded primarily by the Social Sciences and Humanities Research Council of Canada. Their generous support is most gratefully acknowledged, as is the support provided for Dr. Beatty by the National Science and Engineering Research Council of Canada. I would also like to thank the Faculty of Applied Health Sciences, University of Waterloo, for providing a grant to upgrade computer hardware and update software.

A special note of thanks to Arthur Ryman for converting the original *Dictionary* database to XML and developing the XSLT transforms that produced the current edition of this document from it, and to Jonathan Still for restoring the introductory material.

Sincerest appreciation to Lawrence and Miriam Adams of Dance Collection Danse, Jan Garvey, Canadian Administrator, RAD, and David Watchman, formerly Chief Executive, RAD, for their support and encouragement. Finally, thanks to my husband, Jack Kane, for his countless contributions.

*The acronym RAD is used throughout this *Dictionary* to refer to the Royal Academy of Dance.

INTRODUCTION

Purpose and Scope of the Dictionary

This dictionary is designed to provide information about terminology used within the Royal Academy of Dance (RAD), the world's largest examining and teaching body whose syllabus is taught in over 70 countries. It is geared to both teachers and students who wish to understand the precise ways in which ballet terms are used within the RAD. The *Dictionary* therefore lists terms in the variant forms found throughout RAD publications and contains information based primarily on RAD syllabus material:

> Grades Syllabus: Pre-primary to Grade 7, Grade 8 Award for Girls (1991-1994)
> Girls Majors Syllabus: Pre-elementary to Advanced (1986-1994)[1]
> Boys Majors Syllabus: Pre-elementary to Intermediate (1988, 1993)[2]
> Solo Seal Syllabus: Male and Female (1959-1994)

Terms included in the Free Movement or Character sections of the RAD Grades Syllabus are mentioned only as needed, to distinguish them from classical terms.

Each entry contains some or all of the following information:

1. TERM
2. INTERNATIONAL PHONETIC ALPHABET (IPA) PRONUNCIATION
3. ENGLISH ALPHABET PRONUNCIATION
4. PART OF SPEECH, NUMBER, GENDER, MEANING
5. DEFINITION OR DESCRIPTION

1. TERM

Each classical ballet term (e.g., *arabesque*) or composite term (e.g., *arabesque penchée*) is listed alphabetically and presented in italics.

Variant spellings are provided, e.g., *allégro, allegro.* Variant terms are also provided. For example, although the term *arabesque penchée* may be used, the term *penchée in arabesque* is usually used within the RAD. The reader is therefore directed to "See *penchée in arabesque.*"

> ***arabesque penchée*** See *penchée in arabesque.*

Each entry begins with a headword presented in boldface italics (e.g., ***penchée in arabesque***) and is followed by some or all of items 2 to 5.

> ***penchée in arabesque*** [pɑ̃ʃe – aʀabɛsk] pah-SHAY – a-ra-BESK (Fr. tilting action; in arabesque.) A *penchée* action performed with the *working leg* extended in *arabesque en l'air.* Also *arabesque penchée.*

To facilitate finding a term and minimize flipping pages, terms are usually listed in the form and order most often found in syllabus material, e.g., *petit assemblé* is found under "p", *grand jeté* is found under "g". However terms which are numbered, such as arabesques and positions of the arms and feet, have been grouped under the word rather than the number, e.g., *arabesque; position of the arms, 1st; position of the feet, 1st.*

[1] Current title: Vocational Graded Examinations Syllabus: Intermediate Foundation to Advanced 2 Female (1986-1994)

[2] Current title: Vocational Graded Examinations Syllabus: Intermediate Foundation to Advanced 1 Male (1988, 1993)

2. International Phonetic Alphabet (IPA) Pronunciation

Pronunciation is provided within square brackets in a system of internationally used standard symbols, the IPA. These represent a range of sounds extending beyond English usage. When composite terms contain both English and non-English words, the IPA is used for each non-English word; the pronunciation of each English word is not given, and a dash is used in its place, e.g., ***penchée in attitude*** [pɑ̃ʃe – atityd]. In some cases, context determines whether a word is normally pronounced either in English or in French (e.g., *position of the feet, première position*). Alternate pronunciations are given as needed, e.g., ***relevé*** [ʀəlve, ʀləve]. Multiword lexical units are run together when hyphenated, e.g., ***cou-de-pied*** [kudpje] but otherwise separated for easier reading, e.g., ***cou-de-pied devant*** [kudpje d(ə)vɑ̃]. Liaison, the French practice of sounding the unsounded final consonant of a word when it precedes a word which starts with a vowel sound, is observed: the consonant is strung onto the second word, e.g., ***petit assemblé,*** [p(ə)ti tasɑ̃ble]. For an explanation of relevant IPA symbols, see pages xi-xiii.

3. English Alphabet pronunciation

A simplified pronunciation is provided, based on the 26 letters of the English alphabet. This gives a rough approximation of the foreign word, in a form readily recognizable to English-speaking readers. When composite terms contain both English and non-English words, English letters are used for each non-English word; the pronunciation of each English word is not given, and a long dash is used in its place, e.g., ***penchée in attitude,*** p<u>ah</u>-SHAY – a-tee-TUD. Alternate pronunciations are given as needed, e.g., ***petit,*** p(u)-TEE, p'TEE; ***relevé,*** r(u)l-VAY, rl(u)VAY. As explained above, a final unsounded consonant may be linked to the following word, if that word begins with a vowel sound, e.g., ***petit assemblé,*** p(u)-TEE ta-<u>sah</u>-BLAY. For clarification, see pages xii-xiii.

4. Part of speech, number, gender, meaning

Most classical ballet terms are derived from French words. Since the seventeenth century, ballet terminology has evolved continuously along with changes in the French language, and has been adapted wherever ballet has been taught, from Europe to the Americas, Australia, Africa and Asia. Rather than tracing the etymology of each term from its first historical appearance (which would be fascinating, but is beyond the scope of this volume), this dictionary provides a translation of each foreign word as it is understood today.[1]

Part of Speech: Most terms are nouns, or adjectives and past participles of verbs used as nouns. For example, the term *assemblé* (literally "gathered") is the past participle of the verb *assembler* ("to gather"), and is shortened from the composite term *pas assemblé* ("gathered step"). Note that "step" is understood to describe any action performed by the legs, rather than a specific stepping action. Other omitted nouns are understood to include "position" (e.g., *croisé* "a crossed position"), and "action" (e.g., *double fondu* "a double melted action"), although gender agreement is not strictly observed (soon to be discussed).

Number: As in English, the "number" of a noun may be either singular or plural, e.g., *saut* ("jump"), *sauts* ("jumps"). Some nouns have the same singular and plural forms, e.g., *bras,*

---

[1] Paul Robert, *Le Petit Robert Dictionnaire,* Montréal: Les Dictionnaires ROBERT-CANADA S.C.C., 1987. Atkins, Beryl T., Alain Duval, Rosemary C. Milne, and Pierre-Henri Cousin, Hélène M.A.Lewis, Lorna Sinclair, Renée O. Birks, Marie-Noelle Lamy, *Collins Robert French-English, English-French Dictionary,* Toronto; Collins Publishers, 1978.

contretemps, pas, temps. In such cases, the modifier shows the number, e.g., *un pas de bourrée* ("one bourrée step"), *deux pas de bourrée* ("two bourrée steps"). The Anglicized plural form, e.g., *pas de chats, pas de basques, pas de bourrées,* is also seen.

Gender: Unlike English, a French noun has "gender", either masculine or feminine. A French adjective describing a noun agrees in number and gender, and has four forms, e.g., *changé* ms, *changée* fs, *changés* mpl, *changées* fpl ("changed"). Consider, for example, the terms *échappé sauté changé* and *sissonne changée.* For the gender of words in a composite term, consult the entry for each individual word.

Classical ballet terms generally follow rules for the agreement of number and gender. However certain composite terms raise questions, as for example the variants *pointe tendue* versus *pointe tendu.* In the former, the feminine singular form of the adjective *tendue* (pp of v tendre, "to stretch") describes the feminine singular noun *pointe* ("tiptoe"). In the latter, the masculine singular form of the adjective *tendu* may be an abbreviated form of the term *battement tendu,* ("stretched beating action") used as a noun (m) combined with the noun (f) *pointe.* The following are also seen: *arabesque épaulé, petit sissonne, sissonne ordinaire passé, sissonne fermée relevé.* Spelling may on occasion differ from the French (e.g., *temps de flêche*).

Meaning: Although full etymological information is beyond the scope of this volume, a translation of foreign words is provided to stimulate the reader's interest in words and provide helpful associations. See, for example, the entries for *bourrée* and *pas de bourrée.*

> ***bourrée*** [buʀe] boo-RAY (Fr. pp of v bourrer, to cram or stuff; nf a lively 17th century Fr. dance usually in quick duple time; music for that dance or characterized by its rhythmic form, often part of a classical suite.) See *pas de bourrée.*

> ***pas de bourrée*** [pɑ də buʀe] pah d(u) boo-RAY (Fr. bourrée step.) *Terre à terre* steps performed in a continuous movement in any direction, demanding quick, precise footwork. Can vary with the use of either the front or back foot on the initial extension. Taken *devant, derrière, dessus, dessous, en avant, to* 2nd*, en arrière,* and *en tournant.* Usually ends in 5th *position en demi-plié,* but may end *en pointe/s,* in an open position, or in a *lunge.* Variations: *pas de bourrée à cinq pas, pas de bourrée à quatre pas, pas de bourrée couru, pas de bourrée piqué, petit pas de bourrée piqué, running pas de bourrée, wide pas de bourrée en tournant.*

When a French word has come into English usage, its meaning is given under the entry for the word. For composite terms, the word itself may be used as a translation (i.e., provided within round brackets). See, for example, the entries for *arabesque* and *arabesque à dos.*

> ***arabesque*** [ɑʀabɛsk] a-ra-BESK (Arabian <It. arabesc < Arab and esco, -ish; Fr. nf an ornament or style made of an intricate pattern of interlaced lines; a dance pose.) A balanced pose on one leg with the other leg extended *en l'air derrière.* A curved position of the body from the head, through the spine to the tips of the toes of the raised leg. The arms are placed in an extended position with the palms facing downward, creating an elongated line. In all *arabesques,* there is an unbroken line through the arm and hand with no tension in the elbows. There are three basic *arabesques:* 1st, 2nd, and 3rd.

> ***arabesque à dos*** [aʀabɛsk a do] a-ra-BESK a doh (Fr. arabesque; with the back.) An *arabesque,* usually *1st arabesque,* taken in *croisé alignment* of the body with a strong *épaulement* so that the back is visible to the audience. Also called *1st arabesque en croisé* with full *épaulement.*

In French the adjective usually follows the noun it modifies, although some (e.g., *grand, petit)* precede the noun as in English. According to the former convention, a *sissonne relevée* is a *sissonne* (fs) performed with the quality of a *relevé* onto *demi-pointe* (rather than with a jump); according to the latter practice, a *sissonne relevé* is a *relevé* (ms) executed with the form and quality of a *sissonne.* Consider also the terms *sauté pirouette* or *pirouette sauté* (a turning jump) versus *pirouette sautée* (a jumped spin).

Word order may also indicate the sequence of components in a compound action. Consider for example, *glissade piquée* as opposed to a *glissade piqué* or *glissade-piqué.* Within the RAD, the former is a *glissade* performed with a quick, light quality. Outside the RAD, the latter is taken as a *glissade* which then leads into a *piqué* or sharp, stepping action. Similarly, *sissonne tombée* might be interpreted as a "fallen sissonne" whereas *sissonne tombé* is understood to be a composite step consisting of a *sissonne ordinaire* followed by a *tombé.* Consider also *posé passé,* which may indicate either a step executed by a passing action of the stepping leg, or a step followed by a passing action of the free leg. Specific word order may also indicate distinct components, as for example *coupé brisé devant* versus *coupé dessous brisé devant.*

5. Definition or Description

This may comprise a brief definition and/or a longer description as needed. Redundant information is sometimes included, to minimize flipping between entries. When a specifically defined term is used within a definition for the sake of precision, it is presented in italics and defined elsewhere. In some cases the reader is directed beyond the entry.

See	refers the reader to another entry.
Also	provides another spelling or name.
Variations:	is followed by a list of similar positions or actions.

Positions and movements described using the contraction "s/he" are normally performed by both female and male dancers; those described using "she" or "he" are normally performed by women or men only. Positions and movements performed *en pointe/s* are understood to be performed by women either *en pointe/s* or *en demi-pointe/s,* and by men *en demi-pointe/s.*

Each description assumes ballet conventions. For example, unless otherwise stated, the legs are stretched and fully turned-out (the knee joint is extended and the thighs laterally rotated at the hip joints); the body is vertically aligned and lengthened (the pelvis is neutrally balanced, rotated neither forward nor backward, and the spinal curves are functionally diminished); the shoulders are dropped and widened (the shoulder girdle is neither protracted nor retracted), and the arms are configured in long curves extending to the tips of the fingers (the bones of the forearm lie parallel to one another, and the elbow, wrist, and finger joints are not fully extended); and the foot is fully pointed whenever it is not bearing weight (the ankle and metatarsal-phalangeal joints are plantar flexed, and the arches of the foot are increased). It is also understood that, when the legs are fully turned-out, the "front" of the leg refers to the medial surface and the "back" refers to the lateral surface.

ABRREVIATIONS

adj	adjective	inv	invariable
adv	adverb	imp	imperative
art.	article	It.	Italian
def	definite	L.	Latin
excl	exclamation	m	masculine
f	feminine	n	noun
Fr.	French	pl	plural
G.	German	pp	past participle
indef	indefinite	s	singular
infin	infinitive	v	verb

PHONETIC TRANSCRIPTION

A summary of the International Phonetic Alphabet
See also pages xii-xiii.

VOWELS

[a]	**à la**, ch**a**ssé, m**a**nège
[ɑ]	p**a**ssé, p**as**
[ɑ̃]	ch**an**gé, **en**, s**an**s
[e]	coup**é,** pli**é**
[ɛ]	arab**e**sque, derri**è**re
[ɛ̃]	po**in**te, mat**in**
[ə]	l**e**, p**e**tit, pr**e**mier
[i]	pet**i**t, dem**i**
[ɔ]	cl**o**che, p**o**rt
[ɔ̃]	r**on**d, f**on**du, b**on**
[o]	s**au**té, **eau**, piv**ot**
[ø]	d**eux**, p**eu**
[œ]	dans**eu**r, **oeu**vre
[œ̃]	**un**, br**un**
[u]	dess**ou**s, c**ou**
[y]	dess**u**s, s**u**r

SEMI-CONSONANTS

[j]	p**i**ed, derr**i**ère, **y**eux
[w]	pir**ou**ette, garg**oui**llade, **oui**
[ɥ]	c**u**isse, h**u**it

CONSONANTS

[b]	**b**allotté, jam**be**
[d]	**d**e, **d**evant, glissa**de**
[f]	**f**rappé, neu**f**, **ph**rase
[g]	**g**lissé, **g**alop, **g**ar**g**ouillade
[h]	**h**op (exclamation)
[']	**h**aut (no liaison)
[x]	words, borrowed from Spanish, **j**ota, words borrowed from Arabic, **kh**amsin, etc.
[ʒ]	ada**g**e, **j**ambe, **g**igue
[k]	**c**ou-de-pied, fli**c**-fla**c**, **qu**i
[l]	**l**a, **l**ent, so**l**
[m]	**m**anège, fe**mm**e
[n]	**n**oble**, n**om
[ɲ]	li**gn**e, a**gn**eau
[ŋ]	words borrowed from English, campi**ng**
[p]	**p**as, cou**p**é
[ʀ]	**r**eti**r**é, po**r**t
[s]	**s**aut, de**ss**ous, rota**t**ion, d'i**c**i
[ʃ]	**ch**at, pen**ch**ée
[t]	**t**erre, ba**tt**ement
[v]	**v**olé, **v**ous, rê**v**e
[z]	oppo**s**ition, **z**éro

GUIDE TO THE PRONUNCIATION OF FOREIGN WORDS

Most of the foreign terms used in classical ballet are derived from French words, and a few musical terms are borrowed from Italian. In the body of this *Dictionary,* standard French pronunciation is provided in the International Phonetic Alphabet (IPA) after the entry for each term or composite term. As a rough guide for English-speaking readers, simplified French pronunciation is provided in the English alphabet. In this simplified format, nasal sounds are underlined and, although syllables are more evenly accentuated in French than in English, slightly accentuated syllables are shown in upper case letters.

IPA		EXAMPLE	SIMPLIFIED ENGLISH		PRONUNCIATION GUIDE
vowel sounds					
[a]	[a la]	**à la**	(a)	(a la)	As the “a” in “hat”
[ɑ]	[pɑse]	passé	(ah)	(pah-SAY)	As the “a” in “father”
[ɑ̃]	[ʃɑ̃ʒe]	changé	(ah)	(shah-ZHAY)	As the “a” in “father,” but nasal
[e]	[kupe]	coupé	(ay)	(koo-PAY)	As the “ay” in “hay,” but clipped
[ɛ]	[aʀabɛsk]	arabesque	(e)	(a-ra-BESK)	As the “e” in “let”
[ɛ̃]	[pwɛ̃t]	pointe	(e)	(pwet)	As the “e” in “let,” but nasal
[i]	[p(ə)ti]	petit	(ee)	(p(ut)-TEE) (p’TEE)	As the “ee” in “feet”
[ɔ]	[klɔʃ]	cloche	(e)	(klosh)	As the “o” in “hot”
[ɔ̃]	[ʀɔ̃]	**rond**	(o)	(ro)	As “o” in “hot,” but nasal
[o]	[sote]	sauté	(oh)	(soh-TAY)	As the “o” in “over”
[u]	[d(ə)su]	dessous	(oo)	(d(u)-SOO)	As the “oo” in “noon”
[y]	[d(ə)sy]	dessus	(u)	(d(u)-SU)	Between the sounds “ee” as in “feet” and “ou” as in “you”, and clipped
[ə]	[l(ə)]	**le**	((u))	(l(u))	Weakly sounded, as the “e” in “camera”
[ø]	[dø]	**deux**	(uh)	(duh)	Between the sounds “e” as in “pet” and “u” as in “put”, with the lips rounded
[œ]	[dɑ̃sœʀ]	danseur	(eh)	(dah-SEHR)	Between the sounds “e” as in “pet” and “u” as in “put,” but longer
[œ̃]	[œ̃]	**un**	(uh)	(uh)	Between the sounds “e” as in “pet” and “u” as in “put,” but nasal
semi-consonant sounds					
[j]	[pje]	pied	(y)	(pyay)	As the “y” in “yes”
[w]	[piʀwɛt]	pirouette	(w)	(peer-WET)	As the “w” in “wet”
[ɥ]	[kɥis]	cuisse	(uw)	(kuwees)	Between [u] and [w]

GUIDE TO THE PRONUNCIATION OF FOREIGN WORDS (continued)

IPA		EXAMPLE	SIMPLIFIED ENGLISH		PRONUNCIATION GUIDE
consonant sounds					
[b]	[balɔte]	**b**allotté	(b)	(ba-lo-TAY)	As the “b” in “but”
[d]	[də]	**d**e	(d)	(d(u)	As the “d” in “do”
[f]	[fʀape]	**f**rappé	(f)	(fra-PAY)	As the “f” in “for”
[g]	[glise]	**g**lissé	(g)	(glee-SAY)	As the “g” in “go”
[h]	[hɔp]	**h**op	(h)	(hop)	An aspirated “h” as in “hello”
[’]	[‘op]	**h**op	(’)	(’ohp)	An unaspirated or silent “h” as in “honour”
[’]	[ɑ̃ ’o]	en **h**aut	(’)	(ah ’oh)[1]	No *liaison* (no linkage of last consonant of one word to first vowel sound of next)
[x]	[xota]	**j**ota	(ch)	(CHOH-ta)	As the “ch” in “l’chaim” or “loch”
[ʒ]	[adaʒ]	ada**g**e	(zh)	(adazh)	As the “si” in “Asia”
[k]	[kudpje]	**c**ou-de-pied	(k)	(koo-d(u)-pyay)	As the “c” in “cup”
[l]	[la]	**l**a	(l)	(la)	As the “l” in “let”
[m]	[manɛʒ]	**m**anège	(m)	(ma-NEZH)	As the “m” in “me”
[n]	[nɔbl]	**n**oble	(n)	(NO-bl)	As the “n” in “notation”
[ɲ]	[liɲ]	li**gn**e	(ny)	(leeny)	As the “ni” in “onion”
[ŋ]	[dʒʌmpɪŋ]	jumpi**ng**	(ng)	(jumping)	As the “ng” in “jumping”
[p]	[pɑ]	**p**as	(p)	(pah)	As the “p” in “put”
[ʀ]	[ʀ(ə)tiʀe]	**r**eti**r**é	(r)	(r(u)-tee-RAY)	A “rolled r” made in the throat, as if gargling
[s]	[so]	**s**aut	(s)	(soh)	As the “s” in “some”
[ʃ]	[ʃa]	**ch**at	(sh)	(sha)	As the “sh” in “show”
[t]	[tɛʀ]	**t**erre	(t)	(ter)	As the “t” in “to”
[v]	[vɔle]	**v**olé	(v)	(vo-LAY)	As the “v” in “very”
[z]	[ɔpozisjɔ̃]	oppo**s**ition	(z)	(o-poh-zis-YO)	As the “s” in “exercise”

[1] In French, a *liaison* normally occurs when a word ending in a consonant (except c, r, f or q) is followed by a word beginning with a vowel sound: the consonant is normally sounded at the start of the second word, as in *en avant* (ah na-VAH). When (’) is used between words, it eliminates the normal *liaison*, as in *en haut* (ah ’oh). When (’) is used within a word, it indicates a weakly sounded vowel sound, as in *petit* (p’tee).

1st See *arabesque, 1st; position of the arms, 1st; position of the feet, 1st.*

2nd See *arabesque, 2nd; position of the arms, 2nd; position of the feet, 2nd.*

3rd See *arabesque, 3rd; position of the arms, 3rd; position of the feet, 3rd.*

4th See *grand 4th en fondu; position of the arms, 4th; position of the feet, 4th.*

4th derrière [- dɛʀjɛʀ] – der-YER (Fr. 4th behind.) A position of the *working leg* extended to the back. See *position of the feet, 4th.*

4th devant [- d(ə)vɑ̃] – d(u)-VAH (Fr. 4th in front.) A position of the *working leg* extended to the front. See *position of the feet, 4th.*

5th See *position of the arms, 5th; position of the feet, 5th.*

5th derrière [- dɛʀjɛʀ] – der-YER (Fr. 5th behind.) A *5th position* in which the *working foot* is placed behind the other foot. See *position of the feet, 5th.*

5th devant [- d(ə)vɑ̃] - d(u)-VAH (Fr. 5th in front.) A *5th position* in which the *working foot* is placed in front of the other foot. See *position of the feet, 5th.*

à [a] a (Fr. prep on, by, with, to.) See *à dos alignment, attitude à deux bras, arabesque à dos.*

à deux bras [a døbʀa] a duh bra (Fr. with two arms.) Term describing a position taken with both arms curved overhead, corresponding to *5th en haut* (Cecchetti), *en couronne* (French), *5th position* (French, RAD), *3rd position* (Vaganova). See *attitude à deux bras.*

à dos [a do] a doh (Fr. with the back.) 1. Phrase describing a position usually taken *en croisé* with a strong *épaulement* so that the back is visible to the audience, e.g., *arabesque à dos, attitude à dos.* 2. Phrase used in the Solo Seal syllabus to describe positions or movements of the body performed with the back visible to the audience, e.g., *attitude, développé devant ouvert, échappé relevé, pas de bourrée courus;* or with the back directed to the *line of dance,* e.g., *saut de basque.*

à la seconde [a la s(ə)gɔ̃d] a la (su)-GOD (Fr. to the second.) Phrase used to describe the position of the *working leg* extended to the side of the body. See *ballonné, to 2nd.*

à terre [a tɛʀ] a ter (Fr. on the ground.) Phrase used to describe a position in which the *working foot* is in contact with the floor. Term which may be used to modify positions or movements that would otherwise be performed *en l'air,* i.e., with the *working foot* off the floor, as *arabesque.* Also *dégagé, pointe tendu.* See *arabesque à terre, assemblé soutenu à terre, attitude à terre, battement fondu à terre, demi-assemblé soutenu à terre, rond de jambe à terre, rotation à terre, temps lié à terre, terre à terre, tombé à terre.*

adage [adaʒ] adazh (< It. adj adv adagio, slow, slowly, leisurely and with grace; Fr. nm a slow movement in music or ballet.) 1. Term describing a combination of slow, graceful coordinated movements of the arms, feet, body, and head, performed with ease, grace, and fluidity. *Adage* movements are combined to demonstrate beauty of line and form as well as subtlety of expression, and to develop the dancer's sense of equilibrium when the body is supported on one foot. They include controlled leg extensions at varying heights and in a variety of positions supported on the whole foot, *en demi-pointe,* or *en pointe,* and also slow rotary movements on the whole foot. To add contrast and interest, these lyrical actions may be punctuated by the occasional turn or spring. See *fouetté of adage, grand adage.* 2. A generic term for a category of movements performed in the centre, usually after the *Pirouettes* section of a class and before *Allegro.* These may include, at a pre-elementary level: *chassés–en avant, en arrière, passé en avant, passé en arrière, à la seconde; coupés–dessus, dessous; dégagés; rotation à terre; arabesques–1st, 2nd, 3rd; attitude ordinaire, opposition, à deux bras; développés–devant, seconde, derrière; classical walks;* at an elementary level: *chassés–en avant, en arrière, à la seconde, passé en avant, passé en arrière; coupés–dessus, dessous; dégagés; assemblés soutenus en tournant–en dedans with front and back foot; développés–devant, derrière, à la seconde, écarté; demi-grands ronds de jambe; arabesques–1st 2nd 3rd; attitudes–ordinaire, opposition, à deux bras; posés; rotation; fouetté of adage*; at an intermediate level: *glissades–devant, derrière, dessus, dessous; grands ronds de jambe; assemblés soutenus en tournant en dehors with front foot; posés* at 90 degrees; *rises in open positions; développés en fondus; fouettés and rotation en l'air; pivots en dehors and en dedans in attitudes and arabesques; penchée in arabesque; double pirouettes en dehors finish-*

ing in open positions; at an advanced level: *ballottés; arabesque allongée; tombés; grands battements en rond with rise; fouettés and rotation en l'air; grands fouettés relevés en tournant; renversés relevés en dehors; pirouettes en dedans in attitudes and arabesques.*

air [ɛʀ] er (Fr. nm air.) See *en l'air.*

alignment See *body alignment.*

allegro, allégro [a(l)legʀo] a-LAY-groh (It. < L. alacer, adv lively, brisk; Fr. nm a musical composition or movement in allegro tempo, more rapid than allegretto but slower than presto.) 1. Term describing movements performed quickly and with exuberance, highlighting the dancer's speed and agility. *Allegro* movements explore agility and mobility, and push the dancer to his or her physical limits by developing speed and precision in footwork, feline power in jumping, and expansiveness in travelling. While apparently defying the laws of gravity, ballet jumps always conform to basic principles. See *sauté.* There are three basic levels of elevation in jumps to suit different musical tempi, technical goals, and dramatic effects. These are generally categorized as *petit allegro, medium allegro,* and *grand allegro.* Most jumps can be embellished with a beat or beats *(batterie)*, and performed in place *(sur place)* or travelled. 2. A generic term for a category of movements performed in the centre after *Adage* and, for Girls, before *Sur La Pointe*, including sub-categories such as *petit allegro*, *allegro*, *batterie*, and *grand allegro.* 3. A generic term for a sub-category of movements performed during the *Allegro* section of a class, after *petit allegro* and before *batterie*; jumping movements of moderate elevation. These may include, at a pre-elementary level: *assemblés–devant, derrière, dessus, dessous; jetés ordinaires–devant, derrière; pas de chat; assemblé soutenu en tournant en dedans; sissonnes fermées de côté–devant, derrière, dessus, dessous;* at an elementary level: *assemblés–devant, derrière, dessus, dessous; coupés fouettés raccourcis sautés; sissonnes fermées–en avant, en arrière; demi-contretemps; assemblés de côté écarté;* at an intermediate level: *assemblés–en avant, en arrière; assemblés de côté–dessus, dessous; retirés sautés passés; sissonnes ouvertes–en avant, en arrière, de côté; sissonnes doublées–en avant, en arrière, dessus, dessous; ballonnés simples–en avant, de côté; ballonnés composés–en avant, en arrière, de côté; pas de basque sautés–en avant, en arrière; ballottés sautés–dessus, dessous; posé assemblé soutenu en dedans;* at an advanced level: *jetés ronds de jambe sautés; gargouillade* and *gargouillade finishing in dégagé devant; sissonnes ouvertes battues–en avant, en arrière; sissonnes fermées battues de côté–dessus, dessous; sissonnes fermées changées battues–en avant, en arrière, en tournant; emboîtés sautés en tournant; petites cabrioles ouvertes derrière; assemblés battus–dessus, dessous.*

allongé [alɔ̃ʒe] a-lo-ZHAY (Fr. pp of v allonger, to lengthen or extend; adj stretched out.) Term used to describe a lengthened line taken in *arabesque* either *à terre* or *en l'air*, in which the back is released slightly forward and the *eye line* is either along the front arm or lowered. See *arabesque allongée.*

arabesque [aʀabɛsk] a-ra-BESK (Arabian < It. arabesc < Arab and esco, -ish; Fr. nf an ornament or style made of an intricate pattern of interlaced lines; a dance pose.) A balanced pose on one leg with the other leg extended *en l'air derrière.* A curved position of the body from the head, through the spine to the tips of the toes of the raised leg. The arms are placed in an extended position with the palms facing downward, creating an elongated line. In all *arabesques,* there is an unbroken line through the arm and hand with no tension in the elbows. There are three basic *arabesques: 1st, 2nd,* and *3rd.*

arabesque, 1st [aʀabɛsk, -] a-ra-BESK, – A basic *arabesque* taken facing 2 *(stage right)* or 4 *(stage left):* when taken at 90 degrees, the dancer stands on the *upstage* leg, and the *downstage* leg is raised fully stretched behind and in line with the hip; the *upstage* arm is placed in an extended line in front of the shoulder at eye level; the head is slightly lifted and placed so that the *eye line* is directed over and beyond the middle finger; and the *downstage* arm is placed slightly behind and below the shoulder. Also taken in other *alignments.*

arabesque, 2nd [aʀabɛsk, -] a-ra-BESK, – A basic *arabesque* in which the position of the legs is the same as for *1st arabesque,* taken with the front arm placed in opposition to the *supporting leg* just above shoulder level, and with the *eye line* over and beyond the centre finger; the back arm is placed very slightly behind and below the shoulder. In the Cecchetti method, *2nd arabesque en fondu* is known as *4th arabesque.*

arabesque, 3rd [aʀabɛsk, -] a-ra-BESK, – A basic *arabesque* in which the position is as for *1st arabesque*, but with the arm corresponding to the raised leg placed in front of the body at *2nd arabesque* height (slightly below shoulder height). With a projection upward and outward, the *eye line* is over and beyond the centre finger of the higher arm. In the Cecchetti method, *3rd arabesque en fondu* is known as *5th arabesque.*

arabesque à dos [aʀabɛsk a do] a-ra-BESK a doh (Fr. arabesque; with the back.) An *arabesque*, usually *1st arabesque*, taken in *croisé alignment* of the body with a strong *épaulement* so that the back is visible to the audience. Also called *1st arabesque en croisé* with full *épaulement.*

arabesque à dos à terre [aʀabɛsk a do a tɛʀ] a-ra-BESK a doh a ter (Fr. arabesque; with the back; on the ground.) An *arabesque à dos* taken with the tip of the *working foot* contacting the floor.

arabesque à terre [aʀabɛsk a tɛʀ] a-ra-BESK a ter (Fr. arabesque; on the ground.) An *arabesque* taken with the *working foot* on the floor.

arabesque à terre allongée en fondu, 2nd [aʀabɛsk a tɛʀ alɔ̃ʒe ɑ̃ fɔ̃dy, -] a-ra-BESK a ter a-lo̲-ZHAY a̲h̲ fo̲-DU, – (Fr. 2nd arabesque; on the ground; stretched out; melted.) A lengthened *2nd arabesque* taken with the *working leg* on the floor and the *supporting leg* bent. The back is released slightly forward and the *eye line* is either along the front arm or lowered.

arabesque allongée [aʀabɛsk alɔ̃ʒe] a-ra-BESK a-lo̲-ZHAY (Fr. arabesque; stretched out.) Term used to describe a lengthened *arabesque* taken either *à terre* or *en l'air*, in which the back is released slightly forward and the *eye line* is either along the front arm or lowered.

arabesque de côté [aʀabɛsk də kote] a-ra-BESK d(u) koh-TAY (Fr. arabesque; to the side.) An *arabesque* performed with the dancer facing either *stage right* or *stage left.*

arabesque de côté, 1st [aʀabɛsk də kote, -] a-ra-BESK d(u) koh-TAY, – (Fr. arabesque; to the side, 1st.) A *1st arabesque* performed with the dancer facing either *stage right* or *stage left.*

arabesque en fondu [aʀabɛsk ɑ̃ fɔ̃dy] a-ra-BESK a̲h̲ fo̲-DU (Fr. arabesque; by a blended action.) An *arabesque* taken with the *supporting leg en demi-plié.*

arabesque épaulée [aʀabɛsk epole] a-ra-BESK ay-poh-LAY (Fr. arabesque; shouldered.) A *1st arabesque* in which the spine is rotated to lengthen the arm line, complementing the leg line. The sagittal arm line is maintained despite the spinal rotation, i.e., the front arm widens slightly in opposition to the rotation. Variation: *2nd arabesque* with *épaulement.*

arabesque line [aʀabɛsk -] a-ra-BESK – An elongated position of the arm or arms taken with the palms facing downward and the hands and fingers extended to complete the arm line. 1. A position of the arm or arms corresponding to *arabesque*, but taken when the legs are not *en arabesque*, e.g., a *1st arabesque* taken with the *working leg* extended *devant* instead of *derrière*. In a low *arabesque line*, the front arm is below the shoulder. In a raised *arabesque line*, the front arm is raised above the *eye line* and the back arm balances the line. 2. An *écarté* line of the arms with one arm extended sideways above head height and the other arm extended sideways below shoulder height completing a long diagonal line. Sometimes performed with the leg corresponding to the lifted arm extended *to 2nd*, as in *assemblé de côté.*

arabesque line, 2nd [aʀabɛsk -] a-ra-BESK – *Arabesque* in which the arm on the supporting side is extended to the side slightly lower than the shoulder and not taken back, and the arm of the *working leg* is extended in front of and fractionally above its shoulder.

arabesque line, low [aʀabɛsk -] a-ra-BESK – An *arabesque line* in which the front arm is below the shoulder.

arabesque line, raised [aʀabɛsk -] a-ra-BESK – An *arabesque line* in which the front arm is raised above the *eye line* and the back arm balances the line.

arabesque penchée See *penchée in arabesque.*

arms See *position of the arms.*

arrière [aʀjɛʀ] ar-YER (Fr. nm back.) See *en arrière.*

assemblé [asɑ̃ble] a-sa̲h̲-BLAY (Fr. pp of v assembler, to gather; adj gathered; nm in dance, a jump in which one lands on two feet.) A jumping action where the legs are assembled fully stretched in *5th position* in the air before landing on two feet. In a basic *assemblé,* the arms are carried to *demi-seconde* with the outward movement of the leg and return to *bras bas* on alighting. There is a use of *épaulement* which commences with the jump and finishes with the same shoulder forward as the foot which finishes *devant.* Taken *devant, derrière, dessus, en avant, de côté or porté, en arrière, en tournant, battu,* and *piqué.* Variations: *assemblé fermé, assemblé soutenu, grand assemblé, petit assemblé.*

assemblé battu [asɑ̃ble baty] a-sah-BLAY ba-TU (Fr. gathered step; beaten.) An *assemblé* performed with a beating action of the legs, i.e., with both calves crossing and rebounding, on the closing. May be performed *dessus* or *dessous.*

assemblé battu dessous [asɑ̃ble baty d(ə)su] a-sah-BLAY ba-TU d(u)-SOO (Fr. gathered step; beaten; under.) An *assemblé* performed with the front foot sliding *to 2nd* and closing in front to beat without a *change of feet* in the aerial position, before alighting with a *change of feet,* i.e., with the *working foot 5th derrière.*

assemblé battu dessus [asɑ̃ble baty d(ə)sy] a-sah-BLAY ba-TU d(u)-SU (Fr. gathered step; beaten; over.) An *assemblé* performed with the back foot sliding *to 2nd* and closing behind to beat without a *change of feet* in the aerial position before alighting with a *change of feet,* i.e., with the *working foot 5th devant.*

assemblé de côté [asɑ̃ble də kote] a-sah-BLAY d(u) koh-TAY (Fr. gathered step; in a sideways direction.) An *assemblé* which travels to the side of the body, i.e., toward the *working leg.* The legs aim to join at the height of the jump and may be slightly toward the working side. May be performed *devant, derrière, dessus,* or *dessous.* Variation: *assemblé dessus porté de côté.*

assemblé de côté dessous [asɑ̃ble də kote d(ə)su] a-sah-BLAY d(u) koh-TAY d(u)-SOO (Fr. gathered step; in a sideways direction; under.) An *assemblé* in which the *working foot* starts in front, slides *to 2nd*, and closes *5th derrière.* The step travels sideways in the direction of the *working leg.* The legs aim to join at the height of the jump and may be slightly toward the working side.

assemblé de côté dessus [asɑ̃ble də kote d(ə)sy] a-sah-BLAY d(u) koh-TAY d(u)-SU (Fr. gathered step; in a sideways direction; over.) An *assemblé* in which the *working foot* starts behind, slides *to 2nd*, and closes *5th devant.* The step travels sideways in the direction of the *working leg.* The legs aim to join at the height of the jump and may be slightly toward the working side. Also *assemblé dessus porté de côté.*

assemblé derrière [asɑ̃ble dɛʀjɛʀ] a-sah-BLAY der-YER (Fr. gathered step; behind.) An *assemblé* in which the back foot slides out *to 2nd* and finishes *derrière.*

assemblé dessous [asɑ̃ble d(ə)su] a-sah-BLAY d(u)-SOO (Fr. gathered step; under.) An *assemblé* in which the front foot slides out *to 2nd* and finishes *derrière.*

assemblé dessous de côté See *assemblé de côté dessous.*

assemblé dessus [asɑ̃ble d(ə)sy] a-sah-BLAY d(u)-SU (Fr. gathered step; over.) An *assemblé* in which the back foot slides out *to 2nd* and finishes *devant.*

assemblé dessus de côté See *assemblé de côté dessus.*

assemblé dessus en tournant [asɑ̃ble d(ə)sy ɑ̃ tuʀnɑ̃] a-sah-BLAY d(u)-SU ah toor-NAH (Fr. gathered step; over; turning.) An *assemblé dessus* in which the dancer turns while in the air toward the leg which pushed off. Usually preceded by a preparatory movement such as a *running pas de bourrée,* and ended facing *downstage.*

assemblé dessus porté de côté See *assemblé de côté dessus.*

assemblé devant [asɑ̃ble d(ə)vɑ̃] a-sah-BLAY d(u)-VAH (Fr. gathered step; front.) An *assemblé* in which the front foot slides out *to 2nd* and finishes *devant.*

assemblé en arrière [asɑ̃ble ɑ̃ naʀjɛʀ] a-sah-BLAY ah-nar-YER (Fr. gathered step; backward.) An *assemblé* in which the back foot slides out *to 4th derrière* and finishes *derrière.* This step travels backward.

assemblé en avant [asɑ̃ble ɑ̃ navɑ̃] a-sah-BLAY ah na-VAH (Fr. gathered step; forward.) An *assemblé* in which the front foot slides out *to 4th devant* and finishes *devant.* This step travels forward.

assemblé en tournant See *assemblé dessus en tournant.*

assemblé fermé [asɑ̃ble fɛʀme] a-sah-BLAY fer-MAY (Fr. gathered step; closed.) A jump from one foot to two feet. The dancer begins *en fondu* with the *working leg* extended *en l'air,* and ends in *5th position.* May follow a *sissonne ouverte.* May be performed *devant* with the working foot closing in front or *derrière* with the working foot closing behind. Term not used in current RAD syllabus. Variation: *petit assemblé.*

assemblé piqué [asɑ̃ble pike] a-sah-BLAY pee-KAY (Fr. gathered step; pricked.) An action beginning in *5th position en demi-plié,* in which the dancer extends the *working foot to 2nd en fondu* just off the floor, and performs a *relevé* action closing the *working foot 5th position* with a *change of feet en pointes.* May be performed *dessus* or *dessous.*

assemblé piqué dessous [asɑ̃ble pike d(ə)su] a-sah-BLAY pee-KAY d(u)-SOO (Fr. gathered step; pricked; under.) An *assemblé piqué* in which the *working foot* begins *devant,* extends *to 2nd,* and ends *derrière.*

assemblé piqué dessus [asɑ̃ble pike d(ə)sy] a-sah-BLAY pee-KAY d(u)-SU (Fr. gathered step; pricked; over.) An *assemblé piqué* in which the *working foot* begins *derrière,* extends *to 2nd,* and ends *devant.*

assemblé soutenu à terre [asɑ̃ble sutny a tɛʀ] a-sah-BLAY soot-NU a ter (Fr. gathered step; sustained; on the ground.) A circling action of the *working leg* performed with the tip of the foot sliding along the floor before the leg closes *5th position.* May be performed *en dehors* or *en dedans* tracing either a 90-degree arc, i.e., *demi-*, or a 180-degree arc, i.e., *grand.* See *demi-assemblé soutenu à terre, grand assemblé soutenu à terre.*

assemblé soutenu à terre en dedans [asɑ̃ble sutny a tɛʀ ɑ̃ dədɑ̃] a-sah-BLAY soot-NU a ter ah d(u)-DAH (Fr. gathered step; sustained; on the ground; inward.) An *assemblé soutenu à terre* with the *working foot* tracing an arc from back *to 2nd,* from *2nd* to front, or from back through *2nd* to front before closing. See *demi-assemblé soutenu à terre en dedans, grand assemblé à terre en dedans.*

assemblé soutenu à terre en dehors [asɑ̃ble sutny a tɛʀ ɑ̃ dəɔʀ] a-sah-BLAY soot-NU a ter ah d(u)-OR (Fr. gathered step; sustained; on the ground; outward.) An *assemblé soutenu à terre* with the *working foot* tracing an arc from front *to 2nd,* from *2nd* to back, or from front through *2nd* to back before closing. See *demi-assemblé soutenu à terre en dehors, grand assemblé à terre en dehors.*

assemblé soutenu en dedans See *assemblé soutenu à terre en dedans.*

assemblé soutenu en dedans en fondu, grand See *grand assemblé soutenu en dedans.*

assemblé soutenu en dehors See *assemblé soutenu à terre en dehors.*

assemblé soutenu en dehors en fondu, grand See *grand assemblé soutenu en dehors.*

assemblé soutenu en tournant [asɑ̃ble sutny ɑ̃ tuʀnɑ̃] a-sah-BLAY soot-NU ah toor-NAH (Fr. gathered step; sustained; turning.) A sustained gathering movement leading into a turning action on two feet. Incorporates the action of an *assemblé soutenu à terre en dedans* or *en dehors,* and a *détourné* turn. May be preceded by a *posé* and executed with either a *demi-* or a *grand assemblé soutenu* action.

assemblé soutenu en tournant en dedans [asɑ̃ble sutny ɑ̃ tuʀnɑ̃ ɑ̃ dədɑ̃] a-sah-BLAY soot-NU ah toor-NAH ah d(u)-DAH (Fr. gathered step; sustained; turning; inward.) An *assemblé soutenu à terre* turning toward the initial *supporting leg.* From *5th derrière, en face, bras bas,* the back leg extends to a *dégagé in 2nd en fondu,* and the arms make a *basic port de bras* to arrive in *2nd position* along with the leg; remaining *en fondu* and continuing with a *rond de jambe en dedans* through *4th en croisé,* there is an inclination of the body toward the working leg as the arms move through a low *1st position.* The turning movement commences with the arms and legs being gathered into *5th position en pointes* with the initiating foot *devant,* and continues with the *change of feet* occurring after the first 1/2-turn, to finish *en face* with the initiating foot *derrière* before lowering *en demi-plié* with the arms in *2nd position.* Also taken in other *alignments.*

assemblé soutenu en tournant en dehors [asɑ̃ble sutny ɑ̃ tuʀnɑ̃ ɑ̃ dəɔʀ] a-sah-BLAY soot-NU ah toor-NAH ah d(u)-OR (Fr. gathered step; sustained; turning; outward.) An *assemblé soutenu à terre* with a turn away from the initial *supporting leg.* From *5th devant, en face, bras bas,* the front leg extends to a *dégagé to 2nd en fondu,* and the arms make a *basic port de bras* to arrive in *2nd position* along with the leg; remaining *en fondu* and continuing with a *rond de jambe* *en dehors* through *4th en croisé*, there is a slight inclination of the body toward the *supporting leg* as the arms move through a low *1st position.* The turning movement commences with the arms and legs being gathered into *5th en demi-pointes* with the initiating foot *derrière,* and continues with the *change of feet* occurring after the first 1/2-turn, to finish *en face* with the initiating foot *devant* before lowering *en demi-plié* with the arms in *2nd position.* Also taken in other *alignments.* Term not found in current Majors syllabus but may be used for *free work.*

assemblé, petit See *petit assemblé.*

attitude [atityd] a-tee-TUD (Fr. nf a pose or way of holding oneself.) A contained position based on curves. A balanced pose on one leg with the other leg held in a curved position at 90 degrees. The arms in *4th position* together with the line through the upper back and chest and the placing of the raised leg create a strongly poised position. Adapted from Giambologna's bronze statue known as the flying Mercury (1580) and codified in the early 19th century by the Italian ballet master Carlo Blasis. The three basic *attitudes* are *attitude derrière en croisé, attitude devant en croisé,* and *attitude derrière en ouvert*, although many variations are possible. When performed *à terre,* the *working leg* is stretched with the tip of the foot contacting the floor. The arms may be placed in *4th position* (one overhead, the other side) or *5th position* (both overhead), in which case the position is called *attitude à deux bras.* When the same arm as the *working leg* is placed overhead in *4th*, the position is called *attitude* or *attitude ordinaire.* When the arm opposite to the *working leg* is placed overhead in *4th*, the position is called *attitude in opposition* or *attitude opposition.* See *attitude devant, attitude derrière, attitude à terre, attitude en l'air, attitude in opposition, attitude opposition, attitude ordinaire, attitude à deux bras.* Variations: *attitude à dos, attitude grecque.*

attitude à deux bras [atityd a døbʀa] a-tee-TUD a duh bra (Fr. pose; with two arms.) An *attitude* in which both arms are placed overhead in *5th position.*

attitude à dos [atityd a do] a-tee-TUD a doh (Fr. pose; with the back.) An *attitude* taken *en croisé* with a strong *épaulement* so that the back is visible to the audience.

attitude à terre [atityd a tɛʀ] a-tee-TUD a ter (Fr. pose; on the ground.) A position in which the *working leg* is in *pointe tendu* either *devant* or *derrière* and the arms are in *attitude.* See *attitude ordinaire, attitude opposition, attitude à deux bras.*

attitude derrière en croisé [atityd dɛʀjɛʀ ɑ̃ kʀwaze] a-tee-TUD der-YER ah krwa-ZAY (Fr. pose; behind; crossed.) A basic *attitude* taken facing either *downstage* corner, standing on the *downstage* leg, with the arms in *4th position* with the *upstage* arm raised. The head is turned and slightly raised so that the *eye line* is towards the opposite *downstage* corner. The *upstage* leg is held *en l'air* with the thigh at 90 degrees. The lower part of the leg is centred behind the body and parallel to the floor. The knee is at an angle of 90 degrees.

attitude derrière en ouvert [atityd dɛʀjɛʀ ɑ̃ nuvɛʀ] a-tee-TUD der-YER ah noo-VER (Fr. pose; behind; open.) A basic *attitude* taken facing either *downstage* corner, standing on the *upstage* leg, with the arms in *4th position* with the *downstage* arm raised. The head is turned and slightly raised so that the *eye line* is between 1 *(downstage)* and the other *downstage* corner. The *downstage* leg is held *en l'air* with the thigh at 90 degrees. The heel is centred behind the body with the knee less bent than in *attitude derrière en croisé.*

attitude devant en croisé [atityd d(ə)vɑ̃ ɑ̃ kʀwaze] a-tee-TUD d(u)-VAH ah krwa-ZAY (Fr. pose; front; crossed.) A basic *attitude* taken facing either *downstage* corner, standing on the *upstage* leg, with the arms in *4th position* with the *upstage* arm raised. The head is turned and slightly raised so that the eye line is directed towards 1 *(downstage).* The *downstage* leg is held *en l'air* with the thigh at 90 degrees. The lower part of the leg is centred in front of the body with the knee at an angle of 90 degrees, slightly higher than the foot.

attitude devant in opposition [atityd d(ə)vɑ̃ -] a-tee-TUD d(u)-VAH – (Fr. pose; front; opposite.) An *attitude devant* performed with the arms in *4th position*, the arm opposite to the *working leg* placed overhead.

attitude en l'air [atityd ɑ̃ lɛʀ] a-tee-TUD ah ler (Fr. pose; in the air.) An *attitude* in which the *working leg* is lifted in the air either *devant* or *derrière* and the arms are in *attitude.* See *attitude ordinaire, attitude opposition, attitude à deux bras.*

attitude grecque [atityd gʀɛk] a-tee-TUD grek (Fr. pose; Greek.) An *attitude* in which the arms are *4th crossed* and the leg corresponding to the lower arm is *cou-de-pied derrière* fully stretched, the head is turned toward the *working leg* and the *eye line* is slightly lowered. May be performed *en fondu*.

attitude opposition [atityd ɔpozisjɔ̃] a-tee-TUD o-poh-zees-YO (Fr. pose; opposite.) A position taken with the *working leg* in *attitude*, the arm opposite to the *working leg* in *5th*, and the other arm in *2nd*. Also called *attitude in opposition.*

attitude ordinaire [atityd ɔʀdinɛʀ] a-tee-TUD or-dee-NER (Fr. pose; ordinary.) A position taken with the *working leg* in *attitude*, the arm corresponding to the *working leg* in *5th,* and the other arm in *2nd*.

attitude ordinaire à terre [atityd ɔʀdinɛʀ a tɛʀ] a-tee-TUD or-dee-NER a ter (Fr. pose; ordinary.) A position taken with the *working leg* extended *to 4th* either *devant* or *derrière*, with the arm corresponding to the *working leg* in *5th* and the other arm in *2nd.*

attitude ordinaire en l'air See *attitude ordinaire.*

avant [avɑ̃] a-VAH (Fr. nm front.) See *en avant*.

back bend A movement up and slightly backward in the upper back; this movement increases slightly at the Advanced level.

balance A term used to describe the action of maintaining equilibrium in a sustained position without the support of the *barre*, usually when the dancer is *en demi-pointe/s*, *en pointe/s*, or supported on one leg.

balancé [balɑ̃se] ba-lah-SAY (Fr. pp of v balancer, to rock, swing, sway to and fro, find counterbalance or equilibrium; adj rocked, balanced; nm in dance, a balanced step.) A lyrical *terre à terre* movement set on a waltz rhythm where the accent is on the first step. Comprises three transferences of weight, often done in series from side to side or forward and backward. May be performed *en avant*, *en arrière*, *de côté*, or *en tournant*. Also referred to as *pas balancé.*

balancé de côté [balɑ̃se də kote] ba-lah-SAY d(u) koh-TAY (Fr. balanced step; to the side.) A *balancé* from side to side. 1. Performed by girls. From *classical pose,* the movement commences with a *fondu* on the *supporting leg*, extending the *working leg* with a light sliding movement towards *2nd;* the weight is then transferred sideways onto that foot *en fondu*. This action allows the other foot to be released, bringing it momentarily to the *cou-de-pied derrière* before transferring the weight first onto the *half-pointe* of that foot and then again onto the initial *working foot en fondu*. There is a slight sideways bend of the body over the front leg, with the arms flowing from *3rd* to *3rd position* or from *4th* to *4th position* with the initial step, and the head and eyes following the line of the movement. 2. Performed by boys. As for girls, but with a broader movement and deeper use of *fondu*. The incoming foot in *cou-de-pied* has a relaxed ankle. The hand corresponding to the initial *supporting leg* may be held on the hip with fingers forward. The other arm may begin in *1st position,* and open to a wide *demi-bras* on the initial step. When taken in series, the arm may return to *1st* on the initial step of the second *balancé* with the opposite shoulder forward to the front foot (i.e., in opposition), and so on. Variation: *balancé de côté en arrière.*

balancé de côté en arrière [balɑ̃se də kote ɑ̃ naʀjɛʀ] ba-lah-SAY d(u) koh-TAY ah-nar-YER (Fr. balanced step; to the side; backward.) A *balancé* taken sideways and travelling backward. Usually done in series with the first action in each *balancé* taken sideways and slightly backward to create a zig-zag path.

balancé en arrière [balɑ̃se ɑ̃ naʀjɛʀ] ba-lah-SAY ah-nar-YER (Fr. balanced step; backward.) A *balancé* performed with the initial step taken backward.

balancé en avant [balɑ̃se ɑ̃ navɑ] ba-lah-SAY ah na-VAH (Fr. balanced step; forward.) A *balancé* performed with the initial step taken forward.

balancé en tournant [balɑ̃se ɑ̃ tuʀnɑ̃] ba-lah-SAY ah toor-NAH (Fr. balanced step; turning.) A *balancé* performed while turning. Usually performed in series, making a 1/2-turn on each *balancé*. The dancer usually begins by stepping into the *line of dance* and performs the turn through the second and third actions of the *balancé*, with the first *balancé* turning into the *line of dance* and the second completing the turn. May be performed with footwork similar to *pas de valse*.

ballon [balɔ̃] ba-LO (Fr. nm ball or balloon; in dance, buoyant quality.) Resilience in jumping actions, resulting in a buoyant quality.

ballonné [balɔne] ba-lo-NAY (Fr. pp of v ballonner, to blow up like a balloon; adj inflated; nm a light jump on one leg.) A travelling jump from one leg landing on the same leg, combined with an outward extension and inward bending action of the *working leg.* At the height of the jump both legs are fully stretched, with the push-off leg maintaining its line beneath the body. Executed *sur place* with the *working leg* extending *devant, à la seconde,* or *derrière*, or travelled in the direction of the extended *working leg, en avant, de côté,* or *en arrière.* Also called *ballonné simple.* Variation: *ballonné composé.*

ballonné composé [balɔne kɔ̃poze] ba-lo-NAY ko-poh-ZAY (Fr. light jump on one foot; compound.) Composite step consisting of a *ballonné*, a quick extension leading into a step, and a close. May be performed *en avant*, *en arrière*, or *de côté*. Usually performed to one bar of 3/4 music, such as a polonaise or a mazurka.

ballonné composé de côté [balɔne kɔ̃poze də kote] ba-lo-NAY ko-poh-ZAY d(u) koh-TAY (Fr. light jump on one foot; compound; to the side.) A *ballonné composé* consisting of a *ballonné de côté*, a step sideways extending the other leg, then a close into *5th position.* May be performed *devant* or *derrière*, and *passé devant* or *derrière.*

ballonné composé de côté derrière [balɔne kɔ̃poze də kote dɛʀjɛʀ] ba-lo-NAY ko-poh-ZAY d(u) koh-TAY der-YER (Fr. light jump on one foot; compound; to the side; behind.) A *ballonné composé de côté* in which the back foot extends *to 2nd* in the air and ends mid-calf upon alighting.

ballonné composé de côté devant [balɔne kɔ̃poze də kote d(ə)vɑ̃] ba-lo-NAY ko-poh-ZAY d(u) koh-TAY d(u)-VAH (Fr. light jump on one foot; compound; to the side; front.) A *ballonné composé de côté* in which the front foot extends *to 2nd* in the air and ends mid-shin upon alighting.

ballonné composé de côté passé derrière [balɔne kɔ̃poze də kote pɑse dɛʀjɛʀ] ba-lo-NAY ko-poh-ZAY d(u) koh-TAY pah-SAY der-YER (Fr. light jump on one foot; compound; to the side; passing; behind.) A *ballonné composé de côté* in which the front foot extends *to 2nd* in the air and ends mid-calf upon alighting.

ballonné composé de côté passé devant [balɔne kɔ̃poze də kote pɑse d(ə)vɑ̃] ba-lo-NAY ko-poh-ZAY d(u) koh-TAY pah-SAY d(u)-VAH (Fr. light jump on one foot; compound; to the side; passing; front.) A *ballonné composé de côté* in which the back foot extends *to 2nd* in the air and ends mid-shin upon alighting.

ballonné composé en arrière [balɔne kɔ̃poze ɑ̃ naʀjɛʀ] ba-lo-NAY ko-poh-ZAY ah nar-YER (Fr. light jump on one foot; compound; backward.) A *ballonné composé* consisting of a *ballonné en arrière*, a step backward with the front leg extending, then a close into *5th position.*

ballonné composé en avant [balɔne kɔ̃poze ɑ̃ navɑ̃] ba-lo-NAY ko-poh-ZAY ah na-VAH (Fr. light jump on one foot; compound; forward.) A *ballonné composé* consisting of a *ballonné en avant*, a step forward with the back leg extending, then a close into *5th position.*

ballonné de côté [balɔne də kote] ba-lo-NAY d(u) koh-TAY (Fr. light jump on one foot; to the side.) A *ballonné* in which the *working leg* extends *to 2nd* and the movement travels sideways. May be started with either the front foot or the back foot performing the extension, and ended either mid-shin or mid-calf, without a change *(devant* or *derrière)* or with a change *(passé).* Also *ballonné simple de côté.*

ballonné de côté derrière [balɔne də kote dɛʀjɛʀ] ba-lo-NAY d(u) koh-TAY der-YER (Fr. light jump on one foot; to the side; behind.) A *ballonné de côté* in which the back foot extends *to 2nd* in the air and ends mid-calf.

ballonné de côté devant [balɔne də kote d(ə)vɑ̃] ba-lo-NAY d(u) koh-TAY d(u)-VAH (Fr. light jump on one foot; to the side; front.) A *ballonné de côté* in which the front foot extends *to 2nd* in the air and ends mid-shin.

ballonné de côté passé derrière [balɔne də kote pɑse dɛʀjɛʀ] ba-lo-NAY d(u) koh-TAY pah-SAY der-YER (Fr. light jump on one foot; to the side; passed; behind.) A *ballonné de côté* in which the front foot extends *to 2nd* in the air and ends mid-calf.

ballonné de côté passé devant [balɔne də kote pɑse d(ə)vɑ̃] ba-lo-NAY d(u) koh-TAY pah-SAY d(u)-VAH (Fr. light jump on one foot; to the side; passed; front.) A *ballonné de côté* in which the back foot extends *to 2nd* in the air and ends mid-shin.

ballonné derrière [balɔne dɛʀjɛʀ] ba-lo-NAY der-YER (Fr. light jump on one foot; behind.)

A *ballonné* in which the *working leg* extends *derrière* at the height of the jump and the foot is placed mid-calf upon alighting, without travel.

ballonné devant [balɔne d(ə)vɑ̃] ba-lo-NAY d(u)-VAH (Fr. light jump on one foot; front.) A *ballonné* in which the *working leg* extends *devant* at the height of the jump and the foot is placed mid-shin upon alighting, without travel.

ballonné devant en tournant [balɔne d(ə)vɑ̃ ɑ turnɑ̃] ba-lo-NAY d(u)-VAH ah toor-NAH (Fr. light jump on one foot; front; turning.) A *ballonné devant* in which the dancer turns while in the air away from the leg which pushed off.

ballonné en arrière [balɔne ɑ̃ naʀjɛʀ] ba-lo-NAY ah nar-YER (Fr. light jump on one foot; backward.) A ballonné in which the *working leg* extends back and the movement travels backward. With the *working foot* placed *derrière* at mid-calf level, the movement commences with a *fondu,* then springs off the push-off leg coordinating with the extension of the *working leg* to 45 degrees *derrière.* This movement travels backward. Maintaining the height of the working thigh, the leg bends and is brought in to its starting position with the conclusion of the jump. May be taken *en ouvert* with the arms in *3rd position,* the arm opposite the *working leg* forward, with the head and *eye line* to 1 (downstage).

ballonné en avant [balɔne ɑ̃ navɑ̃] ba-lo-NAY ah na-VAH (Fr. light jump on one foot; forward.) A *ballonné* in which the *working leg* extends front and the movement travels forward. With the little toe of the *working foot* placed in contact with the middle of the shin of the *supporting leg,* the movement commences with a *fondu,* then springs off the push-off leg coordinating with the extension of the *working leg* to 45 degrees *devant.* This movement travels forward. Maintaining the height of the working thigh, the leg bends and is brought in to its starting position with the conclusion of the jump. May be taken *en ouvert* with the arms in *3rd position,* the arm opposite the *working leg* forward, with the head and *eye line* to 1 (downstage).

ballonné simple [balɔne sɛ̃pl(ə)] ba-lo-NAY sepl(u) (Fr. light jump on one foot; simple.) See *ballonné.*

ballotté [balɔte] ba-lo-TAY (Fr. pp of v balloter, to toss about; nm a tossed step.) A rocking movement in which the weight is transferred from one foot to another. May be performed with an *adage* quality, *sauté* with an *allegro* quality, or *en pointe.* In the *adage* version, the initial leg may begin *à terre,* then pass through *5th position en demi-pointe;* or *en l'air,* then pass through *retiré,* after which the released leg unfolds. In the *allegro* version, the initial leg may begin *à terre* or *en l'air* with the knees bending and the ankles crossing at the height of the jump, after which the released leg unfolds. Often performed in series *dessous* and *dessus.* Variation: *petit ballotté.*

ballotté dessous [balɔte d(ə)su] ba-lo-TAY d(u)-SOO (Fr. tossed step; under.) A *ballotté* in which the dancer begins with the back leg extended *à terre* or *en l'air;* s/he then draws the foot into *5th en demi-pointes* (passing through *retiré derrière* from an *en l'air* position), releases the front foot and performs a *développé devant* to 90 degrees *en fondu.*

ballotté dessus [balɔte d(ə)sy] ba-lo-TAY d(u)-SU (Fr. tossed step; over.) A *ballotté* in which the dancer begins with the front leg extended *à terre* or *en l'air;* s/he then draws the foot into *5th en demi-pointes* (passing through *retiré devant* from an *en l'air* position), releases the back foot, and performs a *développé derrière* to 90 degrees *en fondu.*

ballotté sauté [balɔte sote] ba-lo-TAY soh-TAY (Fr. tossed step, jumped.) A rocking movement in which the weight is transferred by jumping from one foot to another. The initial leg may begin *à terre* or *en l'air,* with the knees bending and the ankles crossing at the height of the jump, after which the released leg unfolds. Often performed in series *dessous* and *dessus.*

ballotté sauté dessous [balɔte sote d(ə)su] ba-lo-TAY soh-TAY d(u)-SOO (Fr. tossed step; jumped; under.) A *ballotté sauté* in which the dancer begins with the back leg extended *à terre* or *en l'air;* s/he *springs* into the air, with the knees bending and the ankles crossing at the height of the jump, then lands *en fondu* while unfolding the front leg forward through *retiré devant,* often ending *en ouvert* with the arms *3rd opposition.*

ballotté sauté dessus [balɔte sote d(ə)sy] ba-lo-TAY soh-TAY d(u)-SU (Fr. tossed step; jumped; over.) A *ballotté sauté* in which the dancer begins with the front leg extended *à terre* or *en l'air;* s/he *springs* into the air, with the knees bending and the ankles crossing at the height of the jump, then lands *en fondu* while unfolding the back leg backward through *retiré derrière*, often ending *en ouvert* with the arms *3rd opposition*.

barre [ba(ɑ)ʀ] bar (Fr. nf rod or bar.) The horizontal rod used by dancers to steady themselves during a series of basic exercises. When placed on the *barre,* the hands should never be lower than the elbows allowing the dancer to exert a light pressure downward through the palm. Two basic positions of the body at the *barre:* 1. Facing the *barre.* With the hips squared to the *barre,* both hands are placed on the barre at shoulder width apart with the elbows slightly in front of the body and relaxed; the hands are directly in front of the elbows, and the line of the wrists is unbroken; the fingers rest lightly on the top of the *barre.* 2. Sideways to the *barre.* With the body at a right angle to the *barre* the near hand is placed so that the elbow is slightly in front of the body and relaxed, with the line of the wrist unbroken; the palm rests lightly on the top of the barre. In this position, the dancer is able to move slightly forward, sideways, and backward, without displacing the hand unless a complete *transfer of weight* is made. See *barre work.*

barre work [ba(ɑ)ʀ -] bar – (Fr. nf rod or bar; work.) Basic movements which are studied in the first section of a class, when the dancer prepares his or her mind and body through a series of exercises designed to introduce and reinforce the basic components of ballet technique. These exercises warm, tone, strengthen, and stretch the muscles of the entire body, and form the basis for all that follows in *centre practice, adage,* and *allegro.* They are practised almost as a ritual throughout the dancer's life, initially to build basic technical skills and ultimately to keep the dancer's instrument finely tuned.

bas [ba] ba (Fr. adj adv low; nm bottom.) See *position of the arm, bras bas.*

basque [bask] bask (Fr. nmf Basque language or person; adj from the Basque region of France.) See *pas de basque, saut de basque.*

battement [batmɑ̃] bat-MAH (Fr. nm a beat or beating action.) A beating action of the *working leg*, usually involving a movement away from and toward the body. May be performed *devant, to 2nd, derrière, sur le cou-de-pied, en rond.* Variations: *single, double, serrés.* See *battement balancé, battement fondu, battement frappé, battement fouetté, battement frappé fouetté, battement glissé, battement jeté, battement piqué, battement tendu, petit battement, grand battement, jeté battement.*

battement balancé [batmɑ̃ balɑ̃se] bat-MAH ba-lah-SAY (Fr. beating; rocked.) An *adage* action in which the *working leg* swings from front to back or back to front through *1st position.*

battement dégagé [batmɑ̃ degaʒe] bat-MAH day-ga-ZHAY (Fr. beating; disengaged.) A term of the Cecchetti method. See *battement glissé.*

battement en cloche See *grand battement en cloche.*

battement en cloche derrière See *grand battement en cloche derrière.*

battement en cloche devant See *grand battement en cloche devant.*

battement en cloche, grand See *grand battement en cloche.*

battement fondu [batmɑ̃ fɔ̃dy] bat-MAH fo-DU (Fr. beating; melted.) A smoothly coordinated bending and stretching of both the *supporting leg* and the *working leg.* An essential exercise for developing strength and control for jumps. From *5th position* or *dégagé,* the *working foot* is placed *sur le cou-de-pied* while the *supporting leg* bends to the depth of a *demi-plié.* The *working leg* then opens through a small *attitude* to extend to 45 degrees, as the *supporting leg* simultaneously straightens. May be executed with the *working leg* extending *devant, to 2nd,* or *derrière.* Often practised *en croix. May be taken with the supporting foot* remaining flat or rising as the legs straighten. Variation: *battement fondu à terre, double fondu.*

battement fondu à terre [batmɑ̃ fɔ̃dy a tɛʀ] bat-MAH fo-DU a ter (Fr. beating; melted; on the ground.) A *battement fondu* in which the *working leg* extends to *dégagé* (i.e., toes of the fully stretched foot in contact with the floor) as the *supporting leg* simultaneously straightens. Performed *devant, to 2nd,* or *derrière,* with the *supporting foot* remaining flat.

battement fondu à terre derrière [batmɑ̃ fɔ̃dy a tɛʀ dɛʀjɛʀ] bat-MAH fo-DU a ter der-YER (Fr. beating; melted; on the ground; behind.) A *battement fondu* in which the *working leg* extends to *dégagé derrière* as the *supporting leg* simultaneously straightens.

battement fondu à terre devant [batmɑ̃ fɔ̃dy a tɛʀ d(ə)vɑ̃] bat-MAH fo-DU a ter d(u)-VAH (Fr. beating; melted; on the ground; front.) A *battement fondu* in which the *working leg* extends to *dégagé devant* as the *supporting leg* simultaneously straightens.

battement fondu à terre to 2nd [batmɑ̃ fɔ̃dy a tɛʀ -] bat-MAH fo-DU a ter – (Fr. beating; melted; on the ground; to 2nd.) A *battement fondu* in which the *working leg* extends to *dégagé to 2nd* as the *supporting leg* simultaneously straightens.

battement fondu derrière [batmɑ̃ fɔ̃dy dɛʀjɛʀ] bat-MAH fo-DU der-YER (Fr. beating; melted; behind.) A *battement fondu* in which the *working leg* extends to 45 degrees *derrière* as the *supporting leg* simultaneously straightens.

battement fondu devant [batmɑ̃ fɔ̃dy d(ə)vɑ̃] bat-MAH fo-DU d(u)-VAH (Fr. beating; melted; front.) A *battement fondu* in which the *working leg* extends to 45 degrees *devant* as the *supporting leg* simultaneously straightens.

battement fondu to 2nd [batmɑ̃ fɔ̃dy -] bat-MAH fo-DU – (Fr. beating; melted; to 2nd.) A *battement fondu* in which the *working leg* extends to 45 degrees *to 2nd* as the *supporting leg* simultaneously straightens.

battement fouetté [batmɑ̃ fwɛte] bat-MAH fwe-TAY (Fr. beating; whipped.) A whipping action of the *working leg en l'air* 45 degrees between *2nd* and *4th position*. May be performed to *4th devant* or *4th derrière*, and with a *fondu* in *4th*. Variation: *grand battement fouetté*.

battement fouetté to 4th derrière [batmɑ̃ fwɛte - dɛʀjɛʀ] bat-MAH fwe-TAY – der-YER (Fr. beating; whipped; to 4th behind.) A *battement fouetté* in which the dancer begins with the *working leg* extended *to 2nd en l'air*, then strongly moves it to *4th derrière* and again *to 2nd*.

battement fouetté to 4th devant [batmɑ̃ fwɛte - d(ə)vɑ̃] bat-MAH fwe-TAY – d(u)-VAH (Fr. beating; whipped; to 4th front.) A *battement fouetté* in which the dancer begins with the *working leg* extended *to 2nd en l'air*, then strongly moves it to *4th devant* and again *to 2nd*.

battement frappé [batmɑ̃ fʀape] bat-MAH fra-PAY (Fr. beating; hit.) A striking action of the foot directed towards the floor using a strong extension of the leg. An exercise to develop speed and precision in the use of the foot and ankle. The flexed working ankle begins with the heel placed *sur le cou-de-pied,* then the metatarsals strike the floor and the leg and foot finish in a fully stretched position at *glissé height.* When the *supporting leg* is *en demi-pointe*, the ball of the *working foot* does not brush along the floor but extends directly outward. Taken with the extension *to 2nd, to 4th devant,* or *to 4th derrière.* Often performed in series, and practised *en croix.* Also called *single battement frappé*, or *battement frappé sur le cou-de-pied*. Variations: *double battement frappé*, *battement frappé fouetté*.

battement frappé derrière [batmɑ̃ fʀape dɛʀjɛʀ] bat-MAH fra-PAY der-YER (Fr. beating; hit; behind.) A *battement frappé* in which the flexed working ankle begins with the heel placed *sur le cou-de-pied derrière,* then the metatarsals strike the floor and the leg and foot finish in a fully stretched position *derrière* at *glissé height.*

battement frappé devant [batmɑ̃ fʀape d(ə)vɑ̃] bat-MAH fra-PAY d(u)-VAH (Fr. beating; hit; front.) A *battement frappé* in which the flexed working ankle begins with the heel placed *sur le cou-de-pied devant,* then the metatarsals strike the floor and the leg and foot finish in a fully stretched position *devant* at *glissé height.*

battement frappé devant, double See *double battement frappé devant*.

battement frappé fouetté [batmɑ̃ fʀape fwɛte] bat-MAH fra-PAY fwe-TAY (Fr. beating; hit; whipped.) An inward whipping action of the lower leg. Commencing with the leg extended *to 2nd* at 45 degrees, the working knee bends so that the foot is brought sharply into contact with the *supporting leg* either *devant* or *derrière.* The *working foot* is fully pointed throughout. May be performed *devant* or *derrière.*

battement frappé fouetté derrière [batmɑ̃ fʀape fwɛte dɛʀjɛʀ] bat-MAH fra-PAY fwe-TAY der-YER (Fr. beating; hit; whipped; behind.) A *battement frappé fouetté* in which the foot is brought sharply into contact with the back of the *supporting leg.*

battement frappé fouetté devant [batmɑ̃ fʀape fwɛte d(ə)vɑ̃] bat-MAH fra-PAY fwe-TAY d(u)-VAH (Fr. beating; hit; whipped; front.) A *battement frappé fouetté* in which the foot is brought sharply into contact with the front of the *supporting leg.*

battement frappé sur le cou-de-pied See *battement frappé.*

battement frappé to 2nd [batmɑ̃ fʀape -] bat-MAH fra-PAY – (Fr. beating; hit; to 2nd.) A *battement frappé* in which the flexed working ankle begins with the heel placed *sur le cou-de-pied devant* or *derrière,* then the metatarsals strike the floor and the leg and foot finish in a fully stretched position *to 2nd* at *glissé height.*

battement frappé to 2nd, double See *double battement frappé to 2nd.*

battement glissé [batmɑ̃ glise] bat-MAH glee-SAY (Fr. beating; sliding.) An opening and closing of the fully stretched *working leg* with a quick gliding action of the foot which causes the toes to be released just off the floor. Practised to develop speed of footwork. May commence from *1st* or *5th position.* Taken *devant, to 2nd,* or *derrière,* usually with the arms held in *bras bas* or *2nd position.* Variations: *battement glissé en cloche, battement glissé sur la pointe.* In the Cecchetti method, this action is known as *battement dégagé.*

battement glissé derrière [batmɑ̃ glise dɛʀjɛʀ] bat-MAH glee-SAY der-YER (Fr. beating; sliding; behind.) A *battement glissé* in which the *working leg* opens backward.

battement glissé dessous sur la pointe [batmɑ̃ glise d(ə)su syʀ la pwɛ̃t] bat-MAH glee-SAY d(u)-SOO sur la pwet (Fr. beating; sliding; under; on tiptoe.) A *battement glissé* performed *en pointes,* with the *working foot* commencing *5th devant,* opening *to 2nd,* and closing *5th derrière.* See *battement glissé sur la pointe.*

battement glissé dessus sur la pointe [batmɑ̃ glise d(ə)sy syʀ la pwɛ̃t] bat-MAH glee-SAY d(u)-SU sur la pwet (Fr. beating; sliding; over; on tiptoe.) A *battement glissé* performed *en pointes,* with the *working foot* commencing *5th derrière,* opening *to 2nd,* and closing *5th devant.* See *battement glissé sur la pointe.*

battement glissé devant [batmɑ̃ glise d(ə)vɑ̃] bat-MAH glee-SAY d(u)-VAH (Fr. beating; sliding; front.) A *battement glissé* in which the *working leg* opens forward.

battement glissé en cloche [batmɑ̃ glise ɑ̃ klɔʃ] bat-MAH glee-SAY ah klosh (Fr. beating; sliding; like a bell.) A continuous swinging action of the *working leg* forward and backward through *1st position,* opening to the same height as a *battement glissé.* May be performed commencing *devant* and ending *derrière,* commencing *derrière* and ending *devant,* and in series commencing *devant* or *derrière.*

battement glissé en croix [batmɑ̃ glise ɑ̃ kʀwa] bat-MAH glee-SAY ah krwa (Fr. beating; sliding; crosswise.) A series of *battements glissés* performed *devant, to 2nd, derrière,* and again *to 2nd.*

battement glissé relevé [batmɑ̃ glise ʀəlve] bat-MAH glee-SAY r(u)l-VAY (Fr. beating; sliding; pulled up.) A *battement glissé* performed with a *relevé en pointe.* Commencing *5th position en demi-plié,* the *working foot* slides outward along the floor *en fondu* firmly and with speed, extending to *glissé height,* and the *supporting leg* performs a *relevé* action. The leg may close to *5th position* either *en pointes* or *en demi-plié.* May be performed *devant, to 2nd,* or *derrière.*

battement glissé relevé derrière [batmɑ̃ glise ʀəlve dɛʀjɛʀ] bat-MAH glee-SAY r(u)l-VAY der-YER (Fr. beating; sliding; pulled up; behind.) A *battement glissé relevé* performed with the *working leg* beginning *5th derrière* and extending backward.

battement glissé relevé devant [batmɑ̃ glise ʀəlve d(ə)vɑ̃] bat-MAH glee-SAY r(u)l-VAY d(u)-VAH (Fr. beating; sliding; pulled up; front.) A *battement glissé relevé* performed with the *working leg* beginning *5th devant* and extending forward.

battement glissé relevé to 2nd [batmɑ̃ glise ʀəlve -] bat-MAH glee-SAY r(u)l-VAY – (Fr. beating; sliding; pulled up; to 2nd.) A *battement glissé relevé* performed with the *working leg* beginning *5th position* and extending to the side.

battement glissé sur la pointe [batmɑ̃ glise syʀ la pwɛ̃t] bat-MAH glee-SAY sur la pwet (Fr. beating; sliding; on tiptoe.) A *battement glissé* in which the dancer starts in *5th position en pointes,* slides the tip of the *working foot* outward *to 2nd* at *glissé height,* then slides the tip of the foot inward to close *5th position,* usually with a *change of feet.* May be performed *dessus* or *dessous.*

battement glissé sur la pointe dessous [batmɑ̃ glise syʀ la pwɛ̃t d(ə)su] bat-MAH glee-SAY sur la pwet d(u)-SOO (Fr. beating; sliding; on tiptoe;

under.) A *battement glissé* in which the dancer starts in *5th position devant en pointes*, slides the tip of the *working foot* outward *to 2nd* at *glissé height*, then slides the tip of the foot inward to close *5th position derrière*, with a *change of feet*.

battement glissé sur la pointe dessus [batmɑ̃ glise syʀ la pwɛ̃t d(ə)sy] bat-MAH glee-SAY sur la pwet d(u)-SU (Fr. beating; sliding; on tiptoe; over.) A *battement glissé* in which the dancer starts in *5th position derrière en pointes*, slides the tip of the *working foot* outward *to 2nd* at *glissé height*, then slides the tip of the foot inward to close *5th position devant*, with a *change of feet*.

battement glissé to 2nd [batmɑ̃ glise -] bat-MAH glee-SAY – (Fr. beating; sliding; to 2nd.) A *battement glissé* in which the *working leg* opens to the side.

battement jeté [batmɑ̃ ʒ(ə)te] bat-MAH zh(u)-TAY (Fr. beating; thrown.) A sharply thrown action of the *working leg* opening to 45 degrees and returning strongly to a closed position. Used for developing strength and turnout, and important in the preparation of *allegro* steps. The foot slides along the floor as in *battement tendu* and the leg is thrown out in the required direction to a fully stretched position at 45 degrees. The leg returns firmly with strong use of the foot along the floor to a closed position. May be executed beginning from *1st* or *5th position* and opening *devant, to 2nd,* or *derrière.* Variation: *battement jeté en cloche.*

battement jeté derrière [batmɑ̃ ʒ(ə)te dɛʀjɛʀ] bat-MAH zh(u)-TAY der-YER (Fr. beating; thrown; behind.) A *battement jeté* in which the *working leg* is thrown backward.

battement jeté devant [batmɑ̃ ʒ(ə)te d(ə)vɑ̃] bat-MAH zh(u)-TAY d(u)-VAH (Fr. beating; thrown; front.) A *battement jeté* in which the *working leg* is thrown forward.

battement jeté en cloche [batmɑ̃ ʒ(ə)te ɑ̃ klɔʃ] bat-MAH zh(u)-TAY ah klosh (Fr. beating; thrown; like a bell.) A continuous swinging action of the *working leg* forward and backward through *1st position* opening to the same height as a *battement jeté,* i.e., 45 degrees. May be performed commencing *devant* and ending *derrière*, commencing *derrière* and ending *devant*, and in series commencing *devant* or *derrière*.

battement jeté to 2nd [batmɑ̃ ʒ(ə)te -] bat-MAH zh(u)-TAY – (Fr. beating; thrown; to 2nd.) A *battement jeté* in which the *working leg* is thrown outward to the side.

battement piqué [batmɑ̃ pike] bat-MAH pee-KAY (Fr. beating; pricked.) A *battement glissé* action in which the *working foot* opens *to glissé height*, lowers *à terre* remaining fully stretched, and rebounds quickly and lightly to the previous height. May be performed *devant*, *to 2nd*, or *derrière*. Variations: *battement piqué en rond*, *double battement piqué*, *grand battement piqué*.

battement tendu [batmɑ̃ tɑ̃dy] bat-MAH tah-DU (Fr. beating; outstretched.) The opening and closing of a stretched *working leg à terre.* Practised to strengthen the use of the foot and to bring all the foot and leg muscles into play on both the outward and inward movements. From *1st* or *5th position,* the *working leg* is released with an outward sliding action of the foot, continuing through the metatarsals, until the ankle, instep, and toes are fully stretched and well aligned. To close, the working leg is drawn inward, reversing the sliding action of the foot which ends in *1st* or *5th position.* Taken *devant, to 2nd,* or *derrière; en fondu* on the opening action and *en demi-plié* or *en demi-pointes* on the closing action; and in series *en avant* or *en arrière*.

battement tendu derrière [batmɑ̃ tɑ̃dy dɛʀjɛʀ] bat-MAH tah-DU der-YER (Fr. beating; outstretched; behind.) A *battement tendu* in which the *working foot* opens to the back.

battement tendu devant [batmɑ̃ tɑ̃dy d(ə)vɑ̃] bat-MAH tah-DU d(u)-VAH (Fr. beating; outstretched; front.) A *battement tendu* in which the *working foot* opens to the front.

battement tendu relevé [batmɑ̃ tɑ̃dy ʀəlve] bat-MAH tah-DU r(u)l-VAY (Fr. beating; outstretched; pulled up.) A *battement tendu* in which the *working foot* is extended to *dégagé*, then drawn in until the heel contacts the floor, and re-extended sharply before the closing. Usually performed *to 2nd*.

battement tendu to 2nd [batmɑ̃ tɑ̃dy -] bat-MAH tah-DU – (Fr. beating; outstretched; to 2nd.) A *battement tendu* in which the *working foot* opens to the side. When taken from *5th position,* the leg may close with or without *a change of feet.*

battement, grand See *grand battement*.

battement, petit See *petit battement*.

battements tendus en arrière [batmɑ̃ tɑ̃dy zɑ̃ naʀjɛʀ] bat-MAH tah-DU zah-nar-YER (Fr. beatings; outstretched; backward.) A series of *battements tendus to 2nd* alternating legs, with the *working leg* beginning *5th position devant* and closing *5th position derrière* so that the series retreats.

battements tendus en avant [batmɑ̃ tɑ̃dy zɑ̃ navɑ̃] bat-MAH tah-DU zah na-VAH (Fr. beatings; outstretched; forward.) A series of *battements tendus to 2nd* alternating legs, with the *working leg* beginning *5th position derrière* and closing *5th position devant* so that the series advances.

batterie [batʀi] bat-REE, bat-(u)-REE (Fr. nf the act of beating.) 1. Jumps performed with a beating action of the legs, comprising all types of *entrechats, brisés*, and steps that are embellished with a beat. In *batterie,* the legs open slightly with the jump, and the inward beating action causes the legs to open slightly before landing. See *battu, beats.* 2. A generic term for a sub-category of movements performed during the *Allegro* section of a class, after *allegro* and before *grand allegro.*

battu [baty] ba-TU (Fr. pp of v battre, to beat; adj beaten.) Embellished with a beating action of the legs. See *batterie, beats, échappé sauté battu, changement battu, assemblé battu, jeté battu, coupé fouetté raccourci battu, sissonne fermée battue, sissonne ouverte battue, petit battement battu, petit jeté battu, pas de basque battu.*

beats See *batterie, battu.*

bend A movement of the torso initiated by a *port de bras* incorporating use of the back. May be performed forward, to the side, or back. May involve only the upper body or, in the case of a *forward bend,* action at the hip joints. The recovery from bends usually retraces the path of the body.

bend back A movement up and slightly backward in the upper back; this movement increases slightly at the Advanced level.

bend of upper back A movement up and slightly backward in the upper back above the shoulder blades.

bend, forward See *forward bend.*

bend, full forward See *full forward bend.*

bend, side See *side bend.*

body alignment Phrase referring to the direction faced by the dancer in relation to the audience. The three basic *alignments* are *en face, en croisé,* and *en ouvert.* Secondary *alignments* are *de côté* and *en écarté.*

body positions See *poses of the body (9).*

bourrée [buʀe] boo-RAY (Fr. pp of v bourrer, to cram or stuff; nf a lively 17th century Fr. dance usually in quick duple time; music for that dance or characterized by its rhythmic form, often part of a classical suite.) See *pas de bourrée.*

bow See *révérence.*

bras [bʀa] bra (Fr. nm an arm or arms.) See *port de bras, position of the arms.*

bras bas See *position of the arms, bras bas.*

breathing arm Term used to describe the action of an arm or arms opening from *bras bas* toward *demi-seconde* with an inhalation, and closing to *bras bas* with an exhalation. Not found in current RAD syllabus. Described in current syllabus as "arm to *demi-seconde* and *bras bas*."

brisé [bʀize] bree-ZAY (Fr. pp of v briser, to break or shatter; adj broken; nm in dance, a beaten jump.) A travelling, beaten step consisting of an outward brushing motion *en fondu*, a jump with the *supporting leg* beating against the *working leg*, and a landing *en demi-plié* or *en fondu.* The combination of the sliding movement of the *working leg* and the push-off from the *supporting leg* provides the force to spring into the air, bringing the *supporting leg* up to the extended leg to beat before changing to land on one foot or two. The travel occurs in the direction of the sliding movement. Usually involves a slight complementary action in the torso, head, and arms. May start and end in *5th position* (2 to 2); start in *5th position* and end with the initiating foot at the mid-calf or mid-shin (2 to 1), start and end with the initiating foot at the mid-calf or mid-shin (1 to 1), or start with the initiating foot at the mid-calf or mid-shin and end in *5th position* (1 to 2). A *brisé* which ends on two feet is similar to a beaten *assemblé,* except that a *brisé* usually travels, whereas an *assemblé* does not. May be performed *devant, derrière, dessous, dessus, en avant,* or *en arrière.* Variation: *brisé volé, coupé brisé.*

brisé 1 to 1 [bʀize -] bree-ZAY – (Fr. broken step; 1 to 1.) A *brisé* that begins and ends *en fondu* with the *working foot* placed at or slightly above *cou-de-pied.* The dancer starts *en fondu*, brushes the *working foot* above *glissé height,* jumps into the air beating the *supporting leg* against the *working leg*, and lands on the foot that pushed off *en fondu.* Variation: *coupé brisé derrière, coupé brisé devant, brisé volé.*

brisé 1 to 2 [bʀize -] bree-ZAY – (Fr. broken step; 1 to 2.) A *brisé* that begins *en fondu* with the *working foot* placed at or slightly above *cou-de-pied* and ends in *5th position.* The dancer starts *en fondu*, brushes the *working foot* above *glissé height,* jumps into the air beating the *supporting leg* against the *working leg*, and lands *en demi-plié.*

brisé 2 to 1 [bʀize -] bree-ZAY – (Fr. broken step; 2 to 1.) A *brisé* that begins in *5th position* and ends *en fondu* with the *working foot* placed at or slightly above *cou-de-pied.* The dancer starts *en demi-plié*, brushes the *working foot* above *glissé height,* jumps into the air beating the *supporting leg* against the *working leg*, and lands on the foot that pushed off *en fondu.*

brisé 2 to 2 [bʀize -] bree-ZAY – (Fr. broken step; 2 to 2.) A *brisé* that begins and ends in *5th position.* The dancer starts *en demi-plié*, brushes the *working foot* above *glissé height,* jumps into the air beating the *supporting leg* against the *working leg*, and lands *en demi-plié.*

brisé derrière [bʀize dɛʀjɛʀ] bree-ZAY der-YER (Fr. broken step; behind.) A *brisé* travelling sideways in which the *working leg* begins *5th derrière* and ends *5th devant.* As the *demi-plié* commences, the *working leg* begins to slide towards *2nd position* at *glissé height.* The combination of the sliding movement and the push-off from the *supporting leg* provides the force to spring into the air, bringing the *supporting leg* up to the extended leg to beat *devant* before changing to land in *5th position,* with the *working foot devant.*

brisé dessous [bʀize d(ə)su] bree-ZAY d(u)-SOO (Fr. broken step; under.) A *brisé* travelling sideways in which the *working leg* begins and ends *5th devant.* As the *demi-plié* commences, the *working leg* begins to slide towards *2nd position* at *glissé height.* The combination of the sliding movement and the push-off from the *supporting leg* provides the force to spring into the air, bringing the *supporting leg* up to the extended leg to beat *devant* before changing to land in *5th position,* with the *working foot devant.* The arms are usually held in *3rd position,* with the arm corresponding to the working leg placed forward, and with a slight *épaulement* bringing the same shoulder forward.

brisé dessus [bʀize d(ə)sy] bree-ZAY d(u)-SU (Fr. broken step; over.) A *brisé* travelling sideways in which the *working leg* begins and ends *5th derrière.* As the *demi-plié* commences, the *working leg* begins to slide towards *2nd position* at *glissé height.* The combination of the sliding movement and the push-off from the *supporting leg* provides the force to spring into the air, bringing the *supporting leg* up to the extended leg to beat *derrière* before changing to land in *5th position,* with the *working foot derrière.* The arms are usually held in *3rd position,* with the arm corresponding to the *working leg* placed forward, leaning slightly over the front arm, directing the *eye line* out and over the centre of the forearm.

brisé devant [bʀize d(ə)vɑ̃] bree-ZAY d(u)-VAH (Fr. broken step; front.) A *brisé* travelling sideways in which the *working leg* begins *5th devant* and ends *5th derrière.* As the *demi-plié* commences, the *working leg* begins to slide towards *2nd position* at *glissé height.* The combination of the sliding movement and the push-off from the *supporting leg* provides the force to spring into the air, bringing the *supporting leg* up to the extended leg to beat *derrière* before changing to land in *5th position,* with the *working foot derrière.*

brisé en arrière [bʀize ɑ̃ naʀjɛʀ] bree-ZAY ah-nar-YER (Fr. broken step; backward.) A *brisé* travelling backward in which the *working leg* begins *5th derrière* and ends *5th devant.* As the *demi-plié* commences, the *working leg* begins to slide towards *derrière* at *glissé height.* The combination of the sliding movement and the push-off from the *supporting leg* provides the force to spring into the air, bringing the *supporting leg* up to the extended leg to beat *devant* before changing to land in *5th position,* with the *working foot devant.*

brisé en avant [bʀize ɑ̃ navɑ̃] bree-ZAY ah na-VAH (Fr. broken step; forward.) A *brisé* travelling forward in which the *working leg* begins *5th devant* and ends *5th derrière.* As the *demi-plié* commences, the *working leg* begins to slide towards *devant* at *glissé height.* The combination of the sliding movement and the push-off from the *supporting leg* provides the force to spring into the air, bringing the *supporting leg* up to the extended leg to beat *derrière* before changing to land in *5th position*, with the *working foot derrière.*

brisé volé [bʀize vɔle] bree-ZAY vo-LAY (Fr. broken step; flying.) A variation of *brisé* 1 to 1, usually performed *sur place* in series, alternating *brisé volé devant* and *brisé volé derrière.* To start with a *brisé volé devant*, the dancer begins with the *working leg dégagé derrière*, brushes it through *1st position en demi-plié* to *devant* just above *glissé height*, pushes off and beats the *supporting leg* to the *working leg*, and alights on the initiating leg *en fondu*, with the new *working leg* extended *devant* just above *glissé height.* To continue with the *brisé volé derrière*, s/he brushes the foot through *1st position* or performs a *rond de jambe* action just off the floor to *derrière*, beats the *supporting leg* to the *working leg*, and alights on the initiating leg *en fondu*, with the new *working leg* extended *derrière* just above *glissé height*. The arms usually *undersweep* to *1st* on the *brisé volé devant* and open slightly behind *demi-seconde* for the *brisé volé derrière.* A series may travel slightly, moving forward along a diagonal line across the stage.

brisé volé derrière [bʀize vɔle dɛʀjɛʀ] bree-ZAY vo-LAY der-YER (Fr. broken step; flying; behind.) A *brisé volé* in which the dancer begins with the *working leg dégagé devant*, brushes the foot through *1st position* or performs a *rond de jambe* action just off the floor to *4th position derrière*, pushes off and beats the *supporting leg* to the *working leg*, and alights *sur place* on the initiating leg *en fondu*, with the new *working leg* extended *derrière* just above *glissé height.* The arms usually open slightly behind *demi-seconde*.

brisé volé devant [bʀize vɔle d(ə)vɑ̃] bree-ZAY vo-LAY d(u)-VAH (Fr. broken step; flying; front.) A *brisé volé* in which the dancer begins with the *working leg dégagé derrière*, brushes it through *1st position en demi-plié* to *4th position devant* just above *glissé height*, pushes off and beats the *supporting leg* to the *working leg*, and alights *sur place* on the initiating leg *en fondu*, with the new *working leg* extended in front just above *glissé height.*

cabriole [kabʀijɔl] ka-bree-YOL (< It. capriola, leap of a goat; Fr. nf a caper or jump in which the legs beat, one against the other.) A *grand allegro* jump in which one leg beats against the other either in front of, to the side of, or behind the body. The *working leg* may be extended *devant, to 2nd*, or *derrière* between 45 degrees and 90 degrees or above for men, depending on the musical tempo and context. May be performed *ouverte* or *fermée, de côté dessus* or *dessous,* and *fouettée.* When the *working leg* is extended no higher than 45 degrees, the jump is called *petite cabriole.*

cabriole fermée [kabʀijɔl fɛʀme] ka-bree-YOL fer-MAY (Fr. caper; closed.) A *cabriole* in which the dancer begins in *5th position*; s/he then brushes the *working foot en l'air* between 45 degrees and 90 degrees, jumps into the air beating the *supporting leg* against the *working leg* causing it to rebound, and lands on the leg that pushed off, with the extended leg closing *5th position en demi-plié* just after the landing. May be performed *devant, derrière, dessus, dessous*, or *de côté.*

cabriole fermée de côté [kabʀijɔl fɛʀme də kote] ka-bree-YOL fer-MAY d(u) koh-TAY (Fr. caper; closed; to the side.) A *cabriole* in which the dancer begins in *5th position;* s/he then brushes the *working foot to 2nd en l'air* between 45 degrees and 90 degrees, jumps into the air beating the *supporting leg* against the *working leg,* performing the *beat* to the side of the body causing the *working leg* to rebound, and lands on the leg that pushed off, with the extended leg closing *5th position en demi-plié* just after the landing. May be performed *dessus* or *dessous.*

cabriole fermée de côté dessus See *cabriole fermée dessus.*

cabriole fermée derrière [kabʀijɔl fɛʀme dɛʀjɛʀ] ka-bree-YOL fer-MAY der-YER (Fr. caper; closed; behind.) A *cabriole* in which the dancer begins in *5th position* with the *working leg derrière;* s/he brushes the back leg *derrière en l'air* between 45 degrees and 90 degrees, pushes off and beats in front of the *working leg*, performing the *beat* behind the body; s/he then lands on the same foot and immediately closes the extended leg *5th position derrière en demi-plié.*

cabriole fermée dessous [kabʀijɔl fɛʀme d(ə)su] ka-bree-YOL fer-MAY d(u)-SOO (Fr. caper; closed; under.) A *cabriole* in which the dancer begins in *5th position working foot devant;* s/he then brushes the *working foot to 2nd en l'air* between 45 degrees and 90 degrees, pushes off and beats the *supporting leg* in front of the *working leg*, performing the *beat* to the side of the body; s/he then lands on the same foot, and immediately closes the extended leg *5th position derrière en demi-plié.* Also *cabriole fermée de côté dessous.*

cabriole fermée dessus [kabʀijɔl fɛʀme d(ə)sy]

ka-bree-YOL fer-MAY d(u)-SU (Fr. caper; closed; over.) A *cabriole* in which the dancer begins in *5th position* with the *working foot derrière;* s/he brushes the back foot *to 2nd en l'air* between 45 degrees and 90 degrees, pushes off and beats behind the *working leg*, performing the *beat* to the side of the body; s/he then lands on the same foot, and immediately closes the extended leg *5th position devant en demi-plié*.

cabriole fermée devant [kabʀijɔl fɛʀme d(ə)vɑ̃] ka-bree-YOL fer-MAY d(u)-VAH (Fr. caper; closed; front.) A *cabriole* in which the dancer begins in *5th position* with the *working leg devant;* s/he brushes the front leg *devant en l'air* between 45 degrees and 90 degrees, pushes off and beats behind the *working leg*, performing the *beat* in front of the body; s/he then lands on the same foot and immediately closes the extended leg *5th position devant en demi-plié*.

cabriole fouettée [kabʀijɔl fwɛte] ka-bree-YOL fwe-TAY (Fr. caper; whipped.) A *cabriole ouverte devant* in which the dancer performs a half-turn *en dedans* immediately after performing the *beat*, and lands with the extended leg held *derrière en l'air* 45 degrees. May be prepared with a *demi-contretemps*. Similar to a beaten *fouetté sauté*. Not in current Majors syllabus.

cabriole ouverte [kabʀijɔl uvɛʀt] ka-bree-YOL oo-VERT (Fr. caper; open.) A *cabriole* performed commencing *5th position* and ending with the *working leg en l'air*. May be performed *devant*, *derrière*, *dessous*, *dessus*, or *de côté*. Variation: *cabriole fouettée, petite cabriole.*

cabriole ouverte de côté [kabʀijɔl uvɛʀt də kote] ka-bree-YOL oo-VERT d(u) koh-TAY (Fr. caper; open; to the side.) A *cabriole* in which the dancer begins in *5th position;* s/he then brushes the *working foot to 2nd en l'air* between 45 degrees and 90 degrees, jumps into the air beating the *supporting leg* against the *working leg,* performing the *beat* to the side of the body, causing the *working leg* to rebound, and lands on the leg that pushed off, with the extended leg maintaining *2nd position en l'air*.

cabriole ouverte derrière [kabʀijɔl uvɛʀt dɛʀjɛʀ] ka-bree-YOL oo-VERT der-YER (Fr. caper; open; behind.) A *cabriole* in which the dancer begins in *5th position* with the *working leg derrière;* s/he then brushes the *working leg derrière en l'air* between 45 degrees and 90 degrees, jumps into the air beating the *supporting leg* against the *working leg,* performing the *beat* to the side of the body, causing the *working leg* to rebound, and lands on the leg that pushed off, with the extended leg held *derrière en l'air*.

cabriole ouverte dessous [kabʀijɔl uvɛʀt d(ə)su] ka-bree-YOL oo-VERT d(u)-SOO (Fr. caper; open; under.) A *cabriole* in which the dancer begins in *5th position working foot devant;* s/he then brushes the *working foot to 2nd en l'air* between 45 degrees and 90 degrees, jumps into the air beating the *supporting leg* in front of the *working leg*, performing the *beat* to the side of the body, then lands on the same foot, with the extended leg in *2nd position en l'air*.

cabriole ouverte dessus [kabʀijɔl uvɛʀt d(ə)sy] ka-bree-YOL oo-VERT d(u)-SU (Fr. caper; open; over.) A *cabriole* in which the dancer begins in *5th position* with the *working foot derrière;* s/he brushes the back foot *to 2nd en l'air* between 45 degrees and 90 degrees, pushes off and beats behind the *working leg*, performing the *beat* to the side of the body; s/he then lands on the same foot, with the extended leg in *2nd position en l'air*.

cabriole ouverte devant [kabʀijɔl uvɛʀt d(ə)vɑ̃] ka-bree-YOL oo-VERT d(u)-VAH (Fr. caper; open; front.) A *cabriole* in which the dancer begins in *5th position*, usually with the *working leg devant;* s/he brushes the *working leg devant en l'air* between 45 degrees and 90 degrees, pushes off and beats behind the *working leg*, performing the *beat* in front of the body; s/he then lands on the same foot with the extended leg *devant en l'air*. Variation: *cabriole fouetté.*

cabriole, petite See *petite cabriole.*

cambré [kɑ̃bʀe] kah-BRAY (Fr. pp of v cambrer, to arch one's back or throw back one's shoulders; adj arched.) Term of the French school, referring to an arch of the upper body with the head continuing the curved line. Not found in current RAD syllabus.

centre [sɑ̃tʀ] SAH-tr (Fr. nm centre.) 1. That area of the room in which the dancer performs movements without the aid of the *barre*. 2. Term referring to all movements performed without a *barre*. See *centre practice.*

centre practice/centre practise A generic term for a category of *exercises* performed after the *Ports de Bras* section of a class and before the *Pirouettes* section, consisting of *barre exercises* executed without the *barre*. Although *centre* *practice* relates to barre exercises, it is not a complete repetition of barre work. Rather it brings together elements practised in *barre work* and *port de bras* to develop coordination of the whole body working in balanced harmony. Without the constraints of the *barre,* the dancer is free to execute changes of *alignment* and broader *transferences of weight* and to project his/her movements to an audience. Six component actions form the foundations of *centre practice: épaulement, chassé, chassé passé, coupé, posé,* and *pivot.* These in turn form the basis of five fundamental steps: *temps lié, fouetté à terre, rotation à terre, classical walk,* and *classical run.*

centre stage Term used to describe the location of the dancer on the centre of the stage.

chaîné [ʃɛne] shen-AY (Fr. mutated form of pp of v enchaîner, to link or string together; adj linked; nm chain step.) See *chaînés, chaînés en diagonale.*

chaînés [ʃɛne] shen-AY (Fr. nmpl chain steps.) Type of turn often performed in series *en diagonale en pointes.* The dancer begins with the foot *dégagé devant*, steps to the side along the *line of dance* making a 1/2-turn *en dedans*, and steps in *1st position* making a 1/2-turn *en dehors* to complete one full turn. May be prepared with a *chassé* instead of a *posé.* When performed in series, each step is taken in *1st position* along the *line of dance*, with the arms usually held in *pirouette position.* May be practised with fingers on shoulders, the elbows supported and lifted to the sides. May be performed slowly, i.e., stepping on specific musical counts, or as quickly as possible through the music. See *chaînés en diagonale.* Also *chaînés déboulés*, *chaînés pirouettes.*

chaînés déboulés de côté See *chaînés.*

chaînés en diagonale [ʃɛne zɑ̃ djagɔnal] shen-AY zah dya-go-NAL (Fr. chain steps; on the diagonal.) A series of *chaîné* turns performed along a straight path extending from one *upstage* corner to the opposite *downstage* corner.

chaînés pirouettes in series See *chaînés.*

changé [ʃɑ̃ʒe] shah-ZHAY (Fr. pp of v changer, to change; adj changed.) Term used to describe actions performed with a *change of feet.* See *échappé sauté changé, sissonne changée, sissonne fermée changée battue, sissonne ouverte changée.*

change of feet Phrase used to describe a change from *5th position* right foot *devant* to *5th position* left foot *devant*, or the reverse. Used to describe actions which may be performed with or without reversing the *5th position,* such as *temps lié to 2nd*, *échappé sauté*, and *échappé relevé.*

changement [ʃɑ̃ʒmɑ̃] shahzh-MAH (Fr. nm a change or changing.) A jump in which the legs begin in *5th position* and change in the air at the height of the jump, separating as little as possible, to land in the opposite *5th position.* See *changement battu, changement en pointes, petit changement, retiré changement.* Also referred to as *changement de pieds.*

changement battu [ʃɑ̃ʒmɑ̃ baty] shahzh-MAH ba-TU (Fr. changing; beaten.) A *changement* in which the legs beat together in the air. From *5th position,* the legs open slightly sideways on leaving the ground, in order to execute the beating action of the legs without a *change of feet,* before landing with a *change of feet.* In the Cecchetti method this step is called *royal* or *entrechat royal.*

changement en pointes [ʃɑ̃ʒmɑ̃ ɑ̃ pwɛ̃t] shahzh-MAH ah pwet (Fr. changing; on tiptoe.) A small, low *changement* performed on the tips of the feet in *pointe shoes.*

changement, petit See *petit changement.*

chassé [ʃase] sha-SAY (Fr. pp of v chasser, to hunt or chase; adj chased; nm a chased step.) One of the basic elements of *centre practice.* A linking movement with a sliding action of the foot commencing from either an open or a closed position and ending in an open position *en demi-plié.* Can be taken in varying *alignments* and directions. See *chassé temps levé*, *coupé chassé pas de bourrée*, *pas chassé*, *temps levé chassé pas de bourrée.* Variation: *chassé passé.*

chassé à la seconde See *chassé to 2nd.*

chassé en arrière [ʃase ɑ̃ naʀjɛʀ] sha-SAY ahnar-YER (Fr. chased; backward.) A *chassé* commencing with a *demi-plié* in *5th derrière*, in which the back foot slides backward along the floor to *4th opposite 5th position en demi-plié.*

chassé en avant [ʃase ɑ̃ navɑ̃] sha-SAY ah na-VAH (Fr. chased; forward.) A *chassé* commencing with a *demi-plié* in *5th devant*, in which the front foot slides forward along the floor to *4th opposite 5th position en demi-plié.*

chassé en avant, pas See *pas chassé.*

chassé pas de bourrée [ʃase pɑ də buʀe] sha-SAY pah d(u) boo-RAY (Fr. chased; bourrée step.) A composite step consisting of a *chassé* leading into a *pas de bourrée.* See *coupé chassé pas de bourrée, temps levé chassé pas de bourrée.*

chassé passé [ʃase pɑse] sha-SAY pah-SAY (Fr. chased; passed.) A variation of a *chassé* in which the *working foot* passes to *4th position.* May be performed *en avant* or *en arrière*, from either a closed or an open position.

chassé passé en arrière [ʃase pɑse ɑ̃ naʀjɛʀ] sha-SAY pah-SAY ah-nar-YER (Fr. chased; passed; backward.) A *chassé* in which the *working foot* passes backward to *4th position.* May be taken from a closed or an open position. 1. From a closed position, the front foot stretches with the tip of the toe contacting the side of the base of the heel of the *supporting foot* and the floor. It then passes through *5th derrière,* commencing the *demi-plié,* and slides backward along the floor to finish in *4th opposite 5th position en demi-plié.* The arms are lifted to *1st position* with the sliding action. 2. From an open position, the front foot slides backward through *1st position en demi-plié* and tracks a diagonal line to finish *4th opposite 5th position en demi-plié.*

chassé passé en avant [ʃase pɑse ɑ̃ navɑ̃] sha-SAY pah-SAY ah na-VAH (Fr. chased; passed; forward.) A *chassé* in which the *working foot* passes forward to *4th position.* May be taken from a closed or an open position. 1. From a closed position, the back foot stretches with the tip of the toe contacting the side of the base of the heel of the *supporting foot* and the floor. It then passes through *5th devant,* commencing the *demi-plié,* and slides forward along the floor to finish in *4th opposite 5th position en demi-plié.* 2. From an open position, the back foot slides forward through *1st position en demi-plié* and tracks a diagonal line to finish *4th opposite 5th position en demi-plié.*

chassé temps levé in 1st arabesque [ʃase tɑ̃ l(ə)ve - aʀabɛsk] sha-SAY tah l(u)-VAY – a-ra-BESK (Fr. chased; time; linked; in 1st arabesque.) A strong jump in *1st arabesque,* prepared by a transference of weight using a *chassé* action. From an open position, the back foot makes a *chassé passé en avant* into *4th position*, immediately transferring the weight into *1st arabesque,* then the movement continues into the *temps levé.*

chassé to 2nd [ʃase -] sha-SAY – (Fr. chased; to 2nd.) A *chassé* commencing with a *demi-plié* in *5th position*, in which the *working foot* slides outward along the floor to *2nd position en demi-plié.*

chassé, pas See *pas chassé.*

chat [ʃa] sha (Fr. nm cat.) See *grand pas de chat to 4th, pas de chat.*

cheval [ʃ(ə)val] sh(u)-VAL (Fr. nm horse.) See *pas de cheval en pointe, pas de cheval sauté en pointe.*

cinq [sɛ̃k] sek (Fr. nm adj five.) See *entrechat cinq, pas de bourrée à cinq pas.*

cinquième [sɛ̃kjɛm] sek-YEM (Fr. adj fifth.) See *position of the feet, 5th.*

circular port de bras See *port de bras, circular; port de bras in 4th position en fondu, circular; port de bras with transfer of weight, circular.*

classical pose A basic *pose of the body* taken facing 1 *(downstage),* standing on one leg while the other is placed *derrière à terre* with the knee bent and the foot fully stretched. The inside of the knees are in contact with each other and the arms are held in *demi-seconde.*

classical run One of the basic steps of *centre practice.* A smooth running action with a sense of poise and a strong lift through the whole body. Taken *en avant* or *en arrière.*

classical study A short *enchaînement* consisting of classical ballet steps (as opposed to a Free Movement study consisting of non-technical steps).

classical walk One of the basic steps of *centre practice.* A stylised way of walking in classical ballet, a smooth action with a sense of poise and lift through the whole body. Taken *en avant* or *en arrière.*

cloche [klɔʃ] klosh (Fr. nf bell.) See *en cloche.*

composé [kɔ̃poze] ko-poh-ZAY (Fr. adj formed from many different elements; nm a compound or composite.) See *ballonné composé.*

contretemps [kɔ̃tʀətɑ̃] ko-tr(u)-TAH (Fr. nm in music, a complication or off-beat rhythm; in dance, an off-beat step or steps.) See *demi-contretemps, full contretemps.*

contretemps, demi- See *demi-contretemps.*

corps [kɔʀ] kor (Fr. nm a body or bodies.) A body or a group of dancers, as *corps de ballet.*

côté [kote] koh-TAY (Fr. nm side.) See *de côté.*

cou-de-pied [kudpje] koo-d(u)-pyay (Fr. nm neck of the foot.) 1. Term used to describe a specific point just above the ankle bone *devant* or *derrière*. 2. Abbreviated form of *sur le cou-de-pied,* a phrase used to describe the placement of the *working foot* just above the ankle bone of the *supporting leg*. The working and supporting legs are turned out and the *working foot* is either stretched, flexed, or "wrapped," according to the step being performed. See *battement fondu, battement frappé, entrechat cinq, entrechat trois, petit battement, petit jeté, petit retiré, sissonne ordinaire*. Also called *petit retiré position.*

cou-de-pied derrière [kudpje dɛʀjɛʀ] koo-d(u)-pyay der-YER (Fr. neck of the foot; behind.) 1. Term used to describe a specific point just above the outer ankle bone. 2. Abbreviated form of *sur le cou-de-pied devant,* a phrase used to describe the placement of the *working foot* in front, just above the outer ankle bone of the *supporting leg*. The working and supporting legs are turned out and the *working foot* is either stretched, flexed or "wrapped," according to the step being performed. See *battement fondu, battement frappé, entrechat cinq, entrechat trois, petit battement, petit jeté, petit retiré, sissonne ordinaire*. Also called *petit retiré derrière position.*

cou-de-pied devant [kudpje d(ə)vɑ̃] koo-d(u)-pyay d(u)-VAH (Fr. neck of the foot; front.) 1. Term used to describe a specific point just above the inner ankle bone. 2. Abbreviated form of *sur le cou-de-pied devant,* a phrase used to describe the placement of the *working foot* in front, just above the inner ankle bone of the *supporting leg*. The working and supporting legs are turned out and the *working foot* is either stretched, flexed or "wrapped," according to the step being performed. See *battement fondu, battement frappé, entrechat cinq, entrechat trois, petit battement, petit jeté, petit retiré, sissonne ordinaire*. Also called *petit retiré devant position.*

coupé [kupe] koo-PAY (Fr. pp of v couper, to cut; adj cut; nm in dance, a cutting step.) One of the basic elements of *centre practice.* A form of *transfer of weight.* An action in which one foot cuts away the other. Often an intermediary or linking step. May be performed *dessus* or *dessous*, either *terre à terre* or *sauté*. See *coupé brisé, coupé chassé pas de bourrée, coupé fouetté raccourci, coupé fouetté raccourci battu, coupé fouetté raccourci sauté, coupés jetés en tournant en manège, coupé sauté, posé coupé, posé coupé pirouette en dedans.*

coupé brisé [kupe bʀize] koo-PAY bree-ZAY (Fr. cutting step; broken step.) A composite step consisting of a *coupé* and a variation of a *brisé* (from one foot to the other, instead of one foot to the same). May be performed *devant* or *derrière.*

coupé brisé derrière [kupe bʀize dɛʀjɛʀ] koo-PAY bree-ZAY der-YER (Fr. cutting step; broken step; behind.) A composite step consisting of a *coupé dessous* and a variation of a *brisé.* The dancer begins *en fondu* with the *working foot* placed at or slightly above *cou-de-pied derrière;* s/he then steps *sur place,* passing the other foot through *1st position* to extend *derrière* above *glissé height,* jumps into the air beating the *supporting leg* against the front of the *working leg* to perform the *beat* in front of the body, changes feet, and lands in the starting position.

coupé brisé devant [kupe bʀize d(ə)vɑ̃] koo-PAY bree-ZAY d(u)-VAH (Fr. cutting step; broken step; front.) A composite step consisting of a *coupé dessus* and a variation of a *brisé.* The dancer begins *en fondu* with the *working foot* placed at or slightly above *cou-de-pied devant;* s/he then steps *sur place,* passing the other foot through *1st position* to extend *devant* above *glissé height,* jumps into the air beating the *supporting leg* against the back of the *working leg* to perform the *beat* in front of the body, changes feet, and lands in the starting position.

coupé chassé pas de bourrée [kupe ʃase pɑ də buʀe] koo-PAY sha-SAY pah d(u) boo-RAY (Fr. cutting step; chased step; bourrée step.) A composite step consisting of a *coupé dessous*, a *chassé en avant*, and a *pas de bourrée dessous.*

coupé dessous [kupe d(ə)su] koo-PAY d(u)-SOO (Fr. cutting step; under.) A *coupé* in which one foot cuts behind the other.

coupé dessous brisé devant [kupe d(ə)su bʀize d(ə)vɑ̃] koo-PAY d(u)-SOO bree-ZAY d(u)-VAH

(Fr. cutting step; under; broken step; front.) A composite step consisting of a *coupé dessous* and a *brisé devant*.

coupé dessous en tournant [kupe d(ə)su ɑ̃ tuʀnɑ̃] koo-PAY d(u)-SOO ah toor-NAH (Fr. cutting step; over; turning.) A *coupé dessous* with a simultaneous turn in the direction of the foot which is released. Used as a preparation into turning actions of jumps *en manège*. See *coupés jetés en tournant en manège*.

coupé dessous en tournant chassé en avant [kupe d(ə)su ɑ̃ tuʀnɑ̃ ʃase ɑ̃ navɑ̃] koo-PAY d(u)-SOO ah toor-NAH sha-SAY ah na-VAH (Fr. cutting step; under; turning; chased step; forward.) A composite step consisting of a *coupé dessous* and a simultaneous turn in the direction of the foot which is released, followed by a *chassé en avant*. May be performed in series. See *coupés jetés en tournant en manège*.

coupé dessus [kupe d(ə)sy] koo-PAY d(u)-SU (Fr. cutting step; over.) A *coupé* in which one foot cuts in front of the other.

coupé dessus brisé en avant [kupe d(ə)sy bʀize ɑ̃ navɑ̃] koo-PAY d(u)-SU bree-ZAY ah na-VAH (Fr. cutting step; over; broken step; forward.) A composite step consisting of a *coupé dessus*, then a brush of the back foot through *1st position* into a *brisé en avant*.

coupé fouetté raccourci [kupe fwɛte ʀakuʀsi] koo-PAY fwe-TAY ra-koor-SEE (Fr. cutting step; whipped step; shortened.) A composite step in which the dancer steps *en pointe*, cutting behind and replacing the *supporting foot*, strongly extends the *working leg to 2nd en l'air* 45 degrees, and finishes *en fondu*, sharply bringing the *working foot* to mid-calf. Also referred to as *coupé fouetté raccourci relevé*. Variations: *coupé fouetté raccourci battu*, *coupé fouetté raccourci sauté*. May be taken *en tournant*.

coupé fouetté raccourci battu [kupe fwɛte ʀakuʀsi baty] koo-PAY fwe-TAY ra-koor-SEE ba-TU (Fr. cutting step; whipped step; shortened; beaten.) A *coupé fouetté raccourci sauté* in which the legs join in the air to beat in *5th position* without a *change of feet* before the landing. May be taken *en tournant*.

coupé fouetté raccourci sauté [kupe fwɛte ʀakuʀsi sote] koo-PAY fwe-TAY ra-koor-SEE soh-TAY (Fr. cutting step; whipped step; shortened; jumped.) A composite action in which the dancer steps on the whole foot, cutting behind and replacing the *supporting foot*, jumps into the air strongly extending the *working leg to 2nd en l'air* 45 degrees, and lands on the foot that pushed off, sharply bringing the *working foot* to mid-calf.

coupé sauté [kupe sote] koo-PAY soh-TAY (Fr. cutting step; jumped.) A jumped *coupé* in which the dancer springs from one leg to the other with the *working foot* cutting in front of, beside, or behind and replacing the *supporting foot*. Usually an intermediary or linking step. May be performed *dessus* or *dessous*.

coupé sauté dessous [kupe sote d(ə)su] koo-PAY soh-TAY d(u)-SOO (Fr. cutting step; jumped; under.) A jumped *coupé* in which the dancer springs from one leg to the other with the *working foot* cutting behind and replacing the *supporting foot*.

coupé sauté dessus [kupe sote d(ə)sy] koo-PAY soh-TAY d(u)-SU (Fr. cutting step; jumped; over.) A jumped *coupé* in which the dancer springs from one leg to the other with the *working foot* cutting in front of and replacing the *supporting foot*.

coupés jetés en tournant en manège [kupe ʒ(ə)te zɑ̃ tuʀnɑ̃ ɑ̃ manɛʒ] koo-PAY zh(u)-TAY zah toor-NAH ah ma-NEZH (Fr. cutting step; thrown step; turning; in a circle.) A composite step performed in series along a circular path around the room, consisting of a *coupé dessous en tournant*, and a *jeté en avant*.

couru [kuʀy] koo-RU (Fr. pp of v courir, to run; adj run.) See *courus, pas de bourrée couru*.

courus [kuʀy] koo-RU (Fr. nmpl running steps.) A series of very small, rapid, even steps *en pointe* with the feet well crossed in *5th position* and the body remaining poised over the feet. When performed in *1st position*, the legs are usually parallel. May be performed *sur place*, *en tournant*, or travelling *en avant*, *en arrière*, or *de côté*. In the Cecchetti method, this step is called *pas de bourrée couru*.

courus de côté [kuʀy də kote] koo-RU d(u) koh-TAY (Fr. running steps; to the side.) *Courus* which travel sideways. From *5th position*, the dancer commences with the back foot initiating the sideways travel which is usually in the direction corresponding to the front foot. The movement continues with the weight being evenly transferred in minute and rapid steps.

courus en arrière [kuʀy zɑ̃ naʀjɛʀ] koo-RU zah nar-YER (Fr. running steps; backward.) *Courus* which travel backward.

courus en avant [kuʀy zɑ̃ navɑ̃] koo-RU zah na-VAH (Fr. running steps; forward.) *Courus* which travel forward.

courus en diagonale [kuʀy zɑ̃ djagɔnal] koo-RU zah dya-go-NAL (Fr. running steps; on the diagonal.) *Courus* performed while travelling along the line from an *upstage/downstage* corner to the opposite *downstage/upstage* corner.

courus en tournant [kuʀy zɑ̃ tuʀnɑ̃] koo-RU zah toor-NAH (Fr. running steps; turning.) *Courus* performed while turning, usually *sur place*. May be performed with or without a *change of feet*.

courus sur place [kuʀy syʀ plas] koo-RU sur plas (Fr. running steps; on; place.) *Courus* performed without travel.

croisé [kʀwaze] krwa-ZAY (Fr. pp of v croiser, to cross; adj crossed.) See *croisé derrière, croisé devant, en croisé*.

croisé derrière [kʀwaze dɛʀjɛʀ] krwa-ZAY der-YER (Fr. crossed; behind.) A basic *pose of the body* taken facing either *downstage* corner with the *upstage* foot *degagé derrière.* The arms are held in *4th position* with the *upstage* arm raised. There is a lift of the body forward and up. The head turns and is slightly raised so that the *eye line* is towards 1 *(downstage).*

croisé devant [kʀwaze d(ə)vɑ̃] krwa-ZAY d(u)-VAH (Fr. crossed; front.) A basic *pose of the body* taken facing either *downstage* corner with the *downstage* foot *dégagé devant.* The arms are held in *4th position* with the *upstage* arm raised. There is a strong lift in the upper body and the head is turned and raised so that the *eye line* is between 1 *(downstage)* and the other *downstage* corner.

croix [kʀwa] krwa (Fr. nf cross.) See *en croix*.

crossed 4th See *position of the arms, 4th crossed; position of the feet, 4th*.

cuisse [kɥis] kuwees (Fr. nf thigh.) See *temps de cuisse*.

curtsey Simple form of a Girl's *révérence* performed by placing the ball of the *working foot* or the tip of that foot on the floor just behind the *supporting foot* while bending both knees.

dance steps A generic term for a sub-category of *enchaînements* performed during the *Allegro* section of a Pre-Elementary class, after *Batterie*. Including *coupé chassé pas de bourrée*, *pas chassé*, and *pas de valse* for Girls, or *coupé chassé pas de bourrée*, *pas chassé*, *galop*, and *échappés sautés* for Boys.

de [də] d(u) (Fr. prep of, from.) See *de côté, entrechat six de volée de côté, pas de bourrée, rond de jambe*.

de côté [də kote] d(u) koh-TAY (Fr. from; side.) 1. Phrase which refers to a step or series of steps which travel sideways either right or left, in relation to the dancer's body. See *assemblé de côté, balancé de côté, ballonné composé de côté, ballonné de côté, cabriole fermée de côté, cabriole ouverte de côté, courus de côté, demi-contretemps de côté, entrechat six de volée de côté, fouetté relevé de côté, fouetté sauté de côté, jeté devant de côté, pas de bourrée couru de côté, pas de valse de côté, posé coupé de côté, posé de côté, sissonne fermée battue de côté, sissonne fermée de côté, sissonne fermée relevée de côté, sissonne ouverte de côté, sissonne relevée ouverte de côté.* 2. Phrase which describes the dancer facing 2 *(stage right)* or 4 *(stage left).* See *arabesque de côté*.

déboîté [debwate] day-bwa-TAY (Fr. pp of the v déboîter, to dislocate; adj pulled out.) An *emboîté* performed *en arrière*, often in series with each *working leg* beginning in front and closing behind. Term not found in current RAD syllabus.

déboulé [debule] day-boo-LAY (Fr. pp of v débouler, to bolt or tumble down; adj tumbled down.) Term not found in current RAD syllabus. See *chaînés*.

dedans [dədɑ̃] d(u)-DAH (Fr. adj inside; prep in or turned in.) See *en dedans*.

dégagé [degaʒe] day-ga-ZHAY (Fr. pp of v dégager, to free or extricate; adj having freedom and ease; nm a disengaged action or position.) 1. Term used to describe an extended position of the *working leg* where the toes are in contact with the floor, either *devant, to 2nd,* or *derrière.* The *supporting leg* may be straight or *en fondu.* Also *pointe tendu, pointe tendue* (outside the RAD). 2. An action of the *working leg* resulting in a fully extended position with toes contacting the floor. *Battement glissé* is known as *battement dégagé* in the Cecchetti method.

dégagé derrière [degaʒe dɛʀjɛʀ] day-ga-ZHAY der-YER (Fr. disengaged action or position; behind.) A *dégagé* position or action in which the toes contact the floor behind the body in *4th position derrière*.

dégagé derrière en fondu [degaʒe dɛʀjɛʀ ɑ̃ fɔ̃dy] day-ga-ZHAY der-YER ah fo-DU (Fr. disengaged action or position; behind; melted.) A *dégagé* position or action in which the toes of the *working foot* contact the floor behind the body in *4th position derrière* with the *supporting leg* bent.

dégagé devant [degaʒe d(ə)vɑ̃] day-ga-ZHAY d(u)-VAH (Fr. disengaged action or position; front.) A *dégagé* position or action in which the toes of the *working foot* contact the floor in front of the body in *4th position devant*.

dégagé devant en fondu [degaʒe d(ə)vɑ̃ ɑ̃ fɔ̃dy] day-ga-ZHAY d(u)-VAH ah fo-DU (Fr. disengaged action or position; front; melted.) A *dégagé* position or action in which the toes of the *working foot* contact the floor in front of the body in *4th position devant* with the *supporting leg* bent.

dégagé to 2nd [degaʒe -] day-ga-ZHAY – (Fr. disengaged action or position; to 2nd.) A *dégagé* position or action in which the toes of the *working foot* contact the floor to the side of the body in *2nd position*.

dégagé to 2nd en fondu [degaʒe - ɑ̃ fɔ̃dy] day-ga-ZHAY – ah fo-DU (Fr. disengaged action or position; to 2nd; melted.) A *dégagé* position or action in which the toes of the *working foot* contact the floor to the side of the body in *2nd position* with the *supporting leg* bent.

dehors [dəɔʀ] d(u)-OR (Fr. adv outside; prep out, toward the outside, or turned out.) See *en dehors*.

demi [d(ə)mi] d(u)-MEE (Fr. adj half.) See *demi-assemblé soutenu; demi-contretemps; demi-détourné; demi-grand rond de jambe; demi-plié; demi-pointe; demi-rond de jambe en dedans; position of the arms, demi-bras; position of the arms, demi-seconde.*

demi-2nd See *position of the arms, demi-seconde*.

demi-assemblé soutenu à terre [d(ə)miasɑ̃ble sutny a tɛʀ] d(u)-MEE-a-sah-BLAY soot-NU a ter (Fr. half gathered step; sustained; on the ground.) A circling action of the *working leg* moving between *4th* and *2nd* positions with the tip of the foot tracing a 90 degree arc on the floor. May be performed *en dehors* or *en dedans*. May be executed with a *dégagé en fondu* and a stretch of the *supporting leg* during or after the circling action.

demi-assemblé soutenu à terre en dedans [d(ə)miasɑ̃ble sutny a tɛʀ ɑ̃ dədɑ̃] d(u)-MEE-a-sah-BLAY soot-NU a ter ah d(u)-DAH (Fr. half gathered step; sustained; on the ground; inside.) The dancer begins in *5th position* with the *working leg* behind; s/he then performs a *dégagé derrière* or *to 2nd*, moves the leg *en dedans to 2nd* or *devant*, and closes *5th position*.

demi-assemblé soutenu à terre en dehors [d(ə)miasɑ̃ble sutny a tɛʀ ɑ̃ dəɔʀ] d(u)-MEE-a-sah-BLAY soot-NU a ter ah d(u)-OR (Fr. half gathered step; sustained; on the ground; outward.) The dancer begins in *5th position* with the *working leg* in front; s/he then performs a *dégagé devant* or *to 2nd*, moves the leg *en dehors to 2nd* or *derrière*, and closes *5th position*.

demi-assemblé soutenu en dedans See *demi-assemblé soutenu à terre en dedans*.

demi-assemblé soutenu en dehors See *demi-assemblé soutenu à terre en dehors*.

demi-bras See *position of the arms, demi-bras*.

demi-contretemps [d(ə)mikɔ̃tʀətɑ̃] d(u)-MEE-ko-tr(u)-TAH (Fr. half-off-beat step.) A linking step consisting of a *temps levé* and *chassé passé*. Usually performed on an anacrusis beat or beats. Used as a springboard into big actions such as *fouetté sauté* or *fouetté relevé*.

demi-contretemps de côté [d(ə)mikɔ̃tʀətɑ̃ də kote] d(u)-MEE-ko-tr(u)-TAH d(u) koh-TAY (Fr. half-off-beat step; to the side.) A *demi-contretemps* performed with a change of *alignment:* starting *en croisé*, turning on the *temps levé*, and ending *en demi-plié* facing 2 *(stage right)* or 4 *(stage left)*.

demi-détourné [d(ə)mideturne] d(u)-MEE-day-toor-NAY (Fr. half turned away.) A *relevé* on two feet with a 1/2-turn. The body turns simultaneously with the *relevé* action, making a 1/2-turn toward the back foot to finish in *5th position* with the other foot *devant* before lowering *en demi-plié*. Variation: *détourné*.

demi-grand rond de jambe [d(ə)migʀɑ̃ ʀɔ̃ də ʒɑ̃b] d(u)-MEE- grah ro d(u) zhahb (Fr. half big; circle of the leg.) A slow sustained circling action of the leg *en l'air* tracing a 90 degrees arc parallel to the ground. Taken from *4th devant* to *2nd position,* and from *2nd position* to *4th derrière (en dehors);* or from *4th derrière* to *2nd position,* and from *2nd position* to *4th devant (en dedans).*

demi-grand rond de jambe en dedans [d(ə)migʀɑ̃ ʀɔ̃ də ʒɑ̃b ɑ̃ dədɑ̃] d(u)-MEE-grah ro d(u) zhahb ah d(u)-DAH (Fr. half big; circle of the leg; inward.) 1. From *4th derrière to 2nd position.* Commencing *5th derrière,* the *working leg* executes a *développé to 4th derrière* at 90 degrees and is carried to *2nd position.* 2. From *2nd position to 4th devant.* Commencing *5th position,* the *working leg* executes a *développé to 2nd* at 90 degrees and is carried to *4th devant.*

demi-grand rond de jambe en dehors [d(ə)migʀɑ̃ ʀɔ̃ də ʒɑ̃b ɑ̃ dəɔʀ] d(u)-MEE-grah ro d(u) zhahb ah d(u)-OR (Fr. half big; circle of the leg; outward.) 1. From *4th devant to 2nd position.* Commencing *5th devant,* the *working leg* executes a *développé to 4th devant* at 90 degrees and is carried to *2nd position.* 2. From *2nd position to 4th derrière.* Commencing *5th position,* the *working leg* executes a *développé to 2nd* at 90 degrees and is carried to *4th derrière.*

demi-plié [d(ə)miplije] d(u)-MEE-plee-YAY (Fr. nm half-bending action.) A half-bending action of the knees over the toes, with the heels remaining firmly on the floor. Practised to develop a combination of strength and elasticity to facilitate the take-off and landing of jumps. See *en demi-plié.*

demi-plié, en See *en demi-plié.*

demi-pointe, sur la See *sur la demi-pointe.*

demi-pointe/s, en See *en demi-pointe/s.*

demi-rond de jambe en dedans [d(ə)miʀɔ̃ də ʒɑ̃b ɑ̃ dədɑ̃] d(u)-MEE-ro d(u) zhahb ah d(u)-DAH (Fr. half circle of the leg; inward.) Half the circling action of a *rond de jambe à terre en dedans.* The dancer begins with the *working leg* extended to *4th derrière* or to *2nd* with the toes contacting the floor, and traces a 90-degree arc inward to *2nd* or to *4th devant.* Used as a transition between *2nd position* and *4th position.*

demi-rond de jambe en dehors [d(ə)miʀɔ̃ də ʒɑ̃b ɑ̃ dəɔʀ] d(u)-MEE-ro d(u) zhahb ah d(u)-OR (Fr. half circle of the leg; outward.) Half the circling action of a *rond de jambe à terre en dehors.* The dancer begins with the *working leg* extended to *2nd* or to *4th devant* with the toes contacting the floor, and traces a 90-degree arc outward to *4th devant* or to *2nd.* Used as a transition between *2nd position* and *4th position.*

demi-seconde See *position of the arms, demi-seconde.*

derrière [dɛʀjɛʀ] der-YER (Fr. adv prep behind; nm back, rear.) 1. Term used to describe the position of the *working leg* placed behind the other leg or behind the body, as *5th derrière, 4th derrière, croisé derrière,* or *effacé derrière.* See *attitude derrière, cou-de-pied derrière, dégagé derrière, derrière à terre, petit retiré derrière, relevé derrière, relevé passé derrière, retiré derrière, retiré passé derrière.* 2. Term used to describe the direction of an action which occurs behind the body, e.g., *battement fondu derrière, battement frappé derrière, battement frappé fouetté derrière, battement fouetté derrière, battement glissé derrière, battement glissé relevé derrière, battement jeté derrière, battement tendu derrière, brisé volé derrière, cabriole fermée derrière, développé derrière, développé passé derrière, double battement piqué derrière, en cloche derrière, grand battement derrière, grand battement développé derrière, grand battement piqué derrière, grand battement relevé derrière, grand battement retiré derrière, pas soutenu derrière, petit développé passé derrière, piqué derrière, posé passé derrière, sissonne fermée changée battue derrière;* or uses the back foot, e.g., *assemblé derrière, ballonné composé de côté derrière, ballonné composé de côté passé derrière, brisé 2 to 2 derrière, coupé dessous brisé derrière, entrechat trois derrière, entrechat cinq derrière, flic-flac derrière, glissade derrière, jeté ordinaire derrière, pas de bourrée derrière, petit assemblé derrière, petit battement derrière, petit battement battu derrière, posé de côté derrière, retiré sauté passé derrière, sissonne fermée relevée de côté derrière, sissonne fermée de côté derrière, sissonne ordinaire derrière.*

derrière croisé See *croisé derrière; en croisé.*

derrière ouvert See *effacé derrière; en ouvert.*

dessous [d(ə)su] d(u)-SOO (Fr. adv under, underneath; nm bottom, underside.) Term used to describe an action in which the *working leg* closes behind the body, e.g., *coupé dessous*, or in which the *working leg* begins in front of or beside the body and closes behind the body, e.g., *assemblé dessous, battement glissé sur la pointe dessous*. The opposite action is called *dessus*. See *assemblé dessous, assemblé battu dessous, assemblé de côté dessous, ballotté dessous, ballotté sauté dessous, battement glissé sur la pointe dessous, brisé 2 to 2 dessous, brisé* 2 to 1 *dessous, brisé* 1 to 2 *dessous, coupé dessous, glissade dessous, pas de bourrée dessous, pas de bourrée en tournant dessous, pas de bourrée piqué dessous, pas de bourrée piqué en tournant dessous, sissonne doublée dessous, sissonne fermée battue de côté dessous, sissonne fermée de côté dessous, sissonne fermée relevée de côté dessous, temps de cuisse dessous.*

dessus [d(ə)sy] d(u)-SU (Fr. adv over, on top of, above; nm top.) Term used to describe an action in which the *working leg* closes in front of the body, e.g., *coupé dessus*, or in which the *working leg* begins behind or beside the body and closes in front of the body, e.g., *assemblé dessus, battement glissé sur la pointe dessus*. The opposite action is called *dessous*. See *assemblé dessus, assemblé battu dessus, assemblé de côté dessus, ballotté dessus, ballotté sauté dessus, battement glissé sur la pointe dessus, brisé 2 to 2 dessus, brisé* 2 to 1 *dessus, brisé* 1 to 2 *dessus, coupé dessus, glissade dessus, pas de bourrée dessus, pas de bourrée en tournant dessus, pas de bourrée piqué dessus, pas de bourrée piqué en tournant dessus, sissonne doublée dessus, sissonne fermée battue de côté dessus, sissonne fermée de côté dessus, sissonne fermée relevée de côté dessus, temps de cuisse dessus.*

détourné [detuʀne] day-toor-NAY (Fr. probably the mutated form of pp of v se détourner, to turn away or divert; adj turned away.) A *relevé* on two feet with a turn. When taken with a 3/4-turn, the body turns simultaneously with the *relevé* action, turning toward the back foot to finish in *5th position* with a *change of feet* before lowering *en demi-plié*. The *change of feet* occurs after the first 1/4-turn. The pressure from the initial *demi-plié* provides the impetus for the body to turn in one piece, maintaining equilibrium. The head turns with the body, finishing with the *eye line* to the final direction faced. Variation: *demi-détourné*.

deux [dø] duh (Fr. adj nm two.) See *attitude à deux bras*.

devant [d(ə)vɑ̃] d(u)-VAH (Fr. prep in front of; adv in front; nm front.) 1. Term used to describe the position of the *working leg* placed in front of the other leg or in front of the body, as *5th devant, 4th devant, croisé devant,* or *effacé devant.* See *attitude devant, cou-de-pied devant, dégagé devant, devant à terre, petit retiré devant, relevé devant, relevé passé devant, retiré devant, retiré passé devant*. 2. Term used to describe the direction of an action which occurs in front of the body, e.g., *brisé volé devant, cabriole fermée devant, coupé brisé devant, ballonné devant, battement fondu devant, battement frappé devant, battement frappé fouetté devant, battement fouetté devant, battement glissé devant, battement glissé relevé devant, battement jeté devant, battement tendu devant, développé devant, développé passé devant, double battement piqué devant, en cloche devant, grand battement devant, grand battement développé devant, grand battement piqué devant, grand battement relevé devant, grand battement retiré devant, pas soutenu devant, petit développé passé devant, piqué devant, posé passé devant, sissonne fermée changée battue devant;* or uses the front foot, e.g., *assemblé devant, ballonné composé de côté devant, ballonné composé de côté passé devant, brisé 2 to 2 devant, coupé dessous brisé devant, entrechat trois devant, entrechat cinq devant, flic-flac devant, glissade devant, jeté ordinaire devant, pas de bourrée devant, petit assemblé devant, petit battement battu devant, petit battement devant, posé de côté devant, retiré sauté passé devant, sissonne fermée de côté devant, sissonne fermée relevée de côté devant, sissonne ordinaire devant*.

devant croisé See *croisé devant; en croisé.*

devant ouvert See *effacé devant; en ouvert.*

développé [devlɔpe] dayv-loh-PAY (Fr. pp of v développer, to unfold; adj unfolding; nm in dance, an unfolding action of the leg.) A slow and sustained unfolding action of the *working leg.* Can be executed with a *basic port de bras,* the arms and the leg synchronizing throughout the movement. May be performed *devant, to 2nd,* or *derrière,* and *passé.*

développé à la seconde See *développé to 2nd.*

développé derrière [devlɔpe dɛʀjɛʀ] dayv-loh-PAY der-YER (Fr. unfolding action; behind.) From *5th derrière,* the *working leg* is drawn up through *retiré derrière*, the thigh is lifted to *attitude derrière,* and the leg unfolds to its final extension at 90 degrees behind the hip. To complete the action, the leg lowers with control to *5th derrière.*

développé devant [devlɔpe d(ə)vɑ̃] dayv-loh-PAY d(u)-VAH (Fr. unfolding action; front.) From *5th devant,* the *working leg* is drawn up through *retiré devant*, lifts passing through *attitude devant,* and unfolds to its final extension at 90 degrees in front of the hip. To complete the action, the leg lowers with control to *5th devant.*

développé écarté [devlɔpe ekaʀte] dayv-loh-PAY ay-kar-TAY (Fr. unfolding action; spread apart.) A *développé to 2nd* performed in an *écarté alignment* with the leg extending *upstage* or *downstage*.

développé écarté downstage [devlɔpe ekaʀte -] dayv-loh-PAY ay-kar-TAY – (Fr. unfolding action; spread apart; downstage.) A *développé to 2nd* opening to the *écarté devant pose of the body*.

développé écarté upstage [devlɔpe ekaʀte -] dayv-loh-PAY ay-kar-TAY – (Fr. unfolding action; spread apart; upstage.) A *développé to 2nd* opening to the *écarté derrière pose of the body*.

développé passé [devlɔpe pɑse] dayv-loh-PAY pah-SAY (Fr. unfolding action; passed.) Action in which the *working leg* passes from behind the *supporting leg* and unfolds in front of it, or passes from in front of the *supporting leg* and unfolds behind it. May begin in *5th position* or in *4th position en l'air*. May be performed *devant* or *derrière*.

développé passé derrière [devlɔpe pɑse dɛʀjɛʀ] dayv-loh-PAY pah-SAY der-YER (Fr. unfolding action; passed; behind.) The dancer begins with the *working leg* either *5th position* in front, or extended *4th position devant en l'air*; s/he draws the leg through *retiré* and unfolds it to *4th en l'air derrière*.

développé passé devant [devlɔpe pɑse d(ə)vɑ̃] dayv-loh-PAY pah-SAY d(u)-VAH (Fr. unfolding action; passed; front.) The dancer begins with the *working leg* either *5th position* behind, or extended *4th position derrière en l'air*; s/he draws the leg through *retiré* and unfolds it to *4th en l'air devant*.

développé passé devant, petit See *petit développé passé devant*.

développé to 2nd [devlɔpe -] dayv-loh-PAY – (Fr. unfolding action; to the side.) From *5th position,* the *working leg* is drawn up through *retiré,* the thigh is lifted to 90 degrees, and the lower leg unfolds to the height of the thigh in *2nd position.* To complete the action, the leg lowers with control to *5th position.* Also referred to as *développé à la seconde.*

diagonale [djagɔnal] dya-go-NAL (Fr. adj diagonal; nf diagonal line or direction.) See *en diagonale*.

direction numbering A system, introduced in 1997, for assigning a number to the four sides and four corners of the dance space, providing a simple and effective way to indicate body *alignments.* Relates to an imaginary box drawn around the dancer. The audience, or front, is the dancer's predominant point of focus so that the sides of the square commence with number 1, *en face,* proceeding clockwise, and the corners with number 5, *downstage left.* They revolve to the right as this is the most usual way of turning.

dos [do] doh (Fr. nm back.) See *à dos alignment*.

double [dubl] DOO-bl, DOO-bl(u) (Fr. adj double or two times.) See *double assemblé, double demi-plié, double battement frappé, double battement piqué, double fondu, double frappé, double pirouette, double posé pirouette, double rond de jambe, double saut de basque, double tour.*

doublé [duble] doo-BLAY (Fr. adj doubled.) See *sissonne doublée*.

double assemblé [- asɑ̃ble] – a-sah-BLAY (Fr. double; gathered step.) A series of two *assemblés* performed with the same leg brushing *to 2nd.* The first *assemblé* is done without a *change of feet*, and the second with a *change of feet*.

double battement frappé [- batmɑ̃ fʀape] – bat-MAH fra-PAY (Fr. double; beating; struck.) A double beating action of the heel *sur le cou-de-pied,* followed by a *battement frappé* extension. With the *working foot* flexed, the heel passes with a small beating action into *cou-de-pied devant-derrière* or *derrière-devant* before extending. May be taken *to 2nd, to 4th devant,* or *to 4th derrière*.

double battement frappé derrière [- batmɑ̃ fʀape dɛʀjɛʀ] – bat-MAH fra-PAY der-YER (Fr. double; beating; struck; behind.) A double beating action of the heel *sur le cou-de-pied,* followed by a *battement frappé* extension. With the *working foot* flexed, the heel passes with a small beating action into *cou-de-pied devant-derrière* before extending *to 4th derrière.*

double battement frappé devant [- batmɑ̃ fʀape d(ə)vɑ̃] – bat-MAH fra-PAY d(u)-VAH (Fr. double; beating; struck; front.) A double beating action of the heel *sur le cou-de-pied,* followed by a *battement frappé* extension. With the *working foot* flexed, the heel passes with a small beating action into *cou-de-pied derrière-devant* before extending *to 4th devant.*

double battement frappé to 2nd [- batmɑ̃ fʀape -] – bat-MAH fra-PAY – (Fr. double; beating; struck; to 2nd.) A double beating action of the heel *sur le cou-de-pied,* followed by a *battement frappé* extension. With the *working foot* flexed, the heel passes with a small beating action into *cou-de-pied devant-derrière* or *derrière-devant* before extending *to 2nd.*

double battement piqué [- batmɑ̃ pike] – bat-MAH pee-KAY (Fr. double; beating; pricked.) A *battement piqué* in which the *working leg* opens *en l'air* at *glissé height,* lowers *à terre* and rebounds twice, quickly and lightly, to the previous height. May be performed *devant, to 2nd,* or *derrière.*

double battement piqué derrière [- batmɑ̃ pike dɛʀjɛʀ] – bat-MAH pee-KAY der-YER (Fr. double; beating; pricked; behind.) A *battement piqué* in which the *working leg* opens to *4th position derrière en l'air* at *glissé height,* lowers *à terre* and rebounds twice, quickly and lightly, to the previous height.

double battement piqué devant [- batmɑ̃ pike d(ə)vɑ̃] – bat-MAH pee-KAY d(u)-VAH (Fr. double; beating; pricked; front.) A *battement piqué* in which the *working foot* opens to *4th position devant en l'air* at *glissé height,* lowers *à terre* and rebounds twice, quickly and lightly, to the previous height.

double battement piqué to 2nd [- batmɑ̃ pike -] – bat-MAH pee-KAY – (Fr. double; beating; pricked; to 2nd.) A *battement piqué* in which the *working leg* opens to *2nd position en l'air* at *glissé height,* lowers *à terre* and rebounds twice, quickly and lightly, to the previous height.

double demi-plié [- d(ə)miplije] – d(u)-MEE-plee-YAY (Fr. double; half-bending action.) An action in which the dancer closes or ends *en demi-plié* and performs a stretch of the legs followed by another *demi-plié* or a lowering *en demi-plié* to prepare for the next action.

double fondu [- fɔ̃dy] – fo-DU (Fr. double; melted action.) A variation of *battement fondu* in which the dancer begins in *5th position,* or with the working leg either *cou-de-pied devant* or *derrière,* or extended *devant, to 2nd,* or *derrière.* S/he lowers *en fondu* with the working foot *cou-de-pied,* then restretches, maintaining the position of the working leg, performs a second lowering *en fondu* as the working leg begins to extend, and stretches both legs to reach the final position *en l'air.*

double piqué See *double battement piqué.*

double pirouette [- piʀwɛt] – peer-WET (Fr. double; turn.) A *pirouette* in which the dancer's body turns through two revolutions. May be done with just less than or just over two revolutions to start and end in various alignments.

double pirouette en dedans [- piʀwɛt ɑ̃ dədɑ̃] – peer-WET ah d(u)-DAH (Fr. double; turn; inward.) A *pirouette* in which the dancer's body turns toward the *supporting leg* through two revolutions.

double pirouette en dehors [- piʀwɛt ɑ̃ dəɔʀ] – peer-WET ah d(u)-OR (Fr. double; turn; outward.) A *pirouette* in which the dancer's body turns away from the *supporting leg* through two revolutions.

double posé pirouette [- poze piʀwɛt] – poh-ZAY peer-WET (Fr. double; placed; turn.) A *posé pirouette* in which the dancer's body turns through two revolutions.

double posé pirouette en dedans [- poze piʀwɛt ɑ̃ dədɑ̃] – poh-ZAY peer-WET ah d(u)-DAH (Fr. double; placed; turn; inward.) A *posé pirouette en dedans* in which the dancer performs two complete revolutions.

double posé pirouette en dehors [- poze piʀwɛt ɑ̃ dəɔʀ] – poh-ZAY peer-WET ah d(u)-OR (Fr. double; placed; turn; outward.) A *posé pirouette en dehors* in which the dancer performs two complete revolutions.

double rond de jambe See *double rond de jambe en l'air.*

double rond de jambe en l'air [- ʀɔ̃ də ʒɑ̃b ɑ̃ lɛʀ] – ro d(u) zhahb ah ler (Fr. double; circle of the leg; in the air.) A circling action of the lower leg done without disturbing the thigh. The *working foot* traces two small circles in the air beside and slightly in front of the supporting calf, with the *working foot* beginning and ending in *2nd* at 45 degrees. The size of the circle near the calf may be related to that of a tea cup. May be done with the *working leg* beginning and ending 90 degrees and the circling action taken at the height of the knee. May be performed *en dehors* or *en dedans.*

double rond de jambe en l'air en dedans [- ʀɔ̃ də ʒɑ̃b ɑ̃ lɛʀ ɑ̃ dədɑ̃] – ro d(u) zhahb ah ler ah d(u)-DAH (Fr. double; circle of the leg; in the air; inward.) An inward circling action of the lower leg in which the working thigh is held throughout. Starting with the *working leg* extended *to 2nd* at 45 degrees, the lower leg moves with a slight forward arc en route toward the supporting calf until the toe skims the mid-calf, continues outward, then moves again through a slight forward arc toward the calf, and completes the path opening directly *to 2nd*, ending as it began. May be done with the *working leg* beginning and ending 90 degrees and the circling action taken at the height of the knee.

double rond de jambe en l'air en dehors [- ʀɔ̃ də ʒɑ̃b ɑ̃ lɛʀ ɑ̃ dəɔʀ] – ro d(u) zhahb ah ler ah d(u)-OR (Fr. double; circle of the leg; in the air; outward.) An outward circling action of the lower leg in which the working thigh is held throughout. Starting with the *working leg* extended *to 2nd* at 45 degrees, the lower leg moves directly toward the supporting calf until the toe skims the mid-calf, continues through a slight forward arc outward, then moves again toward the calf, and completes the path with a slight forward arc en route *to 2nd*, ending as it began. May be done with the *working leg* beginning and ending 90 degrees and the circling action taken at the height of the knee.

double rond de jambe sauté [- ʀɔ̃ də ʒɑ̃b sote] – ro d(u) zhahb soh-TAY (Fr. double; circle of the leg; jumped.) A jump in which the *working leg* performs a *double rond de jambe* while the *supporting leg* performs a *temps levé.* May be performed *en dehors* or *en dedans.*

double rond de jambe sauté en dedans [- ʀɔ̃ də ʒɑ̃b sote ɑ̃ dədɑ̃] – ro d(u) zhahb soh-TAY ah d(u)-DAH (Fr. double; circle of the leg; jumped; inward.) A jump in which the *working leg* performs a *double rond de jambe en dedans* while the *supporting leg* performs a *temps levé.*

double rond de jambe sauté en dehors [- ʀɔ̃ də ʒɑ̃b sote ɑ̃ dəɔʀ] – ro d(u) zhahb soh-TAY ah d(u)-OR (Fr. double; circle of the leg; jumped; outward.) A jump in which the *working leg* performs a *double rond de jambe en dehors* while the *supporting leg* performs a *temps levé.*

double saut de basque [- so də bask] – soh d(u) bask (Fr. double; jump of the Basque.) A male *grand allegro* step in which the dancer performs a *saut de basque*, completing two revolutions in the air.

double tour [- tuʀ] – toor (Fr. double; turn.) A *tour en l'air* in which the dancer performs two revolutions of the body.

downstage 1. Term used to describe the location of the dancer on the centre front portion of the stage, or anywhere on the front of the stage near the audience. 2. Term used to describe a direction faced in relation to the dancer's body: when a dancer faces *downstage,* s/he is *en face*, facing the audience, or facing 1. See *direction numbering.*

downstage left 1. Term used to describe the location of the dancer on the left front portion of the stage, or near the front left corner. 2. Term used to describe a direction faced in relation to the dancer's body: when a dancer faces *downstage left,* s/he is facing 5. See *direction numbering.*

downstage right 1. Term used to describe the location of the dancer on the right front portion of the stage, or near the front right corner 2. Term used to describe a direction faced in relation to the dancer's body: when a dancer faces *downstage right,* s/he is facing 6. See *direction numbering.*

écarté [ekaʀte] ay-kar-TAY (Fr. pp of v écarter, to separate or move apart; adj spread apart, wide.) A secondary *body alignment* taken facing either *downstage* corner, with the *working leg extended to 2nd* either *upstage* or *downstage.* See *écarté derrière, écarté devant.* Also *en écarté.* Movements performed in this *alignment* include the following steps to or through *2nd position: battement dégagé, battement tendu, développé, posé, glissade, assemblé de côté, grand battement, galop, sissonne doublée.* See *développé écarté, head écarté.*

écarté derrière [ekaʀte dɛʀjɛʀ] ay-kar-TAY der-YER (Fr. spread apart; behind.) A basic *pose of the body* taken facing either *downstage* corner, with the *upstage* foot *dégagé to 2nd.* The arms are in *4th position,* with the *upstage* arm raised. There is a slight inclination of the upper body away from the *working leg* in the extended position from corner to corner. The head is turned and the *eye line* is directed out beyond the *downstage* hand. Also *écarté upstage.*

écarté devant [ekaʀte d(ə)vɑ̃] ay-kar-TAY d(u)-VAH (Fr. spread apart; front.) A basic *pose of the body* taken facing either *downstage* corner with the *downstage* foot *dégagé to 2nd.* A strongly extended position from corner to corner. The arms are in *4th position* with the *downstage* arm raised and slightly opened, and the other arm placed slightly below *2nd position.* The head is turned and raised so that the *eye line* is in front of and beyond the raised forearm. Also *écarté downstage.*

écarté downstage See *écarté devant.*

écarté upstage See *écarté derrière.*

échappé [eʃape] ay-sha-PAY (Fr. pp of v échapper, to escape; adj escaped.) See *échappé relevé, échappé sauté.*

échappé fermé sauté See *échappé sauté fermé.*

échappé relevé [eʃape ʀəlve] ay-sha-PAY r(u)l-VAY (Fr. escaped action; pulled up.) A *relevé* performed with the feet moving from a closed to an open position, and returning to a closed position. From a *demi-plié,* the feet push equally away from the floor with a strong outward action to the open position *en pointes,* before returning to *demi-plié.* Taken to *2nd position* (with or without a *change of feet)* or to *4th position.* Variation: *échappé relevé in 4 counts.*

échappé relevé in 2 counts [eʃape ʀəlve -] ay-sha-PAY r(u)l-VAY – (Fr. escaped action; pulled up; in 2 counts.) An *échappé relevé* consisting of two actions: an opening from *5th position to 2nd* or *4th position en pointes,* and a closing to *5th position en demi-plié.*

échappé relevé in 4 counts [eʃape ʀəlve -] ay-sha-PAY r(u)l-VAY – (Fr. escaped action; pulled up; in 4 counts.) An *échappé relevé* consisting of four actions: an opening from *5th position to 2nd* or *4th position en pointes,* a lowering *en demi-plié* in the open position, a *relevé en pointes* in the open position, and a closing in *5th position en demi-plié.*

échappé relevé to 2nd [eʃape ʀəlve -] ay-sha-PAY r(u)l-VAY – (Fr. escaped; pulled up; to 2nd.) An *échappé relevé* in which the feet begin in *5th position en demi-plié,* push equally away from the floor into *2nd position en pointes,* and return directly to *5th position en demi-plié,* with or without *a change of feet.*

échappé relevé to 2nd en tournant [eʃape ʀəlve - ɑ̃ tuʀnɑ̃] ay-sha-PAY r(u)l-VAY – ah toor-NAH (Fr. escaped action; pulled up; to 2nd turning.) A series of *échappé relevés to 2nd* performed while the body makes a full revolution, with the change of *alignment* occurring on the outward action of the legs.

échappé relevé to 4th [eʃape ʀəlve -] ay-sha-PAY r(u)l-VAY – (Fr. escaped action; pulled up; to 4th.) An *échappé relevé* in which the feet begin in *5th position en demi-plié,* push equally away from the floor with a strong outward action into *4th position en pointes* with the legs and feet aligned one in front of the other, and return directly to *5th position en demi-plié.*

échappé sauté [eʃape sote] ay-sha-PAY soh-TAY (Fr. escaped action; jumped.) A jump from a closed position, either *1st* or *5th,* to an open position, either *2nd* or *4th.* A jump consisting of two *sautés*–from a closed to an open position on the first, then back to a closed position on the second–is now termed *échappé sauté fermé.*

échappé sauté battu See *échappé sauté battu fermé to 2nd with change of feet.*

échappé sauté battu fermé to 2nd with change of feet [eʃape sote baty fɛʀme -] ay-sha-PAY soh-TAY ba-TU fer-MAY – (Fr. escaped action; jumped; beaten; closed; to 2nd with change of feet.) An *échappé sauté to 2nd* embellished with a beat on the closing *sauté.* Beginning *5th devant,* the first action is an *échappé sauté to 2nd position,* and the second is a return to *5th position* with a beating action of the legs together in the air, with the same leg *devant,* before landing with the other leg *devant.*

échappé sauté fermé [eʃape sote fɛʀme] ay-sha-PAY soh-TAY fer-MAY (Fr. escaped action; jumped; closed.) A jump consisting of two *sautés* where the feet move from *5th position,* land in an open position on the first jump, and return to *5th position* on the second jump. Taken to *2nd position* (with or without *a change of feet)* or to *4th position.* Variations: *grand échappé sauté, échappé sauté battu.*

échappé sauté fermé to 2nd [eʃape sote fɛʀme

-] ay-sha-PAY soh-TAY fer-MAY – (Fr. escaped action; jumped; closed; to 2nd.) A jump consisting of two *sautés* where the feet move from *5th position,* open an equal distance to land in *2nd position* on the first jump, and return to *5th position* with or without a *change of feet* on the second jump. From *bras bas,* the arms open to *demi-seconde* at the same time as the legs, and lower to *bras bas* as the feet return to *5th position.*

échappé sauté fermé to 4th [eʃape sote fɛʀme -] ay-sha-PAY soh-TAY fer-MAY – (Fr. escaped action; jumped; closed; to 4th.) A jump consisting of two *sautés* where the feet move from *5th position,* open an equal distance to land in *4th position* on the first jump, and return to *5th position* on the second jump. From *bras bas,* the arms open to *3rd* with the opposite arm forward to the foot on the first jump, and lower to *bras bas* on the second.

effacé [efase] ay-fa-SAY (Fr. pp of v effacer, to hold something sideways on, in order to present as little of the surface as possible (in fencing); adj sideways on.) Term used to describe a *pose of the body* taken *en ouvert.* Also *en effacé.* See *effacé derrière, effacé devant.* In the Grades syllabus prior to 1991, the term *effacé* referred to what is now known as *en ouvert.*

effacé derrière [efase dɛʀjɛʀ] ay-fa-SAY der-YER (Fr. sideways on; behind.) A basic *pose of the body* taken facing either *downstage* corner with the *downstage* foot *dégagé derrière.* The arms are held in *4th position* with the *downstage* arm raised. There is a slight lift and inclination forward in the upper body, while retaining the open line across the chest. The head is turned and lifted so that the *eye line* is in front of and beyond the elbow between 1 *(downstage)* and the other *downstage* corner.

effacé devant [efase d(ə)vɑ̃] ay-fa-SAY d(u)-VAH (Fr. sideways on; front.) A basic *pose of the body* taken facing either *downstage* corner with the *upstage* foot *dégagé devant.* The arms are held in *4th position* with the *downstage* arm raised. Heightened awareness of the opening of the chest and the use of the upper back causes a slight inclination of the upper body, creating a diagonal line from the crown of the head to the tip of the toes. The head is turned and lifted so that the *eye line* is between 1 *(downstage)* and the other *downstage* corner.

élancé [elɑ̃se] ay-lah-SAY (Fr. pp of v s'élancer meaning to shoot, dart, bound, spring; adj darted.) Term used to describe a step which travels in a darting manner. See *jeté élancé en tournant, jeté élancé en avant.*

emboîté [ɑ̃bwate] ah-bwa-TAY (Fr. pp of v emboîter, to fit together; adj fit together; nm in dance, a light step characterized by the passing of the feet, one in front of the other.) Action performed *en pointes* as part of a series of precise, quick transfers of weight under the body line. The dancer begins in *5th position en pointes* with the *working leg* behind; staying *en pointes* throughout, she extends one leg *to 2nd* just off the floor, then closes *5th position* with a *change of feet*; usually performed in series alternating legs; usually initiated with an *assemblé piqué dessus* and performed *en avant*, with each *working leg* beginning behind and closing in front; called *déboîté* when performed *en arrière*, with each *working leg* beginning in front and closing behind.

emboîté relevé en tournant [ɑ̃bwate ʀəlve ɑ̃ tuʀnɑ̃] ah-bwa-TAY r(u)l-VAY ah toor-NAH (Fr. fit together step; pulled up; turning.) A composite step performed *en pointes* consisting of three actions which make a full turn. The dancer begins in *5th position en demi-plié* with the *working foot* behind, arms in *3rd position*; she executes a *relevé passé devant* 2 to 1 travelling slightly along the *line of dance*, bringing the back foot to *retiré devant* and changing the arms to *3rd* while making 1/2-turn *en dedans*; she then steps under the body line and lifts the other leg to *retiré devant* while making 1/2-turn *en dehors* to complete the full turn with the arms changing to *3rd position*; and she finishes *en demi-plié*. Often performed *en diagonale*.

emboîté sauté en tournant [ɑ̃bwate sote ɑ̃ tuʀnɑ̃] ah-bwa-TAY soh-TAY ah toor-NAH (Fr. fit together step; jumped; turning.) Series of three jumping actions making a full turn, often performed *en diagonale*. The dancer begins *5th position en demi-plié;* s/he executes a *sissonne ordinaire passée devant* travelling sideways slightly along the *line of dance* while making a 1/2-turn *en dedans*, does a *petit jeté devant sur place* while making a 1/2-turn *en dehors* to complete the full turn, and executes a *petit assemblé devant* to end as s/he began. The arms often begin in *3rd position*, change to *3rd position* on the *sissonne passée*, and return to *3rd* on the *petit jeté*.

en [ɑ̃] ah (Fr. prep in, on, by, or to.) See *en arrière, en attitude, en avant, en cloche, en croisé, en croix, en dedans, en dehors, en demi-pointe/s, en demi-plié, en diagonale, en écarté, en effacé, en face, en fondu, en l'air, en manège, en ouvert,* *en pointe/s, en première, en tournant.*

en arrière [ɑ̃ naʀjɛʀ] ah nar-YER (Fr. backward.) Phrase denoting movement travelling backward. See *assemblé en arrière, balancé de côté en arrière, ballonné composé en arrière, ballonné en arrière battement tendu en arrière, brisé en arrière, chassé en arrière, chassé passé en arrière, courus en arrière, courus en pointes en arrière, entrechat quatre en arrière, glissade en arrière, jeté battement en arrière, pas de basque glissé en arrière, pas de basque sauté en arrière, pas de bourrée couru en arrière, pas de bourrée en arrière, pas de bourrée en pointe en arrière, pas de valse en arrière, posé coupé en arrière, posé en arrière, posé en pointe/s en arrière, relevé in arabesque en arrière, sissonne doublée en arrière, sissonne fermée changée battue en arrière, sissonne fermée en arrière, sissonne ouverte battue en arrière, sissonne ouverte en arrière, sissonne relevée fermée en arrière, sissonne relevée ouverte en arrière, step en arrière, temps levé posé en arrière, temps lié en arrière, tombé en arrière, walks en arrière.*

en attitude See *attitude.*

en avant [ɑ̃ navɑ̃] ah na-VAH (Fr. forward.) Phrase denoting movement travelling forward. See *assemblé en avant, ballonné composé en avant, ballonné en avant, battement tendu en avant, brisé en avant, chassé en avant, chassé passé en avant, coupé dessous en tournant chassé en avant, coupé dessus brisé en avant, courus en avant, galop en avant, glissade en avant, glissade piquée en avant, grand jeté développé en avant, grand jeté en avant, grand jeté en avant en tournant in attitude en avant, jeté battement en avant, jeté élancé en avant, jeté en avant, pas chassé en avant, pas de basque battu en avant, pas de basque glissé en avant, pas de basque sauté en avant, pas de bourrée couru en avant, pas de bourrée en avant, pas de valse en avant, polka steps en avant, posé coupé en avant, posé en avant, posé grand jeté en avant, posé passé en avant, relevé 1 to 1 en avant, run en avant, sissonne doublée en avant, sissonne fermée changée battue en avant, sissonne fermée changée en avant, sissonne fermée en avant, sissonne fermée relevée en avant, sissonne ouverte battue en avant, sissonne ouverte en avant, sissonne relevée ouverte en avant, skip en avant, soubresaut en avant, temps lié en avant, tombé en avant, walks en avant.*

en cloche [ɑ̃ klɔʃ] ah klosh (Fr. like a bell.) Phrase used to describe a movement of the leg that swings from *4th position à terre* or *en l'air*, brushing through *1st position* to the other *4th position.* The movement is to resemble the pendulum-like action of a bell clapper. See *battement glissé en cloche, battement jeté en cloche, grand battement en cloche, grand battement en cloche in attitude.*

en croisé [ɑ̃ kʀwaze] ah krwa-ZAY (Fr. crossed.) Phrase used to describe a basic *body alignment* taken facing either *downstage* corner, with the *downstage* leg in front: facing 5 *(downstage left)* with the right leg in front, or facing 6 *(downstage right)* with the left leg in front. The *working leg* may be either *devant* or *derrière.* See *croisé derrière, croisé devant.*

en croix [ɑ̃ kʀwa] ah krwa (Fr. in the form of a cross; crosswise.) Phrase used to describe a sequence repeated *devant, to 2nd, derrière,* and again *to 2nd,* or the reverse. *Barre* and *centre* exercises are usually practised *en croix.* Note: when a sequence is performed *devant, to 2nd,* and *derrière,* it is said to be "taken in all positions." See *battement glissé en croix, échappé sauté en croix.*

en dedans [ɑ̃ dədɑ̃] ah d(u)-DAH (Fr. in an inward direction.) 1. Phrase used to describe an inward circling action of the *working leg,* either *à terre* or *en l'air.* With the right leg, this motion is in a counter-clockwise direction. See *assemblé soutenu à terre en dedans, demi-assemblé soutenu à terre en dedans, demi-grand rond de jambe en dedans, grand rond de jambe en l'air en dedans, petit rond de jambe en dedans, rond de jambe à terre en dedans, rond de jambe en l'air en dedans, rond de jambe jeté en dedans.* 2. Phrase used to describe a turn of the body toward the *supporting leg,* e.g., to the right when standing on the right leg. See *flic-flac en dedans, pirouette en dedans, pivot en dedans, posé assemblé soutenu en tournant en dedans, posé pirouette en dedans, sauté pirouette en tournant en dedans.*

en dehors [ɑ̃ dəɔʀ] ah d(u)-OR (Fr. in an outward direction.) 1. Phrase used to describe an outward circling action of the *working leg,* either *à terre* or *en l'air.* With the right leg, this motion is in a clockwise direction. See *assemblé soutenu à terre en dehors, demi-assemblé soutenu à terre en dehors, demi-grand rond de jambe en dehors, grand assemblé soutenu en dehors, grand rond de jambe en l'air en dehors, petit rond de jambe en dehors, rond de jambe à terre en dehors, rond de jambe en l'air en dehors, rond de jambe jeté en dehors.* 2. Phrase used to describe a turn of the body away from the *supporting leg* and toward the *working* *leg*, e.g., to the left when standing on the right leg. See *assemblé soutenu en tournant en dehors, flic-flac en dehors, fouetté rond de jambe en tournant en dehors, pirouette en dehors, pivot en dehors, posé pirouette en dehors.*

en demi-plié [ɑ̃ d(ə)miplije] ah d(u)-MEE-plee-YAY (Fr. in a half bend.) Phrase used to describe a position in which the *supporting legs* are bent and the heels stay in contact with the floor. When only one bent leg supports the body, the term *en fondu* is used.

en demi-pointe/s [ɑ̃ d(ə)mipwɛ̃t] ah d(u)-MEE-pwet (Fr. on half tiptoe.) Phrase used to describe a position in which the ball of the *supporting foot/feet* contact the floor. The ankle is fully extended (plantar flexed). This position was at one time referred to as *"three-quarter pointe."* Movements performed *en demi-pointe/s* may be performed *en pointe/s* when the dancer wears *pointe shoes.*

en diagonale [ɑ̃ djagɔnal] ah dya-go-NAL (Fr. on diagonal.) Phrase describing the line travelled from an *upstage/downstage* corner to the opposite *downstage/upstage* corner, i.e., the longest straight line on the stage. May be used for a series of jumps, steps, or turns which travel broadly. See *pirouettes en diagonale*. The following are performed *en diagonale*: *chaînés, classical walks, courus, emboîté relevé en tournant, glissade, jeté élancé en tournant, pas de valse, petit soutenu, posé pirouette en dedans, posé pirouette en dehors*, runs, *saut de basque*, turns.

en écarté [ɑ̃ nekaʀte] ah nay-kar-TAY (Fr. spread apart.) Phrase referring to a position or movement performed *écarté*. See *écarté.*

en effacé See *en ouvert.*

en face [ɑ̃ fas] ah fas (Fr. facing.) Phrase used to describe a basic *body alignment* taken facing 1 *(downstage)*. The *working leg* can be either *devant, to 2nd*, or *derrière*. See *en face derriere, en face devant.*

en face derrière [ɑ̃ fas dɛʀjɛʀ] ah fas der-YER (Fr. facing: behind.) A basic *pose of the body* taken facing 1 *(downstage)* with the *working leg dégagé derrière* and the arms in *2nd position.* The head is well poised with the *eye line* directly forward, and the shoulders and hips are square.

en face devant [ɑ̃ fas d(ə)vɑ̃] ah fas d(u)-VAH (Fr. facing: front.) A basic *pose of the body* taken facing 1 *(downstage)* with the *working leg dégagé devant* and the arms in *2nd position.* The head is well poised with the *eye line* directly forward, and the shoulders and hips are square.

en fondu [ɑ̃ fɔ̃dy] ah fo-DU (Fr. melted, in a blending action.) Term used to describe a position in which the *supporting leg* is bent and the heel stays in contact with the floor, as *arabesque en fondu.*

en l'air [ɑ̃ lɛʀ] ah ler (Fr. in the air.) Phrase used to describe a position in which the *working foot* is off the floor. This term is used to modify positions or movements that would otherwise be performed *à terre*, i.e., with the *working foot* contacting the floor, as *rond de jambe en l'air*. When the *working leg* is *en l'air* 45 degrees, its foot is below the height of the supporting knee. When the *working leg* is *en l'air* 90 degrees, its foot is in line with the hip.

en manège [ɑ̃ manɛʒ] ah ma-NEZH (Fr. in a circle.) Phrase used to describe a combination of steps or a series of turns which travel around the stage along a circular path, like a merry-go-round or carousel. See *coupés jetés en tournant en manège, petits pas de basque en manège, petits soutenus en manège, pirouettes en manège.*

en ouvert [ɑ̃ nuvɛʀ] ah noo-VER (Fr. open.) Phrase used to describe a basic *body alignment* taken facing either *downstage* corner, with the *upstage* leg in front: facing 5 *(downstage left)* with the left leg in front, or facing 6 *(downstage right)* with the right leg in front. The *working leg* may be either *devant* or *derrière. The effacé poses of the body* are taken *en ouvert.* In the Grades syllabus prior to 1991, the term *effacé* referred to what is now known as *en ouvert.*

en pointe/s [ɑ̃ pwɛ̃t] ah pwet (Fr. on; tiptoe.) Phrase used to describe a position in which the tip of the *supporting foot/feet* contacts the floor. Movements *en pointe/s* must be performed while wearing *pointe shoes;* they are usually practised *en demi-pointe/s*. See *pointe work.* (Note that, in this *Dictionary*, positions and movements described as being performed *en pointe/s* are understood to be done by women either *en pointe/s* or *en demi-pointe/s,* and by men *en demi-pointe/s.)*

en première [ɑ̃ pʀəmjɛʀ] ah pr(u)m-YER (Fr. in; first.) Phrase referring to a step or series of steps which are performed in *1st position of the feet*. See *sauté en première, pas de bourrée en première.*

en première, pas de bourrée See *pas de bourrée en première.*

en première, sauté See *sauté en première.*

en tournant [ɑ̃ tuʀnɑ̃] ah toor-NAH (Fr. by; turning.) Phrase used to refer to an action performed while turning. See *assemblé soutenu en tournant, balancé en tournant, ballonné en tournant, coupé dessous en tournant, courus en tournant, échappé relevé to 2nd en tournant, emboîté relevé en tournant, emboîté sauté en tournant, fouetté relevé en tournant en dehors, fouetté rond de jambe en tournant en dehors, fouetté sauté en tournant, grand fouetté relevé en tournant, grand jeté en tournant, grand pas de basque en tournant, jeté élancé en tournant, pas de bourrée en tournant, pas de bourrée piqué en tournant, pas de valse en tournant, petit pas de basque en tournant, petit jeté en tournant, posé rotation with développé en tournant, sauté pirouette en dedans en tournant, sissonne fermée changée battue en tournant, sissonne ouverte changée en tournant, wide pas de bourrée dessous en tournant.*

enchaînement [ɑ̃ʃɛnmɑ̃] ah-shen-MAH (Fr. nm a sequence of dance steps.) A dance phrase or combination. See *classical study.*

entrechat [ɑ̃tʀəʃa] ah-tr(u)-SHA (< It. intrecciare, to interweave or braid; Fr. nm a jump in which the feet beat rapidly, one against the other.) A jump in which the feet cross and the legs beat in the air. Variations are named according to the number of actions of each leg, e.g., "four" *(quatre)* indicates a jump from two feet to two feet where each leg interweaves twice; "five" *(cinq)* indicates a jump from two feet to one foot where each leg interweaves twice and one foot ends *sur le cou-de-pied devant* or *derrière.* See *entrechat trois, entrechat quatre, entrechat cinq, entrechat six de volée.*

entrechat cinq [ɑ̃tʀəʃa sɛ̃k] ah-tr(u)-SHA sek (Fr. entrechat; five.) A jump in which the legs perform five actions. The dancer begins in *5th position,* jumps into the air, beats with a *change of feet,* performs another *change of feet,* then places the front foot *sur le cou-de-pied devant* or the back foot *sur le cou-de-pied derrière* as s/he lands on the other foot.

entrechat cinq derrière [ɑ̃tʀəʃa sɛ̃k dɛʀjɛʀ] ah-tr(u)-SHA sek der-YER (Fr. entrechat; five; behind.) An *entrechat cinq* in which the dancer begins in *5th position,* jumps into the air, beats with a *change of feet,* performs another *change of feet,* then places the back foot *sur le cou-de-pied derrière* as s/he lands on the other foot.

entrechat cinq devant [ɑ̃tʀəʃa sɛ̃k d(ə)vɑ̃] ah-tr(u)-SHA sek d(u)-VAH (Fr. entrechat; five; front.) An *entrechat cinq* in which the dancer begins in *5th position,* jumps into the air, beats with a *change of feet,* performs another *change of feet,* then places the front foot *sur le cou-de-pied devant* as s/he lands on the other foot.

entrechat quatre [ɑ̃tʀəʃa katʀə] ah-tr(u)-SHA katr(u) (Fr. entrechat; four.) A jump in which the legs change to beat, and return to land with the same leg *devant.* There are four interweaving actions, two with each leg.

entrechat quatre en arrière [ɑ̃tʀəʃa katʀə ɑ̃ naʀjɛʀ] ah-tr(u)-SHA katr(u) ah nar-YER (Fr. entrechat; four; backward.) An *entrechat quatre* performed travelling backward.

entrechat six [ɑ̃tʀəʃa sis] ah-tr(u)-SHA sees (Fr. entrechat; six.) A jump in which the legs change to beat, change again to beat, and land with the other leg *devant.* There are six interweaving actions, three with each leg. Variation: *entrechat six de volée de côté.*

entrechat six de volée de côté [ɑ̃tʀəʃa sis də vɔle də kote] ah-tr(u)-SHA sees d(u) vo-LAY d(u)koh-TAY (Fr. entrechat; six; of flight; to the side.) An *entrechat six* travelled sideways and initiated with a brush *to 2nd.* The dancer begins in *5th position* with the *working leg derrière;* s/he brushes the back foot *to 2nd,* jumps beating the push-off leg behind the *working leg,* then beats twice with a *change of feet* on each beat to land in *5th position* with the *working leg devant.* Often prepared with a *glissade* or *chassé en avant,* with the brush taken *en écarté* with the arms to *open 4th.* Also *entrechat six de côté* (Cecchetti), *entrechat-six de volée* (Russian).

entrechat trois [ɑ̃tʀəʃa tʀwɑ] ah-tr(u)-SHA trwa (Fr. entrechat; three.) A jump in which the legs perform three actions. The dancer begins in *5th position,* jumps into the air, beats without a *change of feet,* performs a *change of feet,* then places the front foot *sur le cou-de-pied devant* or the back foot *sur le cou-de-pied derrière* as s/he alights on the other foot.

entrechat trois derrière [ɑ̃tʀəʃa tʀwɑ dɛʀjɛʀ] ah-tr(u)-SHA trwa der-YER (Fr. entrechat; three;

behind.) An *entrechat trois* in which the dancer begins in *5th position*, jumps into the air, beats without a *change of feet*, performs a *change of feet*, then places the back foot *sur le cou-de-pied derrière* as s/he alights on the other foot.

entrechat trois devant [ɑ̃tʀəʃa tʀwɑ d(ə)vɑ̃] ahtr(u)-SHA trwa d(u)-VAH (Fr. entrechat; three; front.) An *entrechat trois* in which the dancer begins in *5th position*, jumps into the air, beats without a *change of feet*, performs a *change of feet*, then places the front foot *sur le cou-de-pied devant* as s/he alights on the other foot.

enveloppé [ɑ̃vlɔpe] ahv-lo-PAY (Fr. pp of v envelopper, to wrap or shroud; adj encircled; nm an enveloping action.) A reversed *développé* movement, in which the working leg closes from a position *en l'air* through *retiré*. See *grand battement enveloppé*.

épaulé [epole] ay-poh-LAY (Fr. pp likely derived from v épauler, to raise to the shoulder; adj shouldered.) See *arabesque épaulée*.

épaulement [epolmɑ̃] ay-pohl-MAH (Fr. nm likely derived from v épauler, to raise to the shoulder; the use of the shoulder.) One of the basic elements of *centre practice*. A rotary action in the upper torso, combined with the use of head and eyes, which enhances the dancer's line and sense of poise. For example, when closing in *5th position of the feet* with *épaulement*, the spine rotates so that the shoulder corresponding to the front foot comes slightly forward and the *eye line* turns slightly in that direction.

exercise A sequence of basic movements practised to establish fundamental dance skills. See *set exercise*, *training exercise*, *warm up exercise*.

exercise, set See *set exercise*.

exercise, training See *training exercise*.

exercise, warm up See *warm up exercise*.

extended chassé [- ʃase] – sha-SAY (Fr. extended; chased.) A *chassé* in which the sliding action is performed onto an extended leg with the foot fully stretched just prior to the transfer of weight. Executed with a push from the back foot to extend the toe of the front foot beyond the *dégagé* and passing through a small *fondu* on the front leg, releasing the back foot to end *dégagé derrière*. Also referred to as *extended toe chassé*.

eye line Term referring to the use of eyes, whereby the dancer projects his/her gaze into the distance, enhancing the line created through the body and limbs.

face [fas] fas (Fr. nf face.) See *en face*.

failli [faji] fa-YEE (Fr. pp of v faillir, to narrowly miss something; adj narrowly missed; n a narrowly missed action.) A composite step consisting of a *sissonne* showing the *5th position en l'air*, and a *chassé passé en avant*. The dancer starts in *5th position*, jumps into the air holding the *5th position*, separates the legs while travelling very slightly forward, and lands on the front leg with the back leg *en arabesque;* s/he then slides the back leg through *1st position en demi-plié* and continues forward to finish *dégagé derrière* on a straight *supporting leg*; usually performed starting and ending *en croisé*, i.e., turning in *5th position en l'air* and landing *en ouvert*. May be used as a preparatory step for *pas de bourrée*, *assemblé soutenu en dedans*, *assemblé de côté dessus*, *pas de chat*.

feet See *position of the feet*.

fermé [fɛʀme] fer-MAY (Fr. adj closed.) Term used to describe an action which ends with the feet together, in a closed position. See *échappé sauté fermé, sissonne fermée de côté dessus, sissonne fermée de côté dessous, sissonne fermée de côté devant, sissonne fermée de côté derrière, échappé sauté battu fermé without change of feet, échappé sauté battu fermé with change of feet, sissonne fermée en avant, sissonne fermée en arrière, sissonne fermée battue dessus, sissonne fermée relevée de côté devant, sissonne fermée relevée de côté dessous, sissonne fermée relevée de côté dessus, sissonne fermée relevée en avant, sissonne fermée relevée en arrière, sissonne fermée changée battue en tournant, sissonne fermée changée battue devant, sissonne fermée battue de côté dessus, sissonne fermée changée battue en arrière, cabriole fermée devant, cabriole fermée dessus.*

fifth See *position of the arms, 5th; position of the feet, 5th.*

first See *arabesque, 1st; position of the arms, 1st; position of the feet, 1st.*

flac [flak] flak (Fr. excl splash! an onomatopoeic expression, imitating the sound of falling water, or of something falling into water.) See *flic-flac*.

flèche [flɛʃ] flesh (Fr. nf an arrow.) In the RAD, this term is spelled as *flêche*. See *temps de flêche*.

flic-flac [flikflak] fleek-flak (Fr. excl splish splash!) A movement consisting of two quick inward actions of the lower leg. The *working leg* starts in *2nd* at *glissé height*, then the lower leg moves inward with the ball of the foot skimming the floor on each inward action. The working ankle remains stretched throughout and reaches the supporting ankle in front then behind *(devant, derrière)* or behind then in front *(derrière, devant)*, before opening *to 2nd* at *glissé height*. This movement is often performed in conjunction with a *rise*. May be performed *en dehors* or *en dedans*, and *en tournant*.

flic-flac en dedans [flikflak ɑ̃ dədɑ̃] fleek-flak ah d(u)-DAH (Fr. flic-flac; inward.) A *flic-flac* in which the first closing action is in front, and the second is behind. Sometimes referred to as *flic-flac devant derrière*.

flic-flac en dehors [flikflak ɑ̃ dəɔʀ] fleek-flak ah d(u)-OR (Fr. flic-flac; outward.) A *flic-flac* in which the first closing action is behind, and the second is in front. Sometimes referred to as *flic-flac derrière devant*.

flic-flac en tournant [flikflak ɑ̃ tuʀnɑ̃] fleek-flak ah toor-NAH (by turning) A *flic-flac* performed with a simultaneous revolution of the body: on the *flic* (the initial inward action), the first 1/4-turn is taken without a *rise;* at the beginning of the *flac,* the turn continues as the dancer starts to rise; and the turn is completed *en demi-pointe* with leg open. In *flic-flac en dedans en tournant,* the foot closes *devant derrière* and the turn is made toward the *supporting leg;* in *flic-flac en dehors en tournant,* the foot closes *derrière devant* and the turn is made away from the *supporting leg.*

fondu [fɔ̃dy] fo-DU (Fr. pp of v fondre, to melt; adj melted or blurred; nm a blended action.) See *battement fondu*, *en fondu*.

fondu à terre, battement See *battement fondu à terre*.

fondu, en See *en fondu*.

forward bend A relaxed forward curve of the upper back (thoracic spine) with the head line complementing the curve of the spine. Also *port de bras with forward bend.* See *full forward bend, full forward port de bras.*

forward port de bras See *port de bras with forward bend*.

fouetté [fwɛte] fwe-TAY (Fr. pp of v fouetter, to whip or beat; adj whipped; nm a whipping action.) 1. A turn of the body away from the extended leg which often maintains its position in space. May be performed with the *working leg à terre* or *en l'air*, with the *supporting leg* pivoting flat or *en demi-pointe*, or performing a *rise*, *relevé*, or *sauté*. The opposite action is called *rotation*. See *fouetté à terre, fouetté en l'air, fouetté of adage, fouetté relevé, fouetté sauté, grand fouetté relevé en tournant*. 2. A whipping action of the lower leg or of the entire leg, sometimes involving a turn of the body. See *battement frappé fouetté, battement fouetté, coupé fouetté raccourci, fouetté rond de jambe en dehors, fouetté rond de jambe en tournant en dehors, fouetté movement*.

fouetté à terre [fwɛte a tɛʀ] fwe-TAY a ter (Fr. whipped; on the ground.) One of the basic steps of *centre practice.* A fully coordinated movement where the body turns away from the extended leg with a pivoting action of the *supporting leg.* Can be executed with varying use of arms and *alignments*, and with a 1/4-turn or a 1/2-turn. 1. Basic *fouette à terre* with a 1/4-turn. From *dégagé in 2nd en face,* there is a pivoting action of the *supporting leg en dedans,* and the body makes a 1/4-turn away from the extended leg which rotates in its hip socket gradually adjusting its position behind the hip to *1st arabesque* facing 2 *(stage right)* or 4 *(stage left)*. The arms move gradually from *2nd position* to *1st arabesque.* 2. Basic *fouette à terre* with a 1/2-turn. From *dégagé devant* facing 2 *(stage right)* or 4 *(stage left),* there is a pivoting action of the *supporting leg,* and the body makes a 1/2-turn away from the extended leg which rotates in its hip socket passing through *2nd en face* to finish in *1st arabesque* facing the opposite side. The arms move gradually from *1st position,* arriving in *2nd position* by the first 1/4-turn and continuing into *1st arabesque* by the completion of the *fouetté.*

fouetté en l'air [fwɛte ɑ̃ lɛʀ] fwe-TAY ah ler (Fr. whipped; in the air.) A turn of the body away from the extended leg which often maintains its position *en l'air* in space. The opposite action is called *rotation en l'air*. See *fouetté of adage*.

fouetté movement [fwɛte -] fwe-TAY – (Fr. whipped; movement.) A whipping action of the *working leg* sometimes used to initiate a *pirouette en dedans* by moving from *derrière* through *2nd* *en l'air* en route to *pirouette position.*

fouetté of adage [fwɛte - adaʒ] fwe-TAY – adazh (Fr. whipped; at ease.) A slow, smooth *fouetté* action. In its most basic form, the dancer begins in *5th position working leg* front, performs a *dégagé to 2nd*, pivots making a 1/4-turn away from the *working leg* which maintains its position to end *derrière*. This type of *fouetté* may be done *à terre* or *en l'air*. May be prepared with a *dégagé* or a *développé* and performed starting with the leg *devant* and the body making up to a 1/2-turn.

fouetté relevé [fwɛte ʀəlve] fwe-TAY r(u)l-VAY (Fr. whipped; pulled up.) A *relevé* on the *supporting leg* with a simultaneous turn of the body away from the extended leg which strives to maintain its position *en l'air* in space. May be performed either *de côté* or *en tournant*.

fouetté relevé de côté [fwɛte ʀəlve də kote] fwe-TAY r(u)l-VAY d(u) koh-TAY (Fr. whipped; pulled up; to the side.) A *fouetté* in which the dancer begins with the *working leg devant en l'air en fondu en ouvert*, and performs a *relevé* action making a 3/8-turn away from the *working leg* to end *en arabesque de côté*.

fouetté relevé en tournant [fwɛte ʀəlve ɑ̃ tuʀnɑ̃] fwe-TAY r(u)l-VAY ah toor-NAH (Fr. whipped; pulled up; turning.) A *fouetté* in which the dancer performs a *grand battement* action *devant* followed immediately by a *relevé* action making a 1/2-turn away from the *working leg* to end *en arabesque*.

fouetté relevé en tournant, grand See *grand fouetté relevé en tournant.*

fouetté rond de jambe en dedans [fwɛte ʀɔ̃ də ʒɑ̃b ɑ̃ dədɑ̃] fwe-TAY ro d(u) zhahb ah d(u)-DAH (Fr. whipped action; circle of the leg; inward.) A whip-like action of the *working leg.* The dancer begins with the *working leg derrière* at 45 degrees *en fondu,* performs a strong *relevé* while simultaneously whipping the *working leg* through *2nd* to *pirouette position.* When performed in 3/4 rhythm, a stronger emphasis may be placed on the *relevé to 2nd position en l'air.* The arms usually begin in *3rd position,* open to *2nd position* with the *working leg,* and close to *1st position* as the leg reaches *pirouette position.*

fouetté rond de jambe en dehors [fwɛte ʀɔ̃ də ʒɑ̃b ɑ̃ dəɔʀ] fwe-TAY ro d(u) zhahb ah d(u)-OR (Fr. whipped action; circle of the leg; outward.) A whip-like action of the working leg. The dancer begins with the *working leg devant* at 45 degrees *en fondu*, performs a strong *relevé* while simultaneously whipping the *working leg* through *2nd* to *pirouette position.* When performed in 3/4 rhythm, a stronger emphasis may be placed on the *relevé to 2nd position en l'air.* The arms usually begin in *3rd position*, open to *2nd position* with the *working leg,* and close to *1st position* as the leg reaches *pirouette position.* When performed in series with a turn on each *rise,* the step is known as *fouettés ronds de jambe en tournant dehors.*

fouetté rond de jambe en tournant en dehors [fwɛte ʀɔ̃ də ʒɑ̃b ɑ̃ tuʀnɑ̃ ɑ̃ dəɔʀ] fwe-TAY ro d(u) zhahb ah toor-NAH ah d(u)-OR (Fr. whipped action; circle of the leg; turning; outward.) A spin initiated by the whip-like action of the *working leg*. The dancer begins *en fondu* with the *working leg devant en l'air*, performs a strong *relevé* while simultaneously whipping the *working leg* through *2nd* to *pirouette position,* completing a full turn. When performed in 3/4 rhythm, a stronger emphasis may be placed on the *relevé to 2nd position en l'air*. May be performed in series, prepared by a *pirouette en dehors* from *4th position.* The arms usually begin in *3rd position*, open to *2nd position* with the *working leg,* close to *1st position* as the leg reaches *pirouette position,* and return to *3rd position* on the *fondu,* ready to begin the next turn. Sometimes referred to as *fouetté* turns.

fouetté sauté [fwɛte sote] fwe-TAY soh-TAY (Fr. whipped; jumped.) A jump on the *supporting leg* with a simultaneous turn of the body away from the extended leg which strives to maintain its position *en l'air* in space. May be performed either *de côté* or *en tournant*, and embellished with a *beat*.

fouetté sauté de côté [fwɛte sote də kote] fwe-TAY soh-TAY d(u) koh-TAY (Fr. whipped; jumped; to the side.) A *fouetté* in which the dancer begins with the *working leg devant en l'air en fondu en ouvert*, then performs a *temps levé* action making a 3/8-turn away from the *working leg* to land *en arabesque de côté*. Usually prepared with a *grand battement* action.

fouetté sauté en tournant [fwɛte sote ɑ̃ tuʀnɑ̃] fwe-TAY soh-TAY ah toor-NAH (Fr. whipped; jumped; turning.) A *fouetté* in which the dancer performs a *grand battement* action *devant* followed immediately by a *temps levé* making a 1/2-turn away from the *working leg* to land *en arabesque*. Often prepared with a *running pas de bourrée*.

fouetté turns See *fouetté rond de jambe en tournant en dehors.*

fouetté with relevé See *fouetté relevé.*

fourth See *position of the arms, 4th; position of the feet, 4th.*

frappé [fʀape] fra-PAY (Fr. pp of v frapper, to strike; adj struck, hit; a hit action.) See *battement frappé.*

free glissade [- glisad] – glee-SAD (Fr. free; sliding step; forward.) A *glissade* performed in a less technical manner, with the feet bypassing *5th position,* in order to generate the greater momentum needed for *grand allegro.* May be performed *derrière* or *en avant,* and *piquée.* See *glissade.*

free glissade en avant [- glisad ɑ̃ navɑ̃] – glee-SAD ah na-VAH (Fr. free sliding step; forward.) A non-technical *glissade* which travels forward. Used to prepare *allegro* steps such as *posé en avant.*

free glissade piquée en avant [- glisad pike ɑ̃ navɑ̃] – glee-SAD pee-KAY ah na-VAH (Fr. free; sliding action; pricked; forward.) A non-technical *glissade en avant* performed with a quick, light quality.

free work Any *enchaînement* created by a teacher during a class, or by an examiner during an examination. May contain any vocabulary introduced up to and including the student's current level.

full contretemps [- kɔ̃tʀətɑ̃] – ko-tr(u)-TAH (Fr. full off-beat step.) A composite step consisting of a *coupé dessous*, an *extended chassé en avant*, a *temps levé*, and a *chassé passé en avant.* The dancer begins with the weight on one foot, then transfers the weight onto the other foot which cuts behind and replaces the *supporting foot;* s/he then slides the tip of the free foot forward into *4th position en demi-plié*, transfers the weight onto the front foot releasing the back foot *en l'air*, performs a *temps levé en arabesque*, then slides the back foot through *1st position* and forward to end in *4th position en demi-plié*. The *coupé dessous* is usually performed on an anacrusis beat or beats. May be performed with a change in *alignment* on the *coupé dessous.* Often used in *grand allegro enchaînements.*

full forward bend A completely relaxed forward curve of the back (thoracic spine) involving action at the hip joints, with the head line complementing the curve of the spine. The recovery incorporates a lengthening in the torso. Also *full forward port de bras.*

full forward port de bras [- pɔʀ də bʀa] – por d(u) bra (Fr. a full forward carriage of the arm or arms.) A *port de bras with forward bend* performed with a fully relaxed spine at the deepest point. Often performed in a *lunge.* May be taken with an extended line through the spine when horizontal (flat back). Also *full forward bend.*

full grand port de bras See *port de bras, full grand.*

full port de bras See *port de bras, full.*

galop [galo] ga-LOH (Fr. nm a gallop, a lively dance in duple measure, of Hungarian origin.) 1. A term used to describe a non-technical *posé and coupé sauté*, often performed in series. Note: in the Majors syllabus *galop* is also referred to as *posé coupé dessous posé.* 2. Dance study performed to a 2/4 rhythm.

galop en avant [galo ɑ̃ navɑ̃] ga-LOH ah na VAH (Fr. gallop; forward.) A step forward followed by a *coupé sauté dessous.* Often performed in series.

galop en écarté [galo ɑ̃ nekaʀte] ga-LOH ah nay-kar-TAY (Fr. gallop; wide.) A *posé coupé dessous posé* performed sideways *en diagonale* in *écarté alignment,* used to prepare *grand allegro* steps such as *saut de basque.*

gargouillade [gaʀgujad] gar-guwee-YAD (Fr. mutated form of the v gargouiller, to gurgle; nf a gargoyle through which rainwater is projected away from a building; in dance, an embellished step.) An embellished *pas de chat* in which the dancer begins in *5th position* with the *working leg devant*, releases the front foot and leaps sideways performing a *double rond de jambe en l'air* action *en dehors*, and alights on the original *working leg* as the other leg executes the circular action of a single *rond de jambe* action and closes through *retiré* into *5th position devant.* Variation: *gargouillade finishing in dégagé devant.*

gargouillade finishing in dégagé devant [gaʀgujad ɑ̃ dədɑ̃ - degaʒẽ d(ə)vɑ̃] gar-guwee-YAD ah d(u)-DAH – day-ga-ZHAY d(u)-VAH (Fr. embellished step; inward; to disengaged position; in front.) An embellished *pas de chat* in which the dancer begins in *5th position* with the *working leg derrière*, releases the back foot and leaps sideways performing a *double rond de jambe en l'air* action *en dedans*, and alights on the original *working leg*, with the other leg passing through *retiré* to end *dégagé devant en fondu en ouvert*. When prepared from *4th position*, the dancer may performs a *double rond de jambe en l'air* action *en dedans*. Similar to *gargouillade volée* in the Cecchetti method.

glissade [glisad] glee-SAD (Fr. nf a dance step which consists of gliding or sliding along the floor.) A connecting step travelling in any direction and performed *terre à terre*. The basic *glissade* is travelled sideways. From *5th position,* the action commences with a *demi-plié,* extending the *working foot* to a *dégagé in 2nd en fondu;* the *supporting leg* pushes away from the floor and is released so that both legs are momentarily fully stretched; the transfer of weight continues, lowering through the leading foot into a *fondu,* and the freed foot from its *dégagé in 2nd* is drawn firmly into *5th position en demi-plié.* Taken *derrière, devant, dessous,* and *dessus.* When travelled forward *(en avant)* or backward *(en arrière),* the *working foot* extends *to 4th* and the freed foot closes from a *degagé in 4th.* Variations: *free glissade en avant, glissade piquée.*

glissade derrière [glisad dɛʀjɛʀ] glee-SAD der-YER (Fr. sliding step; behind.) A *glissade* sideways initiated by the back foot and done without a *change of feet.* The back foot extends *to 2nd,* and the other foot closes *5th devant.*

glissade dessous [glisad d(ə)su] glee-SAD d(u)-SOO (Fr. sliding step; under.) A *glissade* sideways initiated by the front foot and done with a *change of feet.* The front foot extends *to 2nd,* and the other foot closes *5th devant.*

glissade dessus [glisad d(ə)sy] glee-SAD d(u)-SU (Fr. sliding step; over.) A *glissade* sideways initiated by the back foot and done with a *change of feet.* The back foot extends *to 2nd,* and the other foot closes *5th derrière.*

glissade devant [glisad d(ə)vɑ̃] glee-SAD d(u)-VAH (Fr. sliding step; front.) A *glissade* sideways initiated by the front foot and done without a *change of feet.* The front foot extends *to 2nd,* and the other foot closes *5th derrière.*

glissade en arrière [glisad ɑ̃ naʀjɛʀ] glee-SAD ah-nar-YER (Fr. sliding step; backward.) A *glissade* backward in which the back foot extends *to 4th derrière,* and the other foot closes *5th devant.*

glissade en avant [glisad ɑ̃ navɑ̃] glee-SAD ah na-VAH (Fr. sliding step; forward.) A *glissade* forward in which the front foot extends *to 4th devant,* and the other foot closes *5th derrière.*

glissade piquée [glisad pike] glee-SAD pee-KAY (Fr. sliding step; pricked.) A *glissade* performed with a quick, light quality used to propel the dancer into the next action such as a *posé.* Variations: *free glissade piquée en avant, glissade piquée passée en avant.*

glissade piquée derrière [glisad pike dɛʀjɛʀ] glee-SAD pee-KAY der-YER (Fr. sliding step; pricked; behind.) A *glissade derrière* performed with a quick, light quality.

glissade piquée dessus [glisad pike d(ə)sy] glee-SAD pee-KAY d(u)-SU (Fr. sliding step; pricked; over.) A *glissade dessus* performed with a quick, light quality.

glissade piquée passée en avant [glisad pike pɑse ɑ̃ navɑ̃] glee-SAD pee-KAY pah-SAY ah na-VAH (Fr. sliding step; pricked; passed; forward.) A running *glissade en avant* into *4th position* commencing with the back leg. Always performed on a pick-up beat, with quickness and rhythmic precision.

glissé [glise] glee-SAY (Fr. pp of v glisser to glide or slide; adj sliding; nm a sliding action.) See *battement glissé, glissé height, pas de basque glissé.*

glissé height [glise -] glee-SAY – (Fr. sliding action; height.) Position of the *working leg en l'air* with the toes just off the floor. May be taken *devant, to 2nd,* or *derrière.* See *rond de jambe* at *glissé height* and *battement glissé.*

grand [gʀɑ̃] grah (Fr. adj large or big.) See *grand 4th en fondu; grand allegro; grand assemblé soutenu; grand battement; grand fouetté relevé en tournant; grand jeté développé en avant; grand jeté en avant; grand jeté passé derrière in attitude; grand pas de basque en tournant; grand pas de chat to 4th; grand plié; grand retiré passé; grand rond de jambe en l'air; port de bras, full grand.*

grand 4th en fondu [gʀɑ̃ - ɑ̃ fɔ̃dy] grah – ah fo-DU (Fr. big; 4th; melted.) A wide *4th position,* with the weight well forward and the front leg in a deep *fondu*. This position is commonly used in conjunction with a *port de bras* involving body bends, either circular or forward and back. Sometimes referred to as a *lunge*.

grand adage [grɑ̃ tadaʒ] grah tadazh (Fr. big; adagio.) An *adage enchaînement* of longer duration, with greater emphasis on a sustained, fluid quality of movement.

grand allegro [gʀɑ̃ ta(l)legʀo] grah ta-LAY-groh (Fr. big; lively.) 1. One of three basic categories of elevation, comprising aerial jumps of high elevation. Performed with energy and vigour, it builds power and endurance and is the ultimate test of a male dancer. *Grand allegro* jumps should show the line of the position in the air, and may be embellished with a beating action of the legs. They require the fully coordinated use of feet, legs, and arms in order to generate the greater force needed for high elevation. These may include, at an elementary level: *grands jetés en avant; chassé temps levé; posé temps levé in retiré en manège; full contretemps; pas balancé; tours en l'air, assemblé de côté;* at an intermediate level: *sissonnes ouvertes; sissonnes ouvertes changées; grands jetés en avant; grands jetés en tournant; fouettés sautés; tombés; posé pirouettes en dehors; fouettés ronds de jambe en tournant;* at an advanced level: *pas de bourrées en première; assemblés–dessus en tournant, dessus porté de côté; ballottés sautés–dessus, dessous; sauts de basque; temps de flêche; grands pas de basque en tournant; renversés sautés; sissonnes doublées with développés–dessus, dessous; fouettés sautés en tournant; cabrioles ouvertes and fermées–dessus, dessous, de côté; grands jetés passés derrière in attitude; grands jetés en avant en tournant in attitude; sissonnes ouvertes changées en tournant in attitude; jetés élancés en tournant; coupés jetés en tournant en manège*. 2. A generic term for a sub-category of movements performed during the *Allegro* section of a class, after *batterie*.

grand assemblé soutenu [gʀɑ̃ tasɑ̃ble sutny] grah ta-sah-BLAY soot-NU (Fr. big; gathered step; sustained.) *Assemblé soutenu* in which the *working foot* traces a 180-degree arc along the floor. May be performed *en dehors* or *en dedans*. Often performed *en fondu*.

grand assemblé soutenu en dedans [gʀɑ̃ tasɑ̃ble sutny ɑ̃ dədɑ̃] grah ta-sah-BLAY soot-NU ah d(u)-DAH (Fr. big; gathered step; sustained; inward.) A *grand assemblé soutenu* in which the dancer begins with the *working leg 5th derrière*, extends it *dégagé derrière*, moves it through *2nd* to *devant*, then closes *5th position*. When performed *en fondu*, the *supporting leg* bends as the *working leg* extends, and stretches as it closes.

grand assemblé soutenu en dedans en fondu See *grand assemblé soutenu en dedans*.

grand assemblé soutenu en dehors [gʀɑ̃ tasɑ̃ble sutny ɑ̃ dəɔʀ] grah ta-sah-BLAY soot-NU ah d(u)-OR (Fr. big; gathered step; sustained; outward.) A *grand assemblé soutenu* in which the dancer begins with the *working leg 5th devant*, extends it *dégagé devant*, moves it through *2nd* to *derrière*, then closes *5th position*. When performed *en fondu*, the *supporting leg* bends as the *working leg* extends, and stretches as it closes.

grand assemblé soutenu en dehors en fondu See *grand assemblé soutenu en dehors*.

grand battement [gʀɑ̃ batmɑ̃] grah bat-MAH (Fr. big; beating action.) A strong throwing action of the *working leg*. From *5th position*, the movement is achieved by the use of the floor as in a *battement tendu,* followed by a light flight of the leg to a height of 90 degrees, and a return through the *battement tendu* with control to close in *5th position*. Taken *devant, to 2nd,* and *derrière*. Variations: *grand battement développé*, *grand battement en cloche*, *grand battement en rond*, *grand battement enveloppé, grand battement fouetté*, *grand battement piqué*, *grand battement retiré*.

grand battement derrière [gʀɑ̃ batmɑ̃ dɛʀjɛʀ] grah bat-MAH der-YER (Fr. big; beating; behind.) A *grand battement* in which the *working leg* is thrown backward, starting and ending in *5th derrière*.

grand battement devant [gʀɑ̃ batmɑ̃ d(ə)vɑ̃] grah bat-MAH d(u)-VAH (Fr. big; beating; front.) A *grand battement* in which the *working leg* is thrown forward, starting and ending in *5th devant*.

grand battement développé [gʀɑ̃ batmɑ̃ devlɔpe] grah bat-MAH dayv-loh-PAY (Fr. big; beating action; unfolding.) A *grand battement* performed with a *développé* opening, i.e., the foot passes through *retiré* before extending *en l'air*, instead of sliding the foot along the floor and lifting the leg fully extended. May be performed *devant*, *to 2nd*, or *derrière*. Similar to *grand battement retiré*, but with a strong accent on the extension.

grand battement développé derrière [gʀɑ̃ batmɑ̃ devlɔpe dɛʀjɛʀ] grah bat-MAH dayv-loh-PAY der-YER (Fr. big; beating action; unfolding; behind.) A *grand battement développé* in which the *working leg* opens backward, starting and ending in *5th derrière.*

grand battement développé devant [gʀɑ̃ batmɑ̃ devlɔpe d(ə)vɑ̃] grah bat-MAH dayv-loh-PAY d(u)-VAH (Fr. big; beating action; unfolding; front.) A *grand battement développé* in which the *working leg* opens forward, starting and ending in *5th devant.*

grand battement développé to 2nd [gʀɑ̃ batmɑ̃ devlɔpe -] grah bat-MAH dayv-loh-PAY – (Fr. big; beating action; unfolding; to 2nd.) A *grand battement développé* in which the *working leg* opens outward to the side, starting and ending in *5th position.* May close with or without a *change of feet.*

grand battement en cloche [gʀɑ̃ batmɑ ɑ̃ klɔʃ] grah bat-MAH ah klosh (Fr. big; beating action; like a bell.) A dynamic action in which the *working leg* swings forward and backward through *1st position* like a pendulum, commencing and finishing in an open position *devant* or *derrière.* May be performed commencing *4th derrière* and ending *4th devant*, commencing *4th devant* and ending *4th derrière*, or in a series often commencing *dégagé derrière.* The *working leg* may be lifted fully stretched or *en attitude*, and the *supporting leg* may rise *en demi-pointe* or lower *en fondu* as the *working leg* lifts.

grand battement en cloche derrière [gʀɑ̃ batmɑ̃ ɑ̃ klɔʃ dɛʀjɛʀ] grah bat-MAH ah klosh der-YER (Fr. big; beating; like a bell; behind.) A *grand battement en cloche* beginning in *4th devant* and ending in *4th derrière.*

grand battement en cloche devant [gʀɑ̃ batmɑ̃ ɑ̃ klɔʃ d(ə)vɑ̃] grah bat-MAH ah klosh d(u)-VAH (Fr. big; beating; like a bell; front.) A *grand battement en cloche* beginning in *4th derrière* and ending in *4th devant.*

grand battement en cloche in attitude [gʀɑ̃ batmɑ̃ ɑ̃ klɔʃ - atityd] grah bat-MAH ah klosh – a-tee-TUD (Fr. large; beating; like a bell; in a pose.) A *grand battement en cloche* performed with the *working leg* lifting bent *en attitude.*

grand battement en rond [gʀɑ̃ batmɑ̃ ɑ̃ ʀɔ̃] grah bat-MAH ah ro (Fr. big; beating; in a circle.) A *grand battement* action in which the *working foot* traces a horizontal circular path from front to side *(en dehors)* or from back to side *(en dedans)* before lowering through the opposite *dégagé* into *5th position.* May be performed rising *en demi-pointe* as the leg opens *to 2nd* and ending *4th en fondu.* In *grand battement en rond,* the foot traces a horizontal path between *4th (devant* or *derrière)* and *2nd en l'air,* whereas in *rond de jambe jeté* the foot lifts upward and outward, passing through its apex in *2nd en l'air.*

grand battement en rond en dedans [gʀɑ̃ batmɑ̃ ɑ̃ ʀɔ̃ ɑ̃ dədɑ̃] grah bat-MAH ah ro ah d(u)-DAH (Fr. big; beating; in a circle; inward.) A *grand battement en rond* in which the *working leg* begins in *5th derrière,* is thrown back to 90 degrees, and continues outward through *2nd* at 90 degrees before lowering to *dégagé devant* and closing *5th devant.*

grand battement en rond en dehors [gʀɑ̃ batmɑ̃ ɑ̃ ʀɔ ɑ̃ dəɔʀ] grah bat-MAH ah ro ah d(u)-OR (Fr. big; beating; in a circle; outward.) A *grand battement en rond* in which the *working leg* begins in *5th devant,* is thrown forward to 90 degrees, and continues outward through *2nd* at 90 degrees before lowering to *dégagé derrière* and closing *5th derrière.*

grand battement enveloppé [grɑ̃ batmɑ̃ ɑ̃vlɔpe] grah bat-MAH ahv-lo-PAY (Fr. big; beating action; enveloped.) A *grand battement* performed with an *enveloppé* closing, i.e., the foot passes through *retiré* before closing into *5th position*, instead of sliding along the floor with the leg fully extended. May be performed *devant, to 2nd,* or *derrière.* When taken with a *rise*, the *rise* is performed on the extension, the *demi-pointe* is held on the *retiré,* and the heels lower on the closing.

grand battement fouetté [gʀɑ̃ batmɑ̃ fwɛte] grah bat-MAH fwe-TAY (Fr. big; beating; whipped.) A *battement fouetté* action performed with the *working leg en l'air* at 90 degrees, whipping between *4th* and *2nd position.* May be performed from *4th devant* or *4th derrière.*

grand battement piqué [gʀɑ̃ batmɑ̃ pike] grah bat-MAH pee-KAY (Fr. big; beating; pricked.) A *grand battement* action in which the *working leg* opens *en l'air*, lowers to *dégagé,* and rebounds quickly and lightly to the previous height *en l'air.* May be performed *devant, to 2nd,* or *derrière.*

grand battement piqué derrière [gʀɑ̃ batmɑ̃ pike dɛʀjɛʀ] grah bat-MAH pee-KAY der-YER (Fr.

big; beating; pricked; behind.) A *grand battement piqué* in which the *working leg* is thrown backward.

grand battement piqué devant [gʀɑ̃ batmɑ̃ pike d(ə)vɑ̃] grah bat-MAH pee-KAY d(u)-VAH (Fr. big; beating; pricked; front.) A *grand battement piqué* in which the *working leg* is thrown forward.

grand battement piqué to 2nd [gʀɑ̃ batmɑ̃ pike -] grah bat-MAH pee-KAY – (Fr. big; beating; pricked; to 2nd.) A *grand battement piqué* in which the *working leg* is thrown outward to the side.

grand battement relevé [gʀɑ̃ batmɑ̃ ʀəlve] grah bat-MAH r(u)l-VAY (Fr. big; beating; pulled up.) A *grand battement* action which begins and ends *en demi-plié*, with the *supporting leg* performing a *relevé* action *en pointe* as the *working leg* opens. May be performed *devant*, *to 2nd*, or *derrière*.

grand battement relevé derrière [gʀɑ̃ batmɑ̃ ʀəlve dɛʀjɛʀ] grah bat-MAH r(u)l-VAY der-YER (Fr. big; beating; pulled up; behind.) A *grand battement relevé* in which the *working leg* is thrown backward.

grand battement relevé devant [gʀɑ̃ batmɑ̃ ʀəlve d(ə)vɑ̃] grah bat-MAH r(u)l-VAY d(u)-VAH (Fr. big; beating; pulled up; front.) A *grand battement relevé* in which the *working leg* is thrown forward.

grand battement relevé to 2nd [gʀɑ̃ batmɑ̃ ʀəlve -] grah bat-MAHr(u)l-VAY – (Fr. big; beating; pulled up; to 2nd.) A *grand battement relevé* in which the *working leg* is thrown outward to the side.

grand battement retiré [gʀɑ̃ batmɑ̃ ʀ(ə)tiʀe] grah bat-MAH r(u)-tee-RAY (Fr. big; beating; withdrawn.) A *grand battement* performed with a *développé* opening, taken in 3/4 rhythm with one action per musical beat. The dancer lifts the *working leg* to *retiré*, extends strongly *en l'air*, and closes in *5th*. May be performed *devant*, *to 2nd*, or *derrière*. Similar to *grand battement développé*, but slower and with three even movements.

grand battement retiré derrière [gʀɑ̃ batmɑ̃ ʀ(ə)tiʀe dɛʀjɛʀ] grah bat-MAH r(u)-tee-RAY der-YER (Fr. big; beating; withdrawn; behind.) A *grand battement retiré* in which the *working leg* is thrown backward.

grand battement retiré devant [gʀɑ̃ batmɑ̃ ʀ(ə)tiʀe d(ə)vɑ̃] grah bat-MAH r(u)-tee-RAY d(u)-VAH (Fr. big; beating; withdrawn; front.) A *grand battement retiré* in which the *working leg* is thrown forward.

grand battement retiré to 2nd [gʀɑ̃ batmɑ̃ ʀ(ə)tiʀe -] grah bat-MAH r(u)-tee-RAY – (Fr. big; beating; withdrawn; to 2nd.) A *grand battement retiré* in which the *working leg* is thrown outward to the side.

grand battement to 2nd [gʀɑ̃ batmɑ̃ -] grah bat-MAH – (Fr. big; beating; to 2nd.) A *grand battement* in which the *working leg* is thrown outward to the side, starting and ending in *5th position*. May close with or without a *change of feet*.

grand circular port de bras See *port de bras in 4th position en fondu, circular.*

grand échappé sauté [gʀɑ̃ teʃape sote] grah tay-sha-PAY soh-TAY (Fr. big; escaped action; jumped.) A variation of *échappé sauté fermé to 2nd position,* in which the legs are held in *soubresaut* position to the height of the jump.

grand fouetté relevé en tournant [gʀɑ̃ fwɛte ʀəlve ɑ̃ tuʀnɑ̃] grah fwe-TAY r(u)l-VAY ah toor-NAH (Fr. big; whipped; pulled up; turning.) A virtuoso turn consisting of a *relevé to 2nd en l'air*, followed by a *fouetté relevé en tournant* with the same leg, completing one full revolution. The dancer begins in *dégagé derrière;* s/he performs a *grand battement to 2nd en écarté devant* with a simultaneous *relevé* action, brushes through *1st position en demi-plié* making a 1/4-turn *en dedans* to perform a *grand battement devant* with a *relevé* action, and completes the turn with a *fouetté* to *arabesque* ending *croisé*. To complement the action, the arms move *to 2nd position* with the *battement to 2nd*, *undersweep 1st* to *5th position* with the *battement devant*, and open *to 2nd arabesque* at the conclusion of the *fouetté* action. May be prepared by *chassé en avant en croisé* to *degagé derrière*. May be performed *sauté*, with a *temps levé* in place of the *relevé*.

grand jeté See *grand jeté en avant*.

grand jeté développé en avant [grɑ̃ ʒ(ə)te devlɔpe ɑ̃ navɑ̃] grah zh(u)-TAY dayv-loh-PAY ah na-VAH (Fr. big; thrown action; unfolding; forward.) A *grand jeté en avant* in which the *working leg* performs a *développé* opening instead of a *grand battement* opening.

grand jeté en avant [gʀɑ̃ ʒ(ə)te ɑ̃ navɑ̃] grah zh(u)-TAY ah na-VAH (Fr. big; thrown; forward.) A large leap travelling forward from one foot to the other. Taken to various *arabesque* lines. See *grand jeté en avant in 2nd arabesque*. May be initiated by *coupé dessous posé en avant*, a series of runs, a *glissade*, a *chassé*, or a *posé*. Variations: *grand jeté développé en avant*; *grand jeté en avant in attitude*, *grand jeté en avant en tournant in attitude*.

grand jeté en avant en tournant in attitude [gʀɑ̃ ʒ(ə)te ɑ̃ navɑ̃ ɑ̃ tuʀnɑ̃ - atityd] grah zh(u)-TAY ah na-VAH ah toor-NAH – a-tee-TUD (Fr. big; thrown; forward; turning; in attitude.) A *grand jeté* initiated by a *coupé dessous,* allowing the dancer to turn *en dehors* before leaping forward, appearing to travel in a curved path through space before landing *en attitude*.

grand jeté en avant in 2nd arabesque [gʀɑ̃ ʒ(ə)te ɑ̃ navɑ̃ - arabɛsk] grah zh(u)-TAY ah na-VAH – arabesk (Fr. big; thrown; forward; in 2nd arabesque.) A *grand jeté en avant* taken in an *arabesque* line with the arm opposite to the front leg extended forward. The preparation for the jump usually consists of three runs forward, during which the arms pass in a continuous movement through *bras bas* and *1st positions.* The third step, which is shorter, assisted by the impetus of the arms preparing to take *2nd arabesque,* acts as a spring-board for the jump. Coordinated with a strong *battement* to *4th devant,* the dancer is lifted into the air establishing *2nd arabesque* as soon as possible. There is a sense of suspension during the flight forward before a controlled landing in *2nd arabesque en fondu* with the *eye line* projected forward. Various preparatory movements may be used, but in all combinations the arms are fully coordinated with the jump.

grand jeté en avant in attitude [gʀɑ̃ ʒ(ə)te ɑ̃ navɑ̃ - atityd] grah zh(u)-TAY ah na-VAH – a-tee-TUD (Fr. big; thrown; forward; in attitude.) A *grand jeté en avant* in which the push-off leg is lifted *en attitude*.

grand jeté en tournant [gʀɑ̃ ʒ(ə)te ɑ̃ tuʀnɑ̃] grah zh(u)-TAY ah toor-NAH (Fr. big; thrown; turning.) A large leap which turns. The dancer steps forward, performs a *grand battement devant*, pushes off the *supporting leg* bringing it beside the lifted leg as the whole body rotates in the direction of the push-off leg, then lands *en arabesque* on the leg which performed the *battement*. Usually prepared with a *running pas de bourrée*. The arms pass in a continuous movement through *bras bas* and *1st position* on the *running pas de bourrée* and are retained in *5th position* before opening to *2nd position* on the landing. Also known as *jeté entrelacé* (Vaganova), *tour jeté* (American).

grand jeté passé derrière in attitude [gʀɑ̃ ʒ(ə)te pɑse dɛʀjɛʀ - atityd] grah zh(u)-TAY pah-SAY der-YER – a-tee-TUD (Fr. large; thrown; passed; behind; in a pose.) A large leap in which the bent legs pass one another behind the body. The dancer lifts the *working leg* to *attitude derrière en fondu*, leaps upward, passes the push-off leg backward to *attitude*, and lands on the other leg *en fondu*. May be preceded by a step forward into *attitude derrière en fondu.*

grand pas de basque en tournant [gʀɑ̃ pɑ də bask ɑ̃ tuʀnɑ̃] grah pah d(u) bask ah toor-NAH (Fr. big; step of the Basque; turning.) A large *pas de basque* performed without travelling and with a turn. The dancer begins in *5th position* with the *working foot devant;* s/he performs a *grand battement devant*, pushes off the *supporting leg* which then performs a *grand battement devant*, and lands *sur place en fondu* on the other leg; s/he then draws the feet to *5th en demi-pointes* to perform a *pas de bourrée dessus en tournant*. Often the dancer begins *en croisé*, faces *en face* on the first extension, and lands *en croisé*, with the remaining 3/4-turn occurring during the *pas de bourrée*. The arms usually pass from *2nd position* and *undersweep 1st* to *5th position* on the initial *battement*, open *to 2nd position* on the landing, and lower to *bras bas* during the *pas de bourrée*.

grand pas de chat to 4th [gʀɑ̃ pɑ də ʃa -] grah pah d(u) sha – (Fr. big; step of the cat; to 4th.) A large *pas de chat* ending in *4th position*. The dancer begins by transferring the weight forward onto one foot; s/he then raises the free foot to *retiré*, leaps sideways onto it bringing the other foot to *retiré* and immediately lowers it forward to *4th position en demi-plié*.

grand plié [gʀɑ̃ plije] grah plee-YAY (Fr. big; bending action.) A full bending of the knees over the toes. An exercise used to develop the strength and control of the whole body. In *1st, 4th crossed,* and *5th positions,* the bending action causes the heels to be released from the floor. During the straightening of the legs, the heels are lowered to the floor as soon as possible, making the movement continuous. In *2nd position* and *open 4th* however, because there is a wider base, the heels remain on the floor. Executed in all *positions of the feet.*

grand port de bras, full See *port de bras, full grand*.

grand retiré passé [gʀɑ ʀ(ə)tiʀẽ pɑse] grah r(u)-tee-RAY pah-SAY (Fr. big; withdrawn; passed.) A large *retiré passé*. Executed like a *retiré passé*, but with a stronger quality. May be performed *devant* or *derrière*.

grand rond de jambe See *grand rond de jambe en l'air*.

grand rond de jambe en dedans See *grand rond de jambe en l'air en dedans*.

grand rond de jambe en dehors See *grand rond de jambe en l'air en dehors*.

grand rond de jambe en l'air [gʀɑ̃ ʀɔ̃ də ʒɑ̃b ɑ̃ lɛʀ] grah ro d(u) zhahb ah ler (Fr. big; circle of the leg; in the air.) A slow sustained circling action of the leg *en l'air* tracing a 180-degree arc parallel to the ground. As an exercise, the action begins with a *développé to 4th* at 90 degrees and ends with a closing in *5th position*. Taken from *4th derrière* to *4th devant (en dehors)* and from *4th devant* to *4th derrière (en dedans)*. Also referred to as *grand rond de jambe*.

grand rond de jambe en l'air en dedans [gʀɑ̃ ʀɔ̃ də ʒɑ̃b ɑ̃ lɛʀ ɑ̃ dədɑ̃] grah ro d(u) zhahb ah ler ah d(u)-DAH (Fr. big; circle of the leg; in the air; inward.) A *grand rond de jambe en l'air* tracing an inward arc. From *5th derrière*, the *working leg* executes a *développé to 4th derrière* at 90 degrees and passes through *2nd position* to *4th devant* in one continuous action, before closing *5th devant*. Also referred to as *grand rond de jambe en dedans*.

grand rond de jambe en l'air en dehors [gʀɑ̃ ʀɔ̃ də ʒɑ̃b ɑ̃ lɛʀ ɑ̃ dəɔʀ] grah ro d(u) zhahb ah ler ah d(u)-OR (Fr. big; circle of the leg; in the air; outward.) A *grand rond de jambe en l'air* tracing an outward arc. From *5th devant*, the *working leg* executes a *développé to 4th devant* at 90 degrees and passes through *2nd position* to *4th derrière* in one continuous action, before closing *5th derrière*.

grande pirouette [grɑ̃d piʀwɛt] grahd peer-WET (Fr. big; turn.) A male virtuoso *pirouette en dehors* with the *working leg* extended *en l'air to 2nd*, often prepared by *pirouettes in 2nd with petits sautés*. Also *grande pirouette en seconde*.

grecque [gʀɛk] grek (Fr. adj Greek; nmf Greek person or language.) See *attitude grecque*.

half pointe See *pointe/s, 1/2; en demi-pointe/s; sur la demi-pointe*.

haut ['o] oh (Fr. adj high; nm top.) See *en haut*.

head écarté [- ekaʀte] – ay-kar-TAY A strong turn of the head usually *downstage* so that the chin is over the shoulder and the *eye line* is focused toward the corner of the dancer's square, creating a feeling of width stretching from corner to corner. This head position, usually taken with the body in alignment, may also be taken with the body *en face* and the *eye line* focused toward *stage right* or *left*. May be used in *barre* and *centre exercises* such as *grand battement*, *développé*, and *ballonné composé de côté*.

head erect The head is held centrally over the neck and shoulders with the eyes focused forward and slightly above their natural level.

head in line of direction *Eye line* focused along the *line of dance*. See *spotting*.

head inclined A slight tilt of the head right or left with the eyes focused forward.

head looking into hand A use of the head, when the arm is in *1st* or *2nd position*, where the *eye line* is directed to the palm of the hand.

head over front arm A use of the head, when one arm is placed in *1st position*, with the *eye line* focused over and beyond the forearm.

head to front arm See *head over front arm*.

head to front foot A use of the head, when the *working leg* is *devant*, with the *head turned* in the direction of the front foot.

head to raised hand A use of the head, when one arm is *5th position*, with the *eye line* directed under and beyond the hand.

head to supporting leg A turn of the head in the direction of the *supporting leg*.

head turned A position in with the head is rotated centrally over the neck and shoulders with the eyes focused forward, toward either *downstage* corner when standing *en face*. Generally, the head makes a quarter-turn to face either *downstage* corner, but can turn beyond a quarter when moving the arms from *1st to 2nd*.

head, pirouette See *pirouette head.*

hop A non-technically performed *temps levé*, i.e., a jump from one foot to the same foot. May be used as a preparatory movement.

in opposition See *position of the arms, 4th opposition.*

jambe [ʒɑ̃b] zhahb (Fr. nf a leg.) See *rond de jambe.*

jeté [ʒ(ə)te] zh(u)-TAY (Fr. pp of v jeter, to throw; adj thrown; nm in dance, a jump taking off from one leg and landing on the other.) 1. A thrown action. See *rond de jambe jeté.* 2. A jump from one foot to the other. May be initiated with the *working leg* thrown *devant, to 2nd,* or *derrière* in a variety of *poses* and *alignments,* and landed with the freed leg in a variety of positions. May be performed *sur place,* or travelled *en avant, de côté,* or *en arrière.* See *coupés jetés en tournant en manège, battement jeté, grand jeté en avant, grand jeté en tournant, grand jeté passé derrière in attitude, jeté battement, jeté battu, jeté élancé en tournant, jeté en avant, jeté ordinaire, jeté passé, jeté rond de jambe sauté, petit jeté, petit jeté battu.*

jeté battement [ʒ(ə)te batmɑ̃] bat-MAH zh(u)-TAY (Fr. thrown; beating.) A *petit allegro* step performed *terre à terre*, consisting of a movement similar to a *jeté ordinaire* and the beating action of a *double battement frappé.* Often performed in series. May be performed *en avant* or *en arrière*, and with the accent in (finishing the inward beating action on the musical count) or out (brushing outward *to 2nd position* on the musical count).

jeté battement en arrière [ʒ(ə)te batmɑ̃ ɑ̃ naʀjɛʀ] zh(u)-TAY bat-MAH ah-nar-YER (Fr. thrown; beating; backward.) A *jeté battement* which, when performed in series, travels backward. The dancer begins *5th position derrière*, slides the back leg *to 2nd position* at *glissé height*, performs a low jump *sur place* onto the *working leg* with the other foot *cou-de-pied devant* as in a *battement frappé*, then immediately beats the same foot at ankle height to finish in *cou-de-pied derrière*, as in a *battement frappé.*

jeté battement en avant [ʒ(ə)te batmɑ̃ ɑ̃ navɑ̃] zh(u)-TAY bat-MAH ah na-VAH (Fr. thrown; beating; forward.) A *jeté battement* which, when performed in series, travels forward. The dancer begins *5th position devant*, slides the front leg *to 2nd position* at *glissé height*, performs a low jump *sur place* onto the *working leg* with the other foot *cou-de-pied derrière* as in a *battement frappé*, then immediately beats the same foot at ankle height to finish in *cou-de-pied devant*, as in a *battement frappé.*

jeté battu [ʒ(ə)te baty] zh(u)-TAY ba-TU (Fr. thrown; beaten.) A *jeté ordinaire* in which the legs perform a beat prior to the landing. May be performed *devant* or *derrière.* Variation: *petit jeté battu.*

jeté battu derrière [ʒ(ə)te baty dɛʀjɛʀ] zh(u)-TAY ba-TU der-YER (Fr. thrown; beaten; behind.) A *jeté derrière* initiated with the back foot and performed with a beat. From *5th derrière,* the *working foot* slides along the floor to above *glissé height,* the legs stretch to beat in the air in *5th position* without a *change of feet*, and the jump alights on the initiating foot, with the other foot contacting the mid-calf.

jeté battu devant [ʒ(ə)te baty d(ə)vɑ̃] zh(u)-TAY ba-TU d(u)-VAH (Fr. thrown; beaten; front.) A *jeté devant* initiated with the front foot and performed with a beat. From *5th devant,* the *working foot* slides along the floor to above *glissé height,* the legs stretch to beat in the air in *5th position* without a *change of feet*, and the jump alights on the initiating foot, with the other foot contacting the mid-shin.

jeté coupé élancé See *jeté élancé en tournant.*

jeté derrière [ʒ(ə)te dɛʀjɛʀ] zh(u)-TAY der-YER (Fr. thrown; behind.) A *jeté ordinaire* landing with the freed foot placed *sur le cou-de pied derrière.* From *5th derrière,* the first action is a *demi-plié,* and the back foot slides *to 2nd position* just below 45 degrees, coordinating with the spring off the *supporting leg* from the floor. Before alighting, the extended leg comes in front of the other leg to land with the freed foot *derrière,* the big toe contacting the base of the calf. May also begin *5th devant,* with the front foot initiating the action. In the Cecchetti method, a *jeté ordinaire derrière* initiated with the back foot is called *jeté dessus* or *jeté* over.

jeté derrière de côté [ʒ(ə)te dɛʀjɛʀ̃ də kote] zh(u)-TAY der-YER d(u) koh-TAY (Fr. thrown; behind; to the side.) A *jeté ordinaire* which travels sideways in the direction of the *working foot,* and ends with the other foot contacting the base of the calf.

jeté derrière, petit See *petit jeté derrière.*

jeté dessous [ʒ(ə)te d(ə)su] zh(u)-TAY d(u)-SOO (Fr. thrown; under.) A term of the Cecchetti method. See *jeté devant.*

jeté dessus [ʒ(ə)te d(ə)sy] zh(u)-TAY d(u)-SU (Fr. thrown; over.) A term of the Cecchetti method. See *jeté derrière.*

jeté devant [ʒ(ə)te d(ə)vɑ̃] zh(u)-TAY d(u)-VAH (Fr. thrown; front.) A *jeté ordinaire* landing with the freed foot placed *sur le cou-de pied devant.* From *5th devant,* the first action is a *demi-plié,* and the front foot slides *to 2nd position* just below 45 degrees, coordinating with the spring off the *supporting leg* from the floor. Before alighting, the extended leg comes behind the other leg to land with the freed foot *devant,* the little toe contacting the mid-shin. May also begin *5th derrière,* with the back foot initiating the action. In the Cecchetti method, a *jeté ordinaire devant* initiated with the front foot is called *jeté dessous* or *jeté* under.

jeté devant de côté [ʒ(ə)te d(ə)vɑ̃ də kote] zh(u)-TAY d(u)-VAH d(u) koh-TAY (Fr. thrown; front; to the side.) A *jeté ordinaire* which travels sideways in the direction of the *working foot*, and ends with the other foot contacting the mid-shin.

jeté élancé See *jeté élancé en tournant.*

jeté élancé coupé dessous en tournant See *jeté élancé en tournant.*

jeté élancé en avant See *jeté élancé en tournant.*

jeté élancé en tournant [ʒ(ə)te elɑ̃se ɑ̃ tuʀnɑ̃] zh(u)-TAY ay-lah-SAY ah toor-NAH (Fr. thrown; darted; turning.) A composite step consisting of a *grand jeté en avant* and a *pas de bourrée dessus* or *coupé dessous* performed with a full turn. Often performed in series *en diagonale* or *en manège.* When performed *en diagonale*, the dancer begins in an *upstage* corner *dégagé devant en croisé;* s/he *springs* forward into the line of travel, then performs a *pas de bourrée dessus* or *coupé dessous* making a full turn into the line of travel. The arms usually open to *1st arabesque* on the *jeté* and close to *1st position* with the turn.

jeté en avant [ʒ(ə)te ɑ̃ navɑ̃] zh(u)-TAY ah na-VAH (Fr. thrown; forward.) A *jeté ordinaire* performed travelling forward. May begin *en fondu* and finish *en arabesque* or *en attitude en fondu.* Variation: *grand jeté en avant.*

jeté ordinaire [ʒ(ə)te ɔʀdinɛʀ] zh(u)-TAY or-dee-NER (Fr. thrown; ordinary.) A jump from one foot to the other, landing with the freed foot contacting the base of the shin *(jeté devant)* or the base of the calf *(jeté derrière).* May commence with either the front or the back foot. Usually performed *sur place* but may be travelled, e.g., *jeté devant de côté, jeté en avant, jeté en arrière.* Variations: *grand jeté, jeté battu, petit jeté.*

jeté ordinaire derrière See *jeté derrière.*

jeté ordinaire devant See *jeté devant.*

jeté passé devant [ʒ(ə)te pɑse d(ə)vɑ̃] zh(u)-TAY pah-SAY d(u)-VAH (Fr. thrown; passed; front.) A *spring* in which the legs pass one another in front of the body at the height of the jump. The dancer begins with the *working leg en l'air devant en fondu, springs* into the air, and passes the push-off leg forward *en l'air devant* before alighting on the other leg *en fondu.* The legs may lift straight or *en attitude devant.* In *jeté passé derrière,* the legs pass each other behind the body.

jeté rond de jambe sauté [ʒ(ə)te ʀɔ̃ də ʒɑ̃b sote] zh(u)-TAY ro d(u) zhahb soh-TAY (Fr. thrown; circle of the leg; jumped.) A composite step consisting of a *jeté ordinaire* followed by a *rond de jambe sauté.* May be taken with a *jeté derrière* and a *rond jambe sauté en dedans*, or with a *jeté devant* and a *rond jambe sauté en dehors.*

jeté, grand See *grand jeté en avant.*

jeté, petit See *petit jeté.*

jump An action in which the dancer is propelled off the floor, usually starting and finishing *en demi-plié* or *en fondu.* See *sauté.*

kneel A term used to describe a position in which the dancer is supported on one knee.

l' [l] l (Fr. def art. m or f the.) See *en l'air.*

la [la] la (Fr. def art. f the.) See *à la seconde, sur la demi-pointe, sur la pointe.*

le [l(ə)] l(u) (Fr. def art. m the.) See *sur le cou-de-pied.*

leap A travelling jump from one leg to the other. See *jeté.*

levé [l(ə)ve] l(u)-VAY (Fr. pp of v lever, to lift or raise; adj lifted.) See *temps levé.*

lié [lje] lyay (Fr. pp of v lier, to link; adj linked, connected.) See *temps lié*.

line of dance Path along which the dancer travels while performing a series of steps and/or turns, as in *emboîté relevé en tournant* when the dancer performs a *relevé passé devant* 2 to 1 travelling slightly along the *line of dance*. Also referred to as *line of direction*.

lunge A wide *4th position*, with the weight well forward and the front leg in a deep *fondu*. The back foot can either be flat or fully stretched. This position is commonly used in conjunction with a *port de bras* involving body bends, either circular, or forward and back. Sometimes referred to as *grand 4th en fondu*.

manège [manɛʒ] ma-NEZH (Fr. nm roundabout, merry-go-round, carousel.) See *en manège*.

marché [marʃe] mar-SHAY (Fr. pp of v marcher, to walk or march; adj, marched.) See *pas marchés*.

medium allegro [- a(l)legʀo] – a-LAY-groh One of three basic categories of elevation, comprising jumps slightly higher than *petit allegro*, taken at a less brisk tempo and using ballon, and also incorporates steps of *batterie*. See *allegro*.

multiple pirouette [- piʀwɛt] – peer-WET (Fr. multiple; turn.) A virtuoso *pirouette* in which the dancer performs three or more complete revolutions, at his discretion.

natural 1st See *position of the feet, 1st natural*.

OP corner Opposite prompt corner, also referred to as *stage right* corner.

open 4th See *position of the arms, open 4th; position of the feet, 4th opposite 1st*.

open 5th See *position of the arms, open 5th*.

opposite prompt side See *stage right*.

opposition [ɔpozisjɔ̃] o-poh-zees-YO̲ (Fr. nf opposite.) Term used to describe a *position of the arms* in which the arm placed in front of or above the body is opposite or *"in opposition"* to the *working leg* (when supported on one leg), or to the front foot in a *position of the feet* (with the weight equally distributed). Ordinarily, in *3rd* and *4th position of the arms*, the arm placed in front of or above the body corresponds to the *working leg* or the front foot. See *attitude opposition; position of the arms, 3rd opposition; position of the arms, 4th opposition*.

ordinaire [ɔʀdinɛʀ] or-dee-NER (Fr. adj ordinary or normal.) Term used to describe the usual execution of a position or movement. In *3rd* and *4th position of the arms*, for example, the arm placed in front of or above the body ordinarily corresponds to the *working leg* (when supported on one foot), or to the front foot in a *position of the feet* (with the weight equally distributed). See *attitude ordinaire, jeté ordinaire, sissonne ordinaire*.

ouvert [uvɛʀ] oo-VER (Fr. adj wide or open.) 1. Contraction of the term *en ouvert*, referring to an open body *alignment*. See *en ouvert*. 2. Term used to describe an action which ends with the legs apart, either in an open position or with the *working leg* extended *en l'air*. See *échappé sauté ouvert, sissonne ouverte en avant, sissonne ouverte en arrière, sissonne ouverte de côté, sissonne ouverte battue en avant, sissonne ouverte changée en tournant in attitude ordinaire, cabriole ouverte derrière, petite cabriole ouverte derrière, sissonne relevée ouverte*.

ouvert, en See *en ouvert*.

pas [pɑ] pah (Fr. nm a step or steps.) 1. A dance step or steps. See *grand pas de basque, grand pas de chat, pas balancé, pas chassé, pas de basque, pas de bourrée, pas de valse, pas soutenu, petit pas de basque, petit pas de bourrée*. 2. Term used to describe a dance for a specific number of performers, e.g., "pas de deux" or "pas de trois." 3. A choreographed work, such as Perrot's "Pas de Quatre."

pas balancé See *balancé*.

pas chassé [pɑ ʃase] pah sha-SAY (Fr. step; chased.) A chasing step in which the dancer performs an *extended chassé* into *2nd* or *4th position en fondu*, followed by a *coupé sauté dessous*. Often done in series *en avant*. Whereas *galop* is a step into a spring *(posé, coupé sauté), pas chassé* is a slide into a spring *(chassé, coupé sauté)*.

pas de basque [pɑ də bask] pah d(u) bask (Fr. step of the Basque.) 1. A composite step consisting of transferences of weight. May be performed *glissé* or *sauté*, and *en avant* or *en arrière*. Variations: *grand pas de basque en tournant, petit pas de basque en tournant*. 2. In the Character section of the RAD Grades syllabus, the term *pas de* *basque* refers to a step consisting of three transferences of weight: a spring onto the initiating foot, a step in place onto the ball of the other foot, and a step in place to end on a relaxed leg, ready to perform the next *pas de basque* commencing with the other foot.

pas de basque battu en avant [pɑ də bask baty ɑ̃ navɑ̃] pah d(u) bask ba-TU ah na-VAH (Fr. step of the Basque; beaten; forward.) A *pas de basque sauté en avant* incorporating the beat of an *entrechat trois devant*. During the *spring* sideways, the dancer brings the push-off foot behind the *working foot* to beat in *5th position*, before landing on the *working foot* with the other foot placed mid-shin. A *pas de basque battu en arrière* is a *pas de basque sauté en arrière* incorporating the beat of an *entrechat trois derrière*.

pas de basque glissé [pɑ də bask glise] pah d(u) bask glee-SAY (Fr. step of the Basque; sliding.) A stylised travelling *pas de basque* executed *terre à terre* with a gliding quality. Taken *en avant* or *en arrière.*

pas de basque glissé en arrière [pɑ də bask glise ɑ̃ naʀjɛʀ] pah d(u) bask glee-SAY ah-nar-YER (Fr. step of the Basque; sliding; backward.) A stylised *pas de basque* executed *terre à terre* with a gliding quality and travelling backward. Starting *en croisé, 5th derrière,* the step commences with a *dégagé derrière en fondu;* then, continuing with a circular movement *en dedans,* the weight is transferred onto that leg *en fondu,* while turning towards the other *downstage* corner and bringing the freed leg to *1st* with a fully pointed foot. The freed foot extends to *dégagé derrière* and the weight is transferred backward onto a straight *supporting leg,* extending the other leg to *dégagé devant* before closing in *5th.* The arms commence and end in *demi-bras,* complementing the movement of the legs: they open through *2nd* as the leg extends *derrière* into the circular movement *en dedans,* lower to *bras bas* as the foot passes *1st,* and lift through *1st* to *demi-bras* on the transfer of weight *en arrière.* The *eye line* begins to 1 *(downstage)* and remains there until the foot passes through *1st,* when the head inclines over the *working leg.* On the transfer *en arrière,* the eyes return to 1.

pas de basque glissé en avant [pɑ də bask glise ɑ̃ navɑ̃] pah d(u) bask glee-SAY ah na-VAH (Fr. step of the Basque; sliding; forward.) A stylised *pas de basque* executed *terre à terre* with a gliding quality and travelling forward. Starting *en croisé, 5th devant,* the step commences with a *dégagé devant en fondu;* then, continuing with a circular movement *en dehors,* the weight is transferred onto that leg *en fondu,* while turning towards the other *downstage* corner and bringing the freed leg to *1st* with a fully pointed foot. The freed foot extends to *dégagé devant* and the weight is transferred forward onto a straight *supporting leg,* extending the other leg to *dégagé derrière* before closing in *5th.* The arms complement the movement of the legs: from *3rd position* with the arm corresponding to the front foot placed forward and the *eye line* to 1 *(downstage),* the arm opens to *2nd* with the circular movement of the leg. The other arm passes through *bras bas* as the foot passes though *1st,* and arrives in *3rd position* with the final transfer of weight. The eyes follow the movement of the opening arm, then pick up the track of the other arm as it moves from *bras bas* to *3rd,* and finish with the *eye line* to 1.

pas de basque sauté [pɑ də bask sote] pah d(u) bask soh-TAY (Fr. step of the Basque; jumped.) A stylised travelling *pas de basque* taken with a strong springing action. Taken *en avant* or *en arrière.*

pas de basque sauté en arrière [pɑ də bask sote ɑ̃ naʀjɛʀ] pah d(u) bask soh-TAY ah-nar-YER (Fr. step of the Basque; jumped; backward.) A stylised *pas de basque* taken with a strong springing action and travelling backward. Starting *en croisé, 5th derrière,* the step commences with the *working leg* extending *to 4th derrère en fondu* just above *glissé height,* and continues with a circular movement of the leg *en dedans,* springing onto that leg while turning towards the other *downstage* corner, bringing the freed leg to *retiré position* at the base of the calf. The freed leg then extends backward, followed by a strong transfer of weight onto a straight *supporting leg* with a *dégagé devant,* before closing into *5th.* The arms commence and end in *demi-bras,* as for *pas de basque glissé en arrière.*

pas de basque sauté en avant [pɑ də bask sote ɑ̃ navɑ̃] pah d(u) bask soh-TAY ah na-VAH (Fr. step of the Basque; jumped; forward.) A stylised *pas de basque* taken with a strong springing action and travelling forward. Starting *en croisé, 5th devant,* the step commences with the *working leg* extending to *4th devant* just above *glissé height,* and continues with a circular movement of the leg *en dehors,* springing onto that leg while turning towards the other *downstage* corner, bringing the freed leg to *retiré position* at the base of the calf. The freed leg then extends forward, followed by a strong transfer of weight onto a straight *supporting leg* with a *dégagé derrière,* before closing into *5th.* The arms move from *3rd* to *3rd,* as for *pas de basque glissé en avant.*

pas de bourrée [pɑ də buʀe] pah d(u) boo-RAY (Fr. bourrée step.) *Terre à terre* steps performed in a continuous movement in any direction, demanding quick, precise footwork. Can vary with the use of either the front or back foot on the initial extension. Taken *devant, derrière, dessus, dessous, en avant, en arrière,* and *en tournant.* Usually ends in *5th position en demi-plié,* but may end *en pointe/s,* in an open position, or in a *lunge.* Variations: *pas de bourrée à cinq pas, pas de bourrée à quatre pas, pas de bourrée couru, pas de bourrée piqué, petit pas de bourrée piqué, running pas de bourrée, wide pas de bourrée dessous en tournant.*

pas de bourrée à cinq pas [pɑ də buʀe a sɛ̃k pɑ] pah d(u) boo-RAY a sek pah (Fr. bourrée step; with five steps.) A composite step consisting of a *pas de bourrée dessous* which finishes *en fondu,* and a leg gesture leading into a *posé* to *arabesque.* From *5th derrière,* the action commences with a *demi-plié:* the *working foot* extends to *2nd at glissé height* and closes up to *5th derrière en demi-pointes* (first "step"), the front foot immediately steps to a small *2nd en demi-pointes* (second "step"), lowers *en fondu* with the tip of the initiating foot contacting the floor in front of the instep of the *supporting foot* (third "step"), does a *posé en avant* to *arabesque* (fourth "step"), and closes *5th derrière en demi-plié* (fifth "step"). The *pas de bourrée* is usually performed *en face,* and the *posé* taken *en ouvert.* The arms usually move to *bras bas* on the *pas de bourrée dessous* and pass through *1st position* to *1st arabesque* on the *posé en avant,* with the *arabesque line* held on the closing. The characteristic timing may be counted "and, a, one, y, two," with the *arabesque* reached on the sub-beat "y" just after count "one."

pas de bourrée à quatre pas [pɑ də buʀe a katʀə pɑ] pah d(u) boo-RAY a katr(u) pah (Fr. bourrée step; with four steps.) A composite step consisting of a *pas de bourrée dessous* which finishes *en fondu,* and a *posé* to *arabesque.* From *5th derrière,* the action commences with a *demi-plié:* the *working foot* extends to *2nd at glissé height* and closes up to *5th derrière en demi-pointes* (first "step"), the front foot immediately steps to a small *2nd en pointes* and lowers *en fondu* with the initiating foot closing to *cou-de-pied devant* (second "step"), does a *posé en avant* to *arabesque* (third "step"), and closes *5th derrière en demi-plié* (fourth "step"). The *pas de bourrée* is usually performed *en face,* and the *posé* taken *en ouvert.* The arms usually move to *bras bas* on the *pas de bourrée dessous* and pass through *1st position* to *1st arabesque* on the *posé en avant,* with the *arabesque line* held on the closing. The characteristic timing may be counted "and, a, one, two," with the *arabesque* reached on "one."

pas de bourrée couru [pɑ də buʀe kuʀy] pah d(u) boo-RAY koo-RU (Fr. bourrée step; running.) A *pas de bourrée* which travels in the direction of the initiating foot and finishes in an open position. A linking step consisting of two stepping actions and an open action. The action commences with a *demi-plié:* the dancer extends the *working foot* to *2nd at glissé height* and steps out onto it *en pointe,* closes the other foot *5th position en pointes,* then releases the initiating foot to an open position, either *en demi-plié* or *dégagé en fondu.* May be performed *en avant, en arrière,* or *de côté.* Variation: *running pas de bourrée.* In the Solo Seal syllabus and in the Cecchetti method, the term *pas de bourrée courus* refers to the step now called *courus.*

pas de bourrée couru de côté [pɑ də buʀe kuʀy də kote] pah d(u) boo-RAY koo-RU d(u) koh-TAY (Fr. bourrée step; running; to the side.) A *pas de bourrée couru* travelling sideways. The action commences with a *demi-plié:* the dancer extends the *working foot* to *2nd at glissé height* and steps out onto it *en pointe,* closes the other foot *5th position en pointes,* then releases the initiating foot to an open position, either *en fondu to 2nd à terre,* or *en demi-plié* in *2nd position.* May be initiated with the front or back foot, usually done with no *change of feet.*

pas de bourrée couru de côté to dégagé [pɑ də buʀe kuʀy də kote - degaʒe] pah d(u) boo-RAY koo-RU d(u) koh-TAY – day-ga-ZHAY (Fr. bourrée step; running; to the side; to disengaged position.) A *pas de bourrée couru de côté* which ends in *dégagé to 2nd en fondu.*

pas de bourrée couru en arrière [pɑ də buʀe kuʀy ɑ̃ naʀjɛʀ] pah d(u) boo-RAY koo-RU ah-nar-YER (Fr. bourrée step; running; backward.) A *pas de bourrée couru* travelling backward. The action commences with a *demi-plié:* the dancer extends the *working foot* to *4th derrière at glissé height* and steps backward *en pointe,* closes the other foot *5th devant en pointes,* then releases the back foot *dégagé derrière en fondu* or steps backward into *4th en demi-plié.*

pas de bourrée couru en arrière to dégagé [pɑ də buʀe kuʀy ɑ̃ naʀjɛʀ - degaʒe] pah d(u) boo-RAY koo-RU ah-nar-YER – day-ga-ZHAY (Fr. bourrée step; running; backward; to disengaged position.) A *pas de bourrée couru en arrière* which ends with the back foot releasing to *dégagé derrière en fondu.*

pas de bourrée couru en avant [pɑ də buʀe kuʀy ɑ̃ navɑ̃] pah d(u) boo-RAY koo-RU ah na-VAH (Fr. bourrée step; running; forward.) A *pas de bourrée couru* travelling forward. From *5th devant,* the action commences with a *demi-plié:* the dancer extends the *working foot* to *4th devant at glissé height* and steps forward *en pointe*, closes the other foot *5th derrière en pointes*, then releases the front foot *dégagé devant en fondu* or steps forward into *4th en demi-plié.*

pas de bourrée couru en avant to dégagé [pɑ də buʀe kuʀy ɑ̃ navɑ̃ - degaʒe] pah d(u) boo-RAY koo-RU ah na-VAH – day-ga-ZHAY (Fr. bourrée step; running; forward; to disengaged position.) A *pas de bourrée couru en avant* which ends with the front foot releasing to *dégagé devant en fondu.*

pas de bourrée couru to dégagé [pɑ də buʀe kuʀy - degaʒe] pah d(u) boo-RAY koo-RU – day-ga-ZHAY (Fr. bourrée step; running; to disengaged position.) A *pas de bourrée couru* which ends with the initiating leg released to *dégagé en fondu.* May be performed *en avant*, *en arrière*, or *de côté.*

pas de bourrée couru to demi-plié [pɑ də buʀe kuʀy - d(ə)miplije] pah d(u) boo-RAY koo-RU – d(u)-MEE-plee-YAY (Fr. bourrée step; running; to a half-bend.) A *pas de bourrée couru* which ends *en demi-plié* in an open position, i.e., *2nd* or *4th.* May be performed *en avant* or *en arrière* ending in *4th position*, or *de côté* ending in *2nd position.*

pas de bourrée couru to demi-plié de côté [pɑ də buʀe kuʀy - d(ə)miplije də kote] pah d(u) boo-RAY koo-RU – d(u)-MEE-plee-YAY d(u) koh-TAY (Fr. bourrée step; running; to a half-bend; to the side.) A *pas de bourrée couru* which travels sideways and ends in *2nd position en demi-plié.*

pas de bourrée couru to demi-plié en arrière [pɑ də buʀe kuʀy - d(ə)miplije ɑ̃ naʀjɛʀ] pah d(u) boo-RAY koo-RU – d(u)-MEE-plee-YAY ah-nar-YER (Fr. bourrée step; running; to a half-bend; backward.) A *pas de bourrée couru* which travels backward and ends in *4th position en demi-plié.*

pas de bourrée couru to demi-plié en avant [pɑ də buʀe kuʀy - d(ə)miplije ɑ̃ navɑ̃] pah d(u) boo-RAY koo-RU –d(u)-MEE-plee-YAY ah na-VAH (Fr. bourrée step; running; to a half-bend; forward.) A *pas de bourrée couru* which travels forward and ends in *4th position en demi-plié.*

pas de bourrée de côté See *pas de bourrée couru de côté.*

pas de bourrée derrière [pɑ də buʀe dɛʀjɛʀ] pah d(u) boo-RAY der-YER (Fr. bourrée step; behind.) A *pas de bourrée* travelling sideways with the closing actions taken *derrière-derrière.* From *5th position devant* or *derrière*, the action commences with a *demi-plié:* the *working foot* extends *to 2nd at glissé height* then closes up into *5th derrière en demi-pointes;* the front foot immediately steps to a small *2nd en demi-pointes,* then the other foot closes into *5th derrière en demi-plié.*

pas de bourrée dessous [pɑ də buʀe d(ə)su] pah d(u) boo-RAY d(u)-SOO (Fr. bourrée step; under.) A *pas de bourrée* travelling sideways with the closing actions taken *derrière-devant.* From *5th position devant* or *derrière*, the action commences with a *demi-plié:* the *working foot* extends *to 2nd at glissé height* then closes up into *5th derrière en demi-pointes;* the front foot immediately steps to a small *2nd en demi-pointes,* then the other foot closes into *5th devant en demi-plié.*

pas de bourrée dessous en tournant [pɑ də buʀe d(ə)su ɑ̃ tuʀnɑ̃] pah d(u) boo-RAY d(u)-SOO ah toor-NAH (Fr. bourrée step; under; turning.) A *pas de bourrée dessous* performed *sur place*, with the body turning away from the initial *supporting foot.* The first action may be a *dégagé to 2nd en fondu* or, when initiated with the front foot, an *assemblé soutenu à terre en dehors en fondu.* Variation: *wide pas de bourrée dessous en tournant.*

pas de bourrée dessus [pɑ də buʀe d(ə)sy] pah d(u) boo-RAY d(u)-SU (Fr. bourrée step; over.) A *pas de bourrée* travelling sideways with the closing actions taken *devant-derrière.* From *5th position devant* or *derrière*, the action commences with a *demi-plié:* the *working foot* extends to *2nd at glissé height* then closes up into *5th devant en demi-pointes;* the back foot immediately steps to a small *2nd en demi-pointes,* then the other foot closes into *5th derrière en demi-plié.*

pas de bourrée dessus en tournant [pɑ də buʀe d(ə)sy ɑ̃ tuʀnɑ̃] pah d(u) boo-RAY d(u)-SU ah toor-NAH (Fr. bourrée step; over; turning.) A *pas de bourrée dessus* performed *sur place*, with the body turning toward the initial *supporting foot.* The first action may be a *dégagé to 2nd en fondu* or, when initiated with the back foot, an *assemblé soutenu à terre en dedans en fondu.*

pas de bourrée devant [pɑ də buʀe d(ə)vɑ̃] pah d(u) boo-RAY d(u)-VAH (Fr. bourrée step; front.) A *pas de bourrée* travelling sideways with the closing actions taken *devant-devant.* From *5th position devant* or *derrière*, the action commences with a *demi-plié:* the *working foot* extends to *2nd at glissé height* then closes up into *5th devant en demi-pointes;* the back foot immediately steps to a small *2nd en demi-pointes,* then the other foot closes into *5th devant en demi-plié.*

pas de bourrée en arrière [pɑ də buʀe ɑ̃ naʀjɛʀ] pah d(u) boo-RAY ah-nar-YER (Fr. bourrée step; backward.) A *pas de bourrée* travelling backward. From *5th devant,* the action commences with a *demi-plié:* the *working foot* extends to *4th devant at glissé height* then closes up into *5th devant en demi-pointes;* the back foot immediately steps to a small *4th en demi-pointes,* then the other foot closes into *5th devant en demi-plié.*

pas de bourrée en avant [pɑ də buʀe ɑ̃ navɑ̃] pah d(u) boo-RAY ah na-VAH (Fr. bourrée step; forward.) A *pas de bourrée* travelling forward. From *5th devant,* the action commences with a *demi-plié:* the *working foot* extends to *4th derrière at glissé height* then closes up into *5th derrière en demi-pointes;* the front foot immediately steps to a small *4th en demi-pointes,* then the other foot closes into *5th derrière en demi-plié.*

pas de bourrée en première [pɑ də buʀe ɑ̃ pʀəmjɛʀ] pah d(u) boo-RAY ah pr(u)m-YER (Fr. bourrée step; in first.) A *pas de bourrée* in which the feet pass through *1st position en demi-pointes*, instead of *5th.* The dancer steps onto one foot *en demi-pointe*, passes the other foot through *1st position* to perform a second step *en demi-pointe*, then steps *en fondu*; usually performed *en avant;* used as a preparation into steps such as *grand jeté passé derrière*.

pas de bourrée en tournant [pɑ də buʀe ɑ̃ tuʀnɑ̃] pah d(u) boo-RAY ah toor-NAH (Fr. bourrée step; turning.) A *pas de bourrée* performed *sur place* with a turn occurring smoothly throughout. Often preceded by an *assemblé soutenu.* May be performed *dessus* (turning *en dedans)* or *dessous* (turning *en dehors).*

pas de bourrée piqué [pɑ də buʀe pike] pah d(u) boo-RAY pee-KAY (Fr. bourrée step; pricked.) A *pas de bourrée* which has a sharp, picked up quality. Usually taken *dessous,* but may also be taken *dessus.* May be taken with the freed leg lifting to *retiré position devant* or *derrère,* or to *cou-de-pied (petit pas de bourrée piqué).* May end *en pointes*, in an open position, in a *lunge*, or with a *coupé.* Also taken *en tournant.*

pas de bourrée piqué dessous [pɑ də buʀe pike d(ə)su] pah d(u) boo-RAY pee-KAY d(u)-SOO (Fr. bourrée step; pricked; under.) A *pas de bourrée piqué* in which one foot sharply steps behind the other which is briskly picked up in front. From *5th derrière,* the initiating foot is released *sur le cou-de-pied derrière en fondu;* then, stepping *sur place* onto that foot *en demi-pointe,* the other foot is picked up to *retiré devant;* it then steps to a small *2nd en demi-pointes* with the initiating foot immediately picked up to *retiré devant.* The *pas de bourrée* finishes either by closing to *5th position en demi-pointes* or *en demi-plié,* or by lowering onto the initiating foot *en fondu* with the other foot *sur le cou-de-pied derrière.* When the freed leg is lifted to *cou-de-pied devant* instead of *retiré position devant,* this is known as *petit pas de bourrée piqué dessous.* May be performed *en tournant.*

pas de bourrée piqué dessous en tournant [pɑ də buʀe pike d(ə)su ɑ̃ tuʀnɑ̃] pah d(u) boo-RAY pee-KAY d(u)-SOO ah toor-NAH (Fr. bourrée step; pricked; under; by turning.) A *pas de bourrée piqué dessous* performed *sur place*, with a turn away from the initial *supporting leg* occurring smoothly throughout. Also *pas de bourrée piqué dessous en dehors.*

pas de bourrée piqué dessus [pɑ də buʀe pike d(ə)sy] pah d(u) boo-RAY pee-KAY d(u)-SU (Fr. bourrée step; pricked; over.) A *pas de bourrée piqué* in which one foot sharply steps in front of the other which is briskly picked up behind. May be performed *en tournant.*

pas de bourrée piqué dessus en tournant [pɑ də buʀe pike d(ə)sy ɑ̃ tuʀɑ̃] pah d(u) boo-RAYpee-KAY d(u)-SU ah toor-NAH (Fr. bourrée step; pricked; over; by turning.) A *pas de bourrée piqué dessus* performed *sur place*, with a turn toward the initial *supporting leg* occurring smoothly throughout. Also *pas de bourrée piqué dessus en dedans.*

pas de bourrée piqué en tournant [pɑ də buʀe pike ɑ̃ tuʀnɑ̃] pah d(u) boo-RAY pee-KAY ah toor-NAH (Fr. bourrée step; pricked; turning.) A *pas de bourrée piqué* performed *sur place* with a turn occurring smoothly throughout. Usually performed *dessous en dehors*, but occasionally performed *dessus en dedans*.

pas de bourrée under en tournant, travelled See *wide pas de bourrée dessous en tournant*.

pas de bourrée, running See *running pas de bourrée*.

pas de chat [pɑ də ʃa] pah d(u) sha (Fr. step of the cat.) A light, springing step moving sideways from *5th to 5th,* jumping off one foot and landing on the other foot before closing *en demi-plié.* From *5th derrière en demi-plié,* the back foot is released and commences to lift through *retiré* while at the same time there is a spring upward. At the height of the jump, the leading leg opens slightly in preparation for landing while the push-off leg passes through *retiré devant.* Landing on the leading foot, the other foot swiftly follows to close into *5th devant en demi-plié.* The arms are held in *3rd position* throughout, with the arm corresponding to the leading foot placed in front. The *eye line* is over the forearm to the *downstage* corner. Variation: *grand pas de chat to 4th.*

pas de chat, grand See *grand pas de chat to 4th.*

pas de cheval en pointe [pɑ də ʃ(ə)val ɑ̃ pwɛ̃t] pah d(u) sh(u)-VAL ah pwet (Fr. step of the horse; on tiptoe.) An action of the *working leg*, with the *supporting leg en pointe en fondu,* imitating the motion of a horse pawing the ground. The dancer begins with the *working leg devant à terre*, relaxes the working knee brushing the tip of the *working foot* along the floor, and completes the circular action of the lower leg by extending the leg to end as she began. May be performed in series, either with a *hop* (referred to as *pas de cheval sauté),* or with a *spring* (similar to *spring points).*

pas de cheval sauté en pointe [pɑ də ʃ(ə)val sote ɑ̃ pwɛ̃t] pah d(u) sh(u)-VAL soh-TAY ah pwet (Fr. step of the horse; jumped; on tiptoe.) A *pas de cheval en pointe* performed with a *hop.*

pas de valse [pɑ də vals] pah d(u) vals(u) (Fr. step of the waltz.) A lyrical step done in a *waltz* rhythm, consisting of three transferences of weight from foot to foot, often performed in series. The dancer performs a lilting step onto one foot, the other foot passes through *petit retiré* to step forward or backward, then the dancer transfers the weight onto the first foot with a *coupé* action. May be performed *en avant*, *en arrière*, or *de côté*. Similar to *balancé*. Not included in Boys syllabus.

pas de valse de côté [pɑ də vals də kote] pah d(u) vals(u) d(u) koh-TAY (Fr. step of the waltz; to the side.) A *pas de valse* travelling sideways. When performed in series travelling backward, the first step in each *pas de valse* is taken sideways, the second step is taken backward, and the *coupé* is done *dessus*.

pas de valse en arrière [pɑ də vals ɑ̃ naʀjɛʀ] pah d(u) vals(u) ah-nar-YER (Fr. step of the waltz; backward.) A *pas de valse* travelling backward in which the footwork is similar to a *balancé en arrière* but performed with a broader line.

pas de valse en avant [pɑ də vals ɑ̃ navɑ̃] pah d(u) vals(u) ah na-VAH (Fr. step of the waltz; forward.) A *pas de valse* travelling forward in which the footwork is similar to a *balancé en avant* but performed with a broader line.

pas de valse en tournant [pɑ də vals ɑ̃ tuʀnɑ̃] pah d(u) vals(u) ah toor-NAH (Fr. step of the waltz; turning.) A *pas de valse* performed while turning. When performed in series, each step is taken along the *line of dance* with a 1/2-turn on each *pas de valse*. The first 1/2-turn is done toward the *line of dance* with the second completing the turn.

pas marchés [pɑ marʃe] pah mar-SHAY (Fr. steps; walked.) A series of transfers of weight travelling forward, with each *working leg* performing a *petit développé passé devant* into *4th position en demi-plié.* Performed as stylised walks in the Character section of the Grade 6 syllabus.

pas soutenu [pɑ sutny] pah soot-NU (Fr. step; sustained.) A sustained extension of the leg and foot *à terre* to *dégagé en fondu,* with a coordinated return to a closed position stretching the *supporting leg.* From *5th position,* the *supporting leg* bends at the same time as the *working leg* extends to a *dégagé en fondu.* The return movement is a simultaneous straightening of the *supporting leg* with a closing of the *working leg.* May be executed *devant, to 2nd* (with or without a *change of feet),* and *derrière.* Variation: *pas soutenu with petit développé*.

pas soutenu derrière [pɑ sutny dɛʀjɛʀ] pah soot-NU der-YER (Fr. step; sustained; to the back.) A *pas soutenu* in which the *working leg* starts *5th derrière* and extends to the back.

pas soutenu derrière with petit développé [pɑ sutny dɛʀjɛʀ - p(ə)ti devlɔpe] pah soot-NU der-YER – p(u)-TEE dayv-loh-PAY (Fr. step; sustained; to the back; with small unfolding action.) A *pas soutenu* in which the *working leg* opens to the back with a *petit développé* action instead of a *battement tendu* action.

pas soutenu devant [pɑ sutny d(ə)vɑ̃] pah soot-NU d(u)-VAH (Fr. step; sustained; front.) A *pas soutenu* in which the *working leg* starts *5th devant* and extends to the front.

pas soutenu devant with petit développé [pɑ sutny d(ə)vɑ̃ - p(ə)ti devlɔpe] pah soot-NU d(u)-VAH –p(u)-TEE dayv-loh-PAY (Fr. step; sustained; front; with small unfolding action.) A *pas soutenu* in which the *working leg* opens to the front with a *petit développé* action instead of a *battement tendu* action.

pas soutenu to 2nd [pɑ sutny -] pah soot-NU – (Fr. step; sustained; to 2nd.) A *pas soutenu* in which the *working leg* starts *5th position devant* or *derrière,* extends outward to the side, and closes with or without *a change of feet.*

pas soutenu to 2nd with petit développé [pɑ sutny - p(ə)ti devlɔpe] pah soot-NU – p(u)-TEE dayv-loh-PAY (Fr. step; sustained; to 2nd; with small unfolding action.) A *pas soutenu* in which the *working leg* opens to the side with a *petit développé* action instead of a *battement tendu* action.

pas soutenu with petit développé [pɑ sutny - p(ə)ti devlɔpe] pah soot-NU – p(u)-TEE dayv-loh-PAY (Fr. step; sustained; with small unfolding action.) A *pas soutenu* in which the *working leg* opens with a *petit développé* action instead of a *battement tendu* action.

passé [pɑse] pah-SAY (Fr. pp of v passer, to pass; adj passed; nm a passing action or position.) 1. Term used to describe actions in which the *working leg* passes from front to back or from back to front. See *ballonné composé de côté passé, ballonné de côté passé, chassé passé, développé passé, grand jeté passé, glissade piquée passé, grand retiré passé, jeté passé devant, petit retiré passé, petit développé passé, petit retiré sauté passé, posé passé, relevé passé, retiré passé, retiré sauté passé, sissonne ordinaire passée.* 2. *Retiré position* is sometimes referred to as *passé.*

penchée [pɑ̃ʃe] pah-SHAY (Fr. pp of v pencher, to slant, tilt, tip, or lean over; adj tilted; nf a tilted position or tilting action.) An action taken with the *working leg en l'air* in which the relationship of the body and the *working leg* is sustained while the body tilts or leans away from the *working leg.* Although the *working leg* appears to lift, the motion occurs in the supporting hip. May be performed with the leg extended *to 2nd, attitude derriére,* and *arabesque.*

penchée in 2nd [pɑ̃ʃe -] pah-SHAY – (Fr. tilting action; in 2nd.) A *penchée* action performed with the *working leg* extended in *2nd en l'air.*

penchée in arabesque [pɑ̃ʃe - aʀabɛsk] pah-SHAY – a-ra-BESK (Fr. tilting action; in arabesque.) A *penchée* action performed with the *working leg* extended in *arabesque en l'air.* Also *arabesque penchée.*

penchée in attitude [pɑ̃ʃe - atityd] pah-SHAY – a-tee-TUD (Fr. tilting action; in attitude.) A *penchée* action performed with the *working leg* placed in *attitude derrière en l'air.*

petit [p(ə)ti] p(u)-TEE, p'TEE (Fr. adj small or little.) See *petit allegro, petit assemblé, petit battement, petit changement, petit développé, petit jeté, petit pas de basque en tournant, petit retiré, petit retiré sauté, petit rond de jambe en dehors, petit soutenu, petite cabriole, petite sissonne, petits battements battus, petits battements serrés, petits jetés en tournant, petits pas de basque en manège, petits soutenus en manège.*

petit allegro [p(ə)ti ta(l)legʀo] p(u)-TEE ta-LAY-groh (Fr. small; briskly.) 1. One of three basic categories of elevation, comprising jumps in which the dancer rises sufficiently for the feet to stretch fully in the air. These jumps are often performed with the arms in *bras bas,* since sufficient force for small, low jumps can be applied from the ankles and feet. A sub-category is *terre à terre allegro.* Also comprises linking steps, which may travel in any direction, and steps with a beating action of the legs, known as *batterie.* 2. A generic term for a sub-category of movements performed at the beginning of the *Allegro* section of a class. These may include, at a pre-elementary level: *glissades–devant, derrière, dessus, dessous; pas de bourrées–devant, derrière, dessus, dessous; sautés en première; échappés sautés in 2nd position; changements; soubresauts; sissonnes ordinaires–devant, derrière; petits assemblés–devant, derrière; petits jetés–derrière; coupé sauté–coupé sauté–dessus, dessous;* at an elementary level: *petits changements; pas de bourrée–devant,* *derrière, dessus, dessous; échappés sautés en croix; jeté ordinaires–devant, derrière; pas de basque glissés–en avant, en arrière; sissonnes ordinaires–devant, derrière, passé devant, passé derrière;* at an intermediate level: *jetés battements (accent out)–en avant, en arrière; glissades–en arrière; pas de bourrées–en avant, en arrière; pas de bourrées en tournant–dessus, dessous; pas de bourrées courus to degagé and demi-plié–en avant, en arrière, de côté; pas de bourrées à quatre pas, à cinq pas; faillis; temps de cuisse (French)–dessus, dessous; sissonnes fermées de côté–dessus, dessous.*

petit assemblé [p(ə)ti tasɑ̃ble] p(u)-TEE ta-sah-BLAY (Fr. small; gathered step.) A small jump *sur place* from one foot to two feet. With the *working foot* placed *sur le cou-de-pied devant* or *derrière,* there is a spring off the *supporting leg,* assembling the legs fully stretched in *5th position* in the air before landing in *5th.* May be done *devant* or *derrière*. Variations: *assemblé fermé, petit assemblé en pointes.*

petit assemblé derrière [p(ə)ti tasɑ̃ble dɛʀjɛʀ] p(u)-TEE ta-sah-BLAY der-YER (Fr. small; gathered step; behind.) A *petit assemblé* in which the *working foot* begins *sur le cou-de-pied derrière* and ends *5th derrière.*

petit assemblé derrière en pointes [p(ə)ti tasɑ̃ble dɛʀjɛʀ ɑ̃ pwɛ̃t] p(u)-TEE ta-sah-BLAY der-YER ah pwet (Fr. small; gathered step; behind; on tiptoe.) A *petit assemblé derrière* performed on the tips of the feet. Starting with the *working foot* placed *sur le cou-de-pied derrière*, the dancer performs a low jump into the air, and lands in *5th derrière en pointes.*

petit assemblé devant [p(ə)ti tasɑ̃ble d(ə)vɑ̃] p(u)-TEE ta-sah-BLAY d(u)-VAH (Fr. small; gathered step; front.) A *petit assemblé* in which the *working foot* begins *sur le cou-de-pied devant* and ends *5th devant.*

petit assemblé devant en pointes [p(ə)ti tasɑ̃ble d(ə)vɑ̃ ɑ̃ pwɛ̃t] p(u)-TEE ta-sah-BLAY d(u)-VAH ah pwet (Fr. small; gathered step; front; on tiptoe.) A *petit assemblé devant* performed on the tips of the feet. Starting with the *working foot* placed *sur le cou-de-pied devant*, the dancer performs a low jump into the air, and lands in *5th devant en pointes.*

petit ballotté [p(ə)ti balɔte] p(u)-TEE ba-lo-TAY (Fr. small; tossed step.) A *ballotté* performed *terre à terre.* When performed *en l'air,* the *working leg* extends below 45 degrees. When performed *à terre* it involves a quick action: the *working leg* may extend to *glissé height* with no *développé* action, almost like a *coupé;* or it may open with a *petit développé* action.

petit battement [p(ə)ti batmɑ̃] p(u)-TEE bat-MAH (Fr. small; beating action.) A small sideways beating action of the *working foot* on the *cou-de-pied* of the *supporting leg.* An exercise in accent, speed, and dexterity of the lower leg. From a relaxed knee joint, the lower leg opens sideways, releasing sufficiently for the foot to pass the *supporting leg,* beating *derrière* before opening sideways to beat *devant.* May also commence from a starting position *derrière,* beating *devant* and *derrière.* Practised one movement at a time, in even timing, with an accent *devant* or *derrière*, or rapidly and continuously. Also called *petit battement sur le cou-de pied.* When performed with alternating closings *devant* and *derrière* in series through the music, called *petits battements serrés.* Variation: *petits battements battus.* To find the position of the foot *sur le cou-de-pied devant:* place the feet in *1st position* and draw up the toes of the *working foot* to a fully stretched position at the base of the Achilles tendon; holding the *turn-out* of the working thigh, allow the toes to move slightly back as the heel settles forward, with the sole of the *working foot* in contact with the *supporting leg.* The foot retains this shape through the *exercise.* When taken *en demi-pointe,* this movement may be performed with a fully stretched foot.

petit battement sur le cou-de-pied See *petit battement.*

petit changement [p(ə)ti ʃɑ̃ʒmɑ̃] p(u)-TEE shahzh-MAH (Fr. small; changing.) A small jump with a *change of feet*, performed *terre à terre* and usually in series in order to warm up the feet and ankles.

petit développé [p(ə)ti devlɔpe] p(u)-TEE dayv-loh-PAY (Fr. small; unfolding action.) Action by which a *working leg* may be extended: the foot passes through *petit retiré* to extend *à terre* or just off the floor.

petit développé derrière [p(ə)ti devlɔpe dɛʀjɛʀ] p(u)-TEE dayv-loh-PAY der-YER (Fr. small; unfolding action; behind.) Action by which a *working leg* may be extended to the back: the foot passes through *petit retiré* to extend behind *à terre* or just off the floor.

petit développé devant [p(ə)ti devlɔpe d(ə)vɑ̃] p(u)-TEE dayv-loh-PAY d(u)-VAH (Fr. small; unfolding action; front.) Action by which a *working leg* may be extended to the front: the foot passes through *petit retiré* to extend in front *à terre* or just off the floor.

petit développé passé [p(ə)ti devlɔpe pɑse] p(u)-TEE dayv-loh-PAY pah-SAY (Fr. small; unfolding action; passed.) Small action in which the *working leg* passes from behind the *supporting leg* and unfolds in front of it, or passes from in front of the *supporting leg* and unfolds behind it. May be performed *devant* or *derrière*.

petit développé passé derrière [p(ə)ti devlɔpe pɑse dɛʀjɛʀ] p(u)-TEE dayv-loh-PAY pah-SAY der-YER (Fr. small; unfolding action; passed; behind.) Action by which a *working leg* passes from the front to the back and extends to the back: the foot passes through *petit retiré* to extend behind *à terre* or just off the floor. May be used to initiate steps such as *pas chassé*.

petit développé passé devant [p(ə)ti devlɔpe pɑse d(ə)vɑ̃] p(u)-TEE dayv-loh-PAY pah-SAY d(u)-VAH (Fr. small; unfolding action; passed; front.) Action by which a *working leg* passes from the back to the front and extends to the front: the foot passes through *petit retiré* to extend in front *à terre* or just off the floor. May be used to initiate steps such as *pas chassé*.

petit développé to 2nd [p(ə)ti devlɔpe -] p(u)-TEE dayv-loh-PAY – (Fr. small; unfolding action; to 2nd.) Action by which a *working leg* may be extended to the side: the foot passes through *petit retiré* to extend to the side either *à terre* or just off the floor.

petit développé to 2nd à terre [p(ə)ti devlɔpe - a tɛʀ] p(u)-TEE dayv-loh-PAY – a ter (Fr. small; unfolding action; to 2nd; on the ground.) Action by which a *working leg* may be extended to the side: the foot passes through *petit retiré* to extend to the side *à terre*.

petit développé, reverse See *reverse petit développé*.

petit jeté [p(ə)ti ʒ(ə)te] p(u)-TEE zh(u)-TAY (Fr. small; thrown action.) A small spring *sur place* from one foot onto the other, landing with the foot placed *sur le cou-de pied.* Performed with lightness and precision. Taken *devant* or *derrière, battu,* and *en tournant*. See *petits jetés en tournant*. Variation: *petit jeté battu*.

petit jeté battu [p(ə)ti ʒ(ə)te baty] p(u)-TEE zh(u)-TAY ba-TU (Fr. small; thrown; beaten.) A small *spring* performed with a beat. With one foot placed *sur le cou-de-pied,* the movement commences with a spring into the air stretching both legs to perform a beat in *5th position* without a *change of feet*, then lands on the other foot with the free foot fully stretched *sur le cou-de-pied*. May be performed *devant* or *derrière*.

petit jeté battu derrière [p(ə)ti ʒ(ə)te baty dɛʀjɛʀ] p(u)-TEE zh(u)-TAY ba-TU der-YER (Fr. small; thrown; beaten; behind.) A *petit jeté battu* which starts and ends with the foot placed *sur le cou-de-pied derrière*.

petit jeté battu devant [p(ə)ti ʒ(ə)te baty d(ə)vɑ̃] p(u)-TEE zh(u)-TAY ba-TU d(u)-VAH (Fr. small; thrown; beaten; front.) A *petit jeté battu* which starts and ends with the foot placed *sur le cou-de-pied devant*.

petit jeté derrière [p(ə)ti ʒ(ə)te dɛʀjɛʀ] p(u)-TEE zh(u)-TAY der-YER (Fr. small; thrown; behind.) A *petit jeté* which starts with one foot placed *sur le cou-de-pied derrière,* commences with a spring into the air with the raised foot passing to replace the push-off foot, and lands with the freed foot placed *sur le cou-de-pied derrière*. May be taken *en pointe*.

petit jeté devant [p(ə)ti ʒ(ə)te d(ə)vɑ̃] p(u)-TEE zh(u)-TAY d(u)-VAH (Fr. small; thrown action; front.) A *petit jeté* which starts with one foot placed *sur le cou-de-pied devant,* commences with a spring into the air with the raised foot passing to replace the push-off foot, and lands with the freed foot placed *sur le cou-de-pied devant*. May be taken *en pointe*.

petit jeté devant by 1/2 turn [p(ə)ti ʒ(ə)te d(ə)vɑ̃ -] p(u)-TEE zh(u)-TAY d(u)-VAH – (Fr. small; thrown action; front; by half turn.) A *petit jeté devant* in which the dancer performs a half-turn in the air. Often performed in series *en diagonale,* and also called *petits jetés en tournant*.

petit pas de basque en tournant [p(ə)ti pɑ də bask ɑ̃ tuʀnɑ̃] p(u)-TEE pah d(u) bask ah toor-NAH (Fr. small; step of the Basque; turning.) A type of *pirouette* often performed in series. From *dégagé devant*, there is a *spring* to the side along the *line of dance* landing on the extended foot *en pointe* and circling the other leg to *4th devant* at *glissé height;* then a closing to *5th devant en pointes* with a 1/4-turn to face the *line of dance;*

and a 3/4-turn toward the back foot to complete the turn in *5th position* with the other foot *devant* before lowering onto the back foot *en fondu*. The arms usually begin *3rd ordinaire*, open toward *2nd*, and close in *1st position* as the foot closes in *5th devant*. Similar to *petit soutenu*, except that in *petit pas de basque en tournant* the second leg circles to *4th devant* before closing *5th en pointes*.

petit pas de bourrée piqué dessous [p(ə)ti pɑ də buʀe pike d(ə)su] p(u)-TEE pah d(u) boo-RAY pee-KAY d(u)-SOO (Fr. small; bourrée step; pricked; under.) A *pas de bourrée piqué dessous* performed with the working foot placed *cou-de-pied devant* instead of *retiré devant*.

petit retiré [p(ə)ti ʀ(ə)tiʀe] p(u)-TEE r(u)-tee-RAY (Fr. small; withdrawn action.) A small drawing up action of the *working foot* to a fully pointed position at the height of the ankle bone. See *petit retiré position*. Variations: *petit retiré devant, petit retiré derrière, petit retiré passé, petit retiré sauté*.

petit retiré derrière [p(ə)ti ʀ(ə)tiʀe dɛʀjɛʀ] p(u)-TEE r(u)-tee-RAY der-YER (Fr. small; withdrawn; behind.) A small drawing up action of the *working foot* to a fully pointed position at the height of the outer ankle bone. From *5th derrière*, the back foot peels off the floor as the knee flexes; the toes are drawn to a fully pointed position behind the supporting heel and continue up to *cou-de-pied derrière*. The return to *5th derrière* is through the *working foot*.

petit retiré devant [p(ə)ti ʀ(ə)tiʀe d(ə)vɑ̃] p(u)-TEE r(u)-tee-RAY d(u)-VAH (Fr. small; withdrawn; front.) A small drawing up action of the *working foot* to a fully pointed position at the height of the inner ankle bone. From *5th devant*, the front foot peels off the floor as the knee flexes; the toes are drawn to a fully pointed position in front of the supporting heel and continue up to *cou-de-pied devant*. The return to *5th devant* is through the *working foot*.

petit retiré passé [p(ə)ti ʀ(ə)tiʀe pɑse] p(u)-TEE r(u)-tee-RAY pah-SAY (Fr. small; withdrawn action; passed.) A variation of *petit retiré* in which the *working foot* begins in front and ends behind, or the reverse. Taken *devant* or *derrière*.

petit retiré passé derrière [p(ə)ti ʀ(ə)tiʀe pɑse dɛʀjɛʀ] p(u)-TEE r(u)-tee-RAY pah-SAY der-YER (Fr. small; withdrawn; passed; behind.) A *petit retiré passé* in which the *working foot* begins in front and ends behind. From *5th devant*, the front foot peels off the floor as the knee flexes; the toes are drawn directly to *petit retiré position* before closing through the *working foot* into *5th derrière*.

petit retiré passé devant [p(ə)ti ʀ(ə)tiʀe pɑse d(ə)vɑ̃] p(u)-TEE r(u)-tee-RAY pah-SAY d(u)-VAH (Fr. small; withdrawn; passed; front.) A *petit retiré passé* in which the *working foot* begins behind and ends in front. From *5th derrière*, the back foot peels off the floor as the knee flexes; the toes are drawn directly to *petit retiré position* before closing through the *working foot* into *5th devant*.

petit retiré position [p(ə)ti ʀ(ə)tiʀe -] p(u)-TEE r(u)-tee-RAY – (Fr. small; withdrawn; position.) A position in which the toes of the fully pointed foot are in contact with the *supporting leg* at the base of the Achilles tendon.

petit retiré sauté [p(ə)ti ʀ(ə)tiʀe sote] p(u)-TEE r(u)-tee-RAY soh-TAY (Fr. small; withdrawn action; jumped.) A small withdrawn jumping action. The dancer performs a *retiré sauté passé* with the tip of the *working leg* lifting to the base of the calf instead of to just below knee height. May be performed *passé devant* or *passé derrière*. Often performed in series.

petit retiré sauté passé See *petit retiré sauté*.

petit retiré sauté passé derrière [p(ə)ti ʀ(ə)tiʀe sote pɑse dɛʀjɛʀ] p(u)-TEE r(u)-tee-RAY soh-TAY pah-SAY der-YER (Fr. small; withdrawn; jumped; passed; behind.) A *petit retiré sauté* with the *working foot* beginning *5th devant* and ending *5th derrière*.

petit retiré sauté passé devant [p(ə)ti ʀ(ə)tiʀe sote pɑse d(ə)vɑ̃] p(u)-TEE r(u)-tee-RAY soh-TAY pah-SAY d(u)-VAH (Fr. small; withdrawn; jumped; passed; front.) A *petit retiré sauté* with the *working foot* beginning *5th derrière* and ending *5th devant*.

petit rond de jambe en dedans [p(ə)ti ʀɔ̃ də ʒɑ̃b ɑ̃ dədɑ̃] p(u)-TEE ro d(u) zhahb ah d(u)-DAH (Fr. small; circle of the leg; inward.) A non-technical circular action performed *en dedans*, often leading into another movement such as a *full contretemps* or a *coupé dessus chassé passé en avant*.

petit rond de jambe en dehors [p(ə)ti ʀɔ̃ də ʒɑ̃b ɑ̃ dəɔʀ] p(u)-TEE ro d(u) zhahb ah d(u)-OR (Fr. small; circle of the leg; outward.) A non-technical circular action performed *en dehors*, often leading into another movement such as a *coupé dessous*.

petit rond de jambe en l'air [p(ə)ti ʀɔ̃ də ʒɑ̃b ɑ̃ lɛr] p(u)-TEE ro d(u) zhahb ah ler (Fr. small; circle of the leg; in the air.) The dancer picks up the *working foot,* performs a small circling action of the lower leg beside the *supporting* ankle, extends the leg toward *2nd*, and then closes it. May be performed *en dedans* or *en dehors,* and with a *rise* or a *temps levé*.

petit sauté [p(ə)ti sote] p(u)-TEE soh-TAY (Fr. small; jump.) A hop used as a preparation for turns. See *pirouettes in 2nd with petits sautés.*

petit soutenu [p(ə)ti sutny] p(u)-TEE soot-NU (Fr. small; sustained step.) Type of *pirouette* usually performed briskly in series, often *en diagonale*. With the *working foot* starting *devant*, there is a step to the side *en pointe* along the *line of dance;* then a closing directly into *5th position devant en pointes;* and a turn toward the back foot to complete the turn in *5th position* with the other foot *devant* before lowering onto the back foot *en fondu*. The arms usually begin *3rd ordinaire*, open toward *2nd*, and close in *1st position* as the foot closes in *5th devant*. Similar to *petit pas de basque en tournant,* except that in *petit soutenu* the second leg closes directly to *5th en pointes*.

petite cabriole [p(ə)tit kabʀijɔl] p(u)-TEET ka-bree-YOL (Fr. small; caper.) A small *cabriole* performed with the *working foot en l'air* above *glissé height* and no higher than 45 degrees. The dancer jumps into the air, beating the push-off leg against the extended leg causing the latter to rebound slightly, and lands on the push-off leg, with the extended leg either held *en l'air* or closing just after the landing. May be performed *devant*, *derrière*, *dessus,* and *dessous*.

petite cabriole ouverte derrière [p(ə)tit kabʀijɔl uvɛʀt dɛʀjɛʀ] p(u)-TEET ka-bree-YOL oo-VERT der-YER (Fr. small; caper; open; behind.) A *petite cabriole* in which the dancer begins with the *working foot derrière en l'air* above *glissé height* and no higher than 45 degrees, jumps into the air beating the push-off leg against the extended leg causing the latter to rebound slightly, and lands on the push-off leg, with the extended leg held *en l'air*.

petite sissonne [p(ə)tit sisɔn] p(u)-TEET see-SON (Fr. small; sissonne.) A small jump from two feet to one, similar to *sissonne ordinaire*, but performed quickly, often as a preparatory action. The dancer begins in *5th position;* s/he springs into the air stretching both legs, and lands *en fondu* with the *working foot* fully stretched at or slightly above *cou-de-pied*. May be done *devant* or *derrière*, and *passée*.

petite sissonne derrière [p(ə)tit sisɔn dɛʀjɛʀ] p(u)-TEET see-SON der-YER (Fr. small; sissonne; behind.) A small *sissonne ordinaire derrière* performed quickly, often as a preparatory action.

petite sissonne devant [p(ə)tit sisɔn d(ə)vɑ̃] p(u)-TEET see-SON d(u)-VAH (Fr. small; sissonne; front.) A small *sissonne ordinaire devant* performed quickly, often as a preparatory action.

petits battements battus [p(ə)ti batmɑ̃ baty] p(u)-TEE bat-MAH ba-TU (Fr. small; beating actions; beaten.) A variation of *petit battement* performed in series through the music, without alternating closings. The *working foot* begins *cou-de-pied devant* and, from a relaxed knee joint, the lower leg opens sideways, releasing sufficiently for the foot to beat *cou-de-pied devant.* May also be taken beating continuously *cou-de-pied derrière.*

petits battements serrés [p(ə)ti batmɑ̃ seʀe] p(u)-TEE bat-MAH say-RAY (Fr. small; beating actions; tight.) A series of *petits battements* performed continuously through the music, alternating closings *devant* and *derrière*. See *petit battement*.

petits jetés en tournant [p(ə)ti ʒ(ə)te zɑ̃ tuʀnɑ̃] p(u)-TEE zh(u)-TAY zah toor-NAH (Fr. small; thrown actions; turning.) *Petit jeté devant by 1/2 turn* performed in series, often travelling *en diagonale* or *en manège*. From *dégagé devant,* the first *petit jeté devant* travels sideways along the *line of dance*, making a 1/2-turn in the air toward the *line of dance;* the second *petit jeté devant* is done *sur place*, with a 1/2-turn to complete one full revolution. The arms usually move to *3rd ordinaire* on each landing. When begun in *5th devant,* the initial action is a *sissonne ordinaire passé devant* instead of a *petit jeté devant.*

petits pas de basque en manège [p(ə)ti pɑ də bask ɑ̃ manɛʒ] p(u)-TEE pah d(u) bask ah ma-NEZH (Fr. small; steps of the Basque; in a circle.) *Petits pas de basque en tournant* performed in series along a circular path around the stage.

petits soutenus en manège [p(ə)ti sutny zɑ̃ manɛʒ] p(u)-TEE soot-NU zah ma-NEZH (Fr. small; sustained actions; in a circle.) A series of *petit soutenu* turns performed along a circular path around the stage.

pied [pje] pyay (Fr. nm foot.) See *cou-de-pied, sur le cou-de-pied.*

pieds, position des See *position of the feet.*

piqué [pike] pee-KAY (Fr. pp of v piquer, to prick, jab, or stab; adj pricked; nm a pricking action.) 1. Term referring to an action performed with a sharp, quick quality. See *assemblé piqué, battement piqué, battement piqué en rond, glissade piquée, grand battement piqué, pas de bourrée piqué, petit pas de bourrée piqué.* 2. Outside the RAD, a sharp step *en pointe.*

piqué derrière See *battement piqué.*

piqué devant See *battement piqué.*

pirouette [piʀwɛt] peer-WET (Fr. nf in dance, a turn done around oneself, often while balancing on one foot.) A spinning action performed on one leg either *en dehors* or *en dedans.* The aim is to whirl *en demi-pointe* or *en pointe* with the body in one single piece except for the head, which moves independently according to a practice known as spotting. The turn may be taken away from the *supporting leg (en dehors)* or toward it *(en dedans),* with the *working leg* in a position such as *retiré devant (pirouette position), arabesque,* or *attitude.* May incorporate one or many revolutions. Basic *pirouettes* include *pirouette en dehors from 4th position, pirouette en dehors from 2nd for boys, pirouette en dedans with fouetté, pirouette en dedans without fouetté, posé pirouette.* May be done on the spot, or in series travelling *en diagonale* or *en manège.* See *grande pirouette, pirouette en dedans, pirouette en dehors, pirouette head, pirouette position, pirouette position of the arms, pirouettes en manège, pirouettes en diagonale, pirouettes in 2nd with petits sautés.* Variations: *pirouettes in 2nd with petits sautés, posé pirouette, sauté pirouette.*

pirouette by posé See *posé pirouette.*

pirouette en dedans [piʀwɛt ɑ̃ dədɑ̃] peer-WET ah d(u)-DAH (Fr. turn; inward.) A *pirouette* which spins toward the *supporting leg.* Usually begins from *4th position,* but may be taken from *5th position* with the *working leg derrière* or *2nd position.* With a simultaneous *relevé* on the *supporting leg,* the *working leg* may be brought to *retiré devant, 2nd en l'air, attititude,* or *arabesque* during one or more spins, and may end by closing *en demi-plié,* or extending *en l'air en fondu.* Usually begun with the arms in *3rd position,* with the arm corresponding to the *supporting leg* placed forward. See *pirouette en dedans in 2nd, pirouette en dedans in attitude, pirouette en dedans in 1st arabesque, pirouette en dedans with fouetté, pirouette en dedans without fouetté.* Variation: *posé pirouette en dedans.*

pirouette en dedans by posé See *posé pirouette en dedans.*

pirouette en dedans from 4th position See *pirouette en dedans with fouetté, pirouette en dedans without fouetté.*

pirouette en dedans in 1st arabesque [piʀwɛt ɑ̃ dədɑ̃ - aʀabɛsk] peer-WET ah d(u)-DAH – a-ra-BESK (Fr. turn; inward; in 1st arabesque.) A *pirouette en dedans* in which the spin is taken in *1st arabesque.* Starting *4th position en fondu,* arms *3rd position* with the arm corresponding to the front leg placed forward: the back leg is lifted to *arabesque* and the arm moved to *1st arabesque* line, with a simultaneous *relevé* on the *supporting leg* and a spin toward it. Usually ends in an open position, with the *working leg en l'air* and the *supporting foot* flat or *en fondu.*

pirouette en dedans in 2nd [piʀwɛt ɑ̃ dədɑ̃ -] peer-WET ah d(u)-DAH – (Fr. turn; inward; in 2nd.) A *pirouette en dedans* in which the *working leg* is extended *to 2nd en l'air* during the spin. Starting *4th position en fondu,* arms *3rd position* with the arm corresponding to the front leg placed forward: the back leg is lifted *to 2nd en l'air* and the arms are opened *to 2nd,* with a simultaneous *relevé* on the *supporting leg* and a spin toward it. Usually ends in an open position, with the *working leg en l'air* and the *supporting foot* flat or *en fondu.*

pirouette en dedans in attitude [piʀwɛt ɑ̃ dədɑ̃ - atityd] peer-WET ah d(u)-DAH – a-tee-TUD (Fr. turn; inward; in a pose.) A *pirouette en dedans* in which the *working leg* is raised *en attitude* during the spin. Starting *4th position en fondu,* arms *3rd position* with the arm corresponding to the front leg placed forward: the back leg is lifted to *attitude derrière* and the arms move directly to *4th* or through *3rd* to *4th,* with a simultaneous *relevé* on the *supporting leg* and a spin toward it. Usually ends in an open position, with the *working leg en l'air* and the *supporting foot* flat or *en fondu.*

pirouette en dedans in attitude ordinaire See *pirouette en dedans in attitude.*

pirouette en dedans with fouetté [piʀwɛt ɑ̃ dədɑ̃ - fwɛte] peer-WET ah d(u)-DAH – fwe-TAY (Fr. turn; inward; with; whipping action.) A *pirouette en dedans* initiated with a whipping action of the *working leg.* Starting *en croisé, 4th position en fondu,* arms *3rd position* with the arm corresponding to the front foot placed forward: the back leg is raised off the ground, passing through *2nd en l'air* and whipping into *retiré devant* with a strong *relevé* on the *supporting leg.* At the same time as the leg is raised off the ground, the leading arm opens towards *2nd* and is immediately joined by the other to form *1st position.* The *pirouette position* is fully established by the first quarter of the turn, and at this point the head and eye focus remain to 1 *(downstage).* The *pirouette* is completed by a swift turning action of the head, with the eyes refocusing to 1 as soon as possible. The balance is retained until the end of the turn, before a controlled closing to *5th devant en demi-plié* facing the other *downstage* corner. The turn may be taken with the arms in *5th* instead of *1st.*

pirouette en dedans with tombé [piʀwɛt ɑ̃ dədɑ̃ - tɔ̃be] peer-WET ah d(u)-DAH – to-BAY (Fr. turn; inward; with; fallen.) A *pirouette en dedans* in which the working leg does not close *en demi-plié* but rather initiates a *tombé en avant* to finish *4th en fondu.*

pirouette en dedans without fouetté [piʀwɛt ɑ̃ dədɑ̃ - fwɛte] peer-WET ah d(u)-DAH – fwe-TAY (Fr. turn; inward; without; whipping action.) A *pirouette en dedans* initiated with the *working leg* moving directly to *retiré devant.* Starting *en croisé, 4th position en fondu:* the impetus for the turn comes from a strong *relevé* on the front leg and a simultaneous gathering of the side arm to *1st position* and the back leg to *retiré devant;* the *pirouette position* is fully established by the first quarter of the turn, and the balance is retained until the end of the turn, before a controlled closing to *5th devant en demi-plié* facing the other *downstage* corner. The arms may be raised directly to any position with the *relevé* action.

pirouette en dedans, double [piʀwɛt ɑ̃ dədɑ, -] peer-WET ah d(u)-DAH, – (Fr. turn; inward, double.) A *pirouette en dedans* performed with two revolutions of the body.

pirouette en dedans, single [piʀwɛt ɑ̃ dədɑ̃, -] peer-WET ah d(u)-DAH, – (Fr. turn; inward; single.) A *pirouette en dedans* performed with one revolution of the body.

pirouette en dedans, triple [piʀwɛt ɑ̃ dədɑ̃, -] peer-WET ah d(u)-DAH, – (Fr. turn; inward; triple.) A *pirouette en dedans* performed with three revolutions of the body.

pirouette en dehors [piʀwɛt ɑ̃ dəɔʀ] peer-WET ah d(u)-OR (Fr. turn; outward.) A *pirouette* which spins away from the *supporting leg.* May begin *en demi-plié*, either in *4th position* with the *working leg derrière*, *5th position* with the *working leg devant*, or *2nd position.* With a simultaneous *relevé* on the *supporting leg,* the *working leg* may be brought to *retiré devant, 2nd en l'air, attititude,* or *arabesque* during one or more spins, and may end by closing *en demi-plié,* or extending *en l'air en fondu.* Usually begun with the arms in *3rd position,* with the arm corresponding to the *working leg* placed forward. See *pirouette en dehors in attitude, pirouette en dehors finishing in attitude, pirouette en dehors finishing in arabesque, pirouette en dehors finishing in open positions, pirouette en dehors from 2nd, pirouette en dehors from 4th.* Variation: *posé pirouette en dehors.*

pirouette en dehors by posé See *posé pirouette en dehors.*

pirouette en dehors from 2nd [piʀwɛt ɑ̃ dəɔʀ -] peer-WET ah d(u)-OR – (Fr. turn; outward; from 2nd.) A *pirouette en dehors* for male dancers. Starting *en face, 2nd position en demi-plié,* arms *3rd position* with the arm corresponding to the *working foot* placed forward: the force for the turn comes from a combination of pressure from the *demi-plié,* a strong rise on the *supporting leg,* and the drawing of the *working leg* quickly to *retiré devant.* The *pirouette position* is fully established by the first quarter of the turn, and at this point the head and eye focus remain to 1 *(downstage).* The *pirouette* is completed by a swift turning action of the head, with the eyes refocusing to 1 as soon as possible. The balance is retained until the end of the turn, before a controlled closing to *5th derrière en demi-plié.*

pirouette en dehors from 4th [piʀwɛt ɑ̃ dəɔʀ -] peer-WET ah d(u)-OR – (Fr. turn; outward; from 4th.) A basic *pirouette en dehors.* Starting *en face, 4th position en demi-plié,* arms *3rd position* with the arm corresponding to the *working foot* (the back foot) placed forward: the impetus for the turn is a combination of a push off both feet and a strong *relevé* bringing the *working foot* to *retiré devant.* The *pirouette position* is fully established by the first quarter of the turn, and at this point the head and eye focus remain to 1 *(downstage).* The *pirouette* is completed by a swift turning action of the head, with the eyes refocusing to 1 as soon as possible. The balance is retained until the end of the turn, before a controlled closing to *5th derrière en demi-plié.*

pirouette en dehors from 5th position See *pirouette en dehors.*

pirouette en dehors in attitude à deux bras [piʀwɛt ɑ̃ dəɔʀ - atityd a døbʀa] peer-WET ah d(u)-OR – a-tee-TUD a duh bra (Fr. turn; outward; in a pose; with two arms.) A *pirouette en dehors* in which the *working leg* is raised *en attitude* with the arms in *5th* during the spin. Starting *4th position en demi-plié,* arms *3rd position* with the arm corresponding to the back leg placed forward: the back leg is lifted to *attitude derrière* and the arms move through *2nd* to *5th position*, with a simultaneous *relevé* on the *supporting leg* and a spin away from it. Usually ends in an open position, with the *working leg en l'air* and the *supporting foot* flat or *en fondu.*

pirouette en dehors to 4th en fondu See *pirouette en dehors.*

pirouette en dehors, double [piʀwɛt ɑ̃ dəɔʀ, -] peer-WET ah d(u)-OR, – (Fr. turn; outward; double.) A *pirouette en dehors* performed with two revolutions of the body.

pirouette en dehors, single [piʀwɛt ɑ̃ dəɔʀ, -] peer-WET ah d(u)-OR, – (Fr. turn; outward; single.) A *pirouette en dehors* performed with one revolution of the body.

pirouette en dehors, triple [piʀwɛt ɑ̃ dəɔʀ, -] peer-WET ah d(u)-OR, – (Fr. turn; outward; triple.) A *pirouette en dehors* performed with three revolutions of the body.

pirouette en manège See *pirouettes en manège.*

pirouette finishing in arabesque en l'air [piʀwɛt - aʀabɛsk ɑ̃ lɛʀ] peer-WET – a-ra-BESK ah ler (Fr. turn; finishing in arabesque; in the air.) A *pirouette*, *en dehors* or *en dedans*, usually taken in *pirouette position* and ending with the *supporting foot* flat or *en fondu* and the *working leg* in *arabesque en l'air.*

pirouette finishing in attitude en l'air [piʀwɛt - atityd ɑ̃ lɛʀ] peer-WET – a-tee-TUD ah ler (Fr. turn; finishing in attitude; in the air.) A *pirouette*, *en dehors* or *en dedans*, usually taken in *pirouette position* and ending with the *supporting foot* flat or *en fondu* and the *working leg* in *attitude en l'air.*

pirouette finishing in open positions [piʀwɛt -] peer-WET – A *pirouette* which ends with the *working leg* either *à terre*, i.e., in a *lunge,* or *en l'air.* See *pirouette finishing in arabesque en l'air, pirouette finishing in attitude en l'air.*

pirouette head [piʀwɛt -] peer-WET – Term used to describe the use of head and *eye line* in turning actions, to maintain balance and control the rate of turn. In turns *sur place,* the gaze is momentarily fixed so that the eyes can focus at a given spot during the first quarter of the turn, then the head swiftly turns around, allowing the eyes to refocus as soon as possible. In a series of travelling turns, the gaze is directed along the *line of dance.* This practice of keeping the head vertically aligned while fixing the gaze helps maintain equilibrium and prevents dizziness during the turn, and the swift turning action adds accent and brilliance. Also known as *spotting.*

pirouette position [piʀwɛt -] peer-WET – A compact position often used in pirouettes since it facilitates a rapid spin: *retiré position devant* with the arms in *1st position.*

pirouette position of the arms [piʀwɛt -] peer-WET – A *1st position* of the arms, held firmly to facilitate a balanced, compact position during turns.

pirouettes en diagonale [piʀwɛt ɑ̃ djagɔnal] peer-WET ah dya-go-NAL (Fr. turns; on the diagonal.) Turns performed in series along the longest line on the stage, a diagonal line extending between the *upstage* and *downstage* corners.

pirouettes en manège [piʀwɛt ɑ̃ manɛʒ] peer-WET ah ma-NEZH (Fr. turns; in a circle.) A series of turns which travel around the stage along a large circular path, like a merry-go-round or carousel.

pirouettes in 2nd with petits sautés [piʀwɛt - p(ə)ti sote] peer-WET – p(u)-TEE soh-TAY (Fr. turns; in; 2nd; with; small; jumps.) A male virtuoso turn performed *en dehors* with the arms and *working leg* extended *to 2nd* while the supporting leg does a series of small, low hops, usually taking two hops to complete one turn. Often prepared by a *pirouette en dehors* finished in *2nd en fondu,* and ended by pulling into a *pirouette en dehors* closing in *5th en demi-plié* or *4th en fondu.* Also called *grande pirouette sautillé* (Vaganova). Variation: *sauté pirouette in 2nd.*

pivot [pivo] pee-VOH (Fr. nm a swivelling action.) 1. One of the basic elements of *centre practice.* A small controlled rotating movement on one leg, where the *pivot* action takes place through the foot, turning either *en dedans* or *en dehors*. In the Cecchetti method, *pivots* in a held position are called *promenades.* 2. In the RAD Grades syllabus, the term *pivots* refers to a series of transferences of weight taken in *3rd position* with the front foot *en fondu* and the back foot on the ball of the foot, often performed turning, as in Character Steps.

pivot en dedans [pivo ɑ̃ dədɑ̃] pee-VOH ah d(u)-DAH (Fr. pivot; inward.) A *pivot* in which the heel releases, moves forward, and lowers in a series of small movements which turn the body in the direction of the *supporting leg.*

pivot en dehors [pivo ɑ̃ dəɔʀ] pee-VOH – ah d(u)-OR (Fr. pivot; outward.) A *pivot* in which the heel releases and lowers in a series of small movements which turn the body in the opposite direction to the *supporting leg*.

place [plas] plas (Fr. nf place or spot.) See *sur place*.

plié [plije] plee-YAY (Fr. pp of v plier, to bend; adj bent; nm bend or bending action.) A bending of the knees. See *demi-plié, double demi-plié, en demi-plié, grand plié, quarter plié.*

plié, demi See *demi-plié.*

plié, grand See *grand plié.*

plié, quarter See *quarter plié.*

pointe [pwɛ̃t] pwet (Fr. nf tiptoe.) The distal end of the foot. Variations: *1/4 pointe/s, 1/2 pointe/s, 3/4 pointe/s.* See *en pointe/s, en demi-pointe/s, pointe shoes, pointe tendu, pointe work, sur la demi-pointe, sur la pointe.*

pointe shoes [pwɛ̃t -] pwet – Specially designed shoes which allow the dancer to support her body weight on the tips of the feet, in order to perform movements included in the *Sur La Pointe* section of a class.

pointe tendu [pwɛ̃t tɑ̃dy] pwet tah-DU (Fr. tiptoe; outstretched.) Phrase formerly used to describe an extended position of the *working leg* where the toes are in contact with the floor, either *devant, to 2nd,* or *derrière.* The term *dégagé* is now used. Outside the RAD, the feminine form of the adjective is used, i.e., *pointe tendue*.

pointe work [pwɛ̃t] pwet A category of movements performed by the female dancer, in which the body weight is borne on the tips of the big toe, the second toe, and possibly the middle toe, depending on the shape of the foot. The position *en pointe* produces a straight line through the tibia, ankle, metatarsals, and toes. The central line of balance over the tips of the toes creates an extension of the dancer's line through the leg and foot. *Pointe work* is the ultimate achievement for the female dancer, the culmination of her classical training which brings a further dimension to her dancing.

pointe, sur la See *sur la pointe*.

pointe/s, 1/2 [pwɛ̃t -] pwet - (Fr. tiptoe, half.) Term used in the Grades syllabus to describe a position of the feet in which the weight is supported on the balls of the feet and the heels are raised off the floor as high as possible, i.e., with the ankle/s fully extended. Also *en demi-pointe/s, sur la demi-pointe*. In the Cecchetti method, this position is called *pied à trois quarts* or *three-quarter pointe*, since it is 3/4 of the distance between the sole and point positions.

pointe/s, 1/4 [pwɛ̃t -] pwet – (Fr. tiptoe, quarter.) Term used in the Grades syllabus to describe a position of the feet in which the weight is supported on the balls of the feet and the heels are raised slightly off the floor, half-way between flat and *1/2 pointe/s*.

pointe/s, 3/4 [pwɛ̃t -] pwet - (Fr. tiptoe, three-quarter.) Term used in the Boys Intermediate syllabus to describe a position of the foot or feet in which the pads of the toes are flat on the floor, with the ankle/s fully stretched. Usually taken with the working foot extended *devant, to 2nd,* or *derrière.* When taken with the foot/feet weight-bearing, this position is commonly referred to as *en demi-pointe/s.* In the Cecchetti method, this position is called *pied à trois quarts* or *three-quarter pointe*, since it is 3/4 of the distance between the sole and point positions.

pointe/s, en See *en pointe/s.*

poisson [pwasɔ̃] pwa-SO (Fr. nm a fish.) See *temps de poisson.*

polka 1. A lively dance of Bohemian origin, performed in duple time; or the music for such a dance. See *polka step.* 2. Dance study performed to a 2/4 rhythm.

polka step A composite step consisting of a *hop* followed by three transfers of weight, performed in a 2/4 rhythm: *hop,* step, close, step or *spring.* The *hop* is done on the up-beat or anacrusis. Often performed in series, alternating legs. May be performed *en avant, de côté,* or *en arrière*, and stepping *en pointe/s.*

polka step en avant [- ɑ̃ navɑ̃] – ah na-VAH The dancer performs a small *temps levé* with a *petit développé devant*; she then does a *posé en avant* to *petit retiré derrière*, a *coupé dessous*, and another *posé en avant* to *petit retiré derrière*; the entire step is performed *en pointe/s.*

port [pɔʀ] por (Fr. nm the act of carrying something, or one's carriage or bearing.) See *port de bras.*

port de bras [pɔʀ də bʀa] por d(u) bra (Fr. a carriage of the arm or arms.) 1. A range of arm movements performed within the conventions of classical ballet, always in balanced harmony with the movements of each other and the rest of the body. Its simplest forms are the *basic port de bras* and the *full port de bras.* See *port de bras, basic; port de bras, full.* Variation: *port de bras, reverse.* May involve movement in the torso. See *port de bras in 4th position en fondu, circular; port de bras with forward bend; port de bras with side bend; port de bras, circular.* 2. A term for a category of *barre* or *centre exercises* or an individual *exercise* that concentrates on graceful, flowing movements of the arms, body, head, and *eye line.*

port de bras away from the barre, circular [pɔʀ də bʀa - ba(ɑ)ʀ, -] por d(u) bra – bar, – An action in which the dancer stands at the *barre* in *5th position* with the working arm in *2nd position,* circles the upper body away from the *barre* into a *back bend*, continues to circle the upper body into a *side bend* over the *barre* with the arm moving into *5th position;* completes the circle by lowering the upper body into a full forward bend with the working arm framing the face in *5th position*, then recovers lifting the arm to *2nd position.* Often preceded by a *port de bras* to *1st* then *2nd position.*

port de bras in 4th position en fondu, circular [pɔʀ də bʀa - ɑ̃ fɔ̃dy -] por d(u) bra – ah fo-DU – A movement in which the dancer stands in a deep *lunge* facing *croisé* with the arms in *4th in opposition* (i.e., the upstage arm is overhead): s/he begins by performing a full *forward bend,* proceeds by circling the upper body toward the *upstage* corner into a *side bend* while sweeping the arms across the body to the opposite *4th position*, continues to circle the arms and upper body into a *back bend*, and completes the circling action by bringing the body erect with the arms in the same position as they started.

port de bras to 2nd, reverse [pɔʀ də bʀa -] por d(u) bra – A movement of the arms that passes from *bras bas* through the *demi-seconde* to *2nd position.*

port de bras toward the barre, circular [pɔʀ də bʀa - ba(ɑ)ʀ, -] por d(u) bra – bar, – An action in which the dancer stands at the *barre* in *5th position* with the working arm in *2nd position*, performs a *full forward bend* with the working arm moving to frame the face in *5th position;* s/he then recovers by circling the body toward the *barre* into a *side bend*, continues to circle the upper body into a *back bend*, then a slight *side bend* away from the *barre* as the arm opens toward *2nd position*, and finally brings the body erect as the arm arrives in *2nd position.* See *port de bras, circular.*

port de bras with back bend [pɔʀ də bʀa -] por d(u) bra – See *back bend.*

port de bras with forward bend [pɔʀ də bʀa -] por d(u) bra – An action in which the dancer stands in *5th position* with the arms in *2nd* or *5th position;* s/he then performs a *full forward bend* with the arms moving to frame the face in *5th position*, then recovers by lifting the back, lengthening it until s/he stands upright again in *5th position.* See *full forward port de bras.*

port de bras with side bend [pɔʀ də bʀa, -] por d(u) bra, – A movement in which the dancer begins with one arm in *2nd position;* s/he lifts it to *5th position*, with the head turning away from the arm in profile as the upper body bends sideways; then recovers with the arm in *2nd position* and the upper body erect.

port de bras with transfer of weight, circular

[pɔʀ də bʀa -] por d(u) bra – An action beginning in *attitude ordinaire à terre derrière* facing *croisé:* the dancer performs a *demi-plié* in *4th position*, bending the upper body forward, and circles the upper body into a *side bend* that reaches *upstage*, with the arms changing overhead to *4th position;* from there s/he transfers the weight back, stretching the *supporting leg*, and finishing *pointe tendu devant* as the upper body continues to circle into a *back bend;* s/he completes the circle into a *side bend* that reaches *downstage*, with the arms changing overhead to *4th position*, and finally brings the body erect to finish in *attitude devant opposition à terre*. See *port de bras, circular*.

port de bras, basic [pɔʀ də bʀa, -] por d(u) bra, – The simplest form of *port de bras,* consisting of one continuous movement in which the arms are lifted from *bras bas* to *1st position,* opened out to *2nd position,* and lowered to *bras bas.* Usually taken *en croisé.* As the movement commences, the head slightly turns, inclines, and lowers simultaneously, with the eyes following the hands as the arms are lifted to *1st position,* and one hand thereafter. The eyes follow the *downstage* hand as the arms start to open, and the head and *eye line* are raised and turned towards that corner, coordinating with the opening of the arms to *2nd position.* To lower, the wrists softly turn so that the palms face down with the fingers slightly lengthened; the curve in the elbow is maintained and the fingers are the last to arrive in *bras bas.* As the arms lower to *bras bas,* the head and eyes follow the *downstage* hand; on the completion of the movement, they are raised to 1 *(downstage).*

port de bras, circular [pɔʀ də bʀa, -] por d(u) bra,– A movement of the torso initiated by a *port de bras* and involving forward, side, and back bends, so that the torso and arms trace a circular path. May be performed circling either toward the *barre*, away from the *barre*, or when in *centre en croisé* away from the front foot. Variations: *port de bras in 4th position en fondu, circular; port de bras with transfer of weight, circular.*

port de bras, full [pɔʀ də bʀa, -] por d(u) bra, – A *port de bras* consisting of one continuous movement in which the arms are lifted from *bras bas* through *1st* to *5th position,* and opened to *2nd* before lowering to *bras bas.* Usually taken *en croisé.* As the movement commences, the head slightly turns, inclines, and lowers simultaneously, with the eyes following the hands as the arms are lifted to *1st position.* Retaining a slight inclination, the head is turned and raised with the *eye line* directed to 1 *(downstage)* as the arms are lifted to *5th position.* With an increased lift out of the body, the arms, maintaining their curve, open through a wide *5th position* and are carried to *2nd.* The head lifts and turns to follow the line made by the *downstage* hand and, as the arms arrive in *2nd,* the *eye line* is directed to the *downstage* corner. To lower, the wrists softly turn so that the palms face down with the fingers slightly lengthened; the curve in the elbows is maintained and the fingers are the last to arrive in *bras bas.* As the arms lower to *bras bas,* the head and eyes follow the *downstage* hand and are then raised to 1 on the completion of the movement. For boys: from *1st position* the head lifts and turns directly to 1.

port de bras, full circular See *port de bras, circular*.

port de bras, full forward See *full forward port de bras*.

port de bras, full grand [pɔʀ də bʀa, - gʀɑ̃] por d(u) bra, – grah A movement in which the dancer stands in a deep *lunge* facing *croisé* with the arms in *2nd position;* s/he begins by performing a full forward bend with the upper body, so that the arms sweep across in front of the body and gather into *5th position;* then lifts the upper body through an erect position and continues into a full backward bend; and finally s/he brings the upper body back to an erect position and opens the arms from *5th* to *2nd position.*

port de bras, reverse [pɔʀ də bʀa -] por d(u) bra – (Fr. carriage of the arms; reverse.) 1. A movement of the arms which changes in direction and, in some cases, intermediary positions. Arms usually open through *1st position* and close through *2nd position*. When the action is reversed, they often open through *2nd position* and close through *1st position*. 2. A movement of the arms that begins in *4th crossed in opposition*, moves through *1st position* to finish in another arm position.

port de bras, simple See *port de bras, basic*.

porté [pɔʀte] por-TAY (Fr. pp of v porter, to carry; adj carried.) Term used to describe a travelled step. See *assemblé de côté dessus (assemblé dessus porté de côté)*.

posé [poze] poh-ZAY (Fr. pp of v poser to set or put; adj placed; nm a placed step.) One of the basic elements of *centre practice.* A movement involving a transfer of weight onto the whole foot, *demi-pointe,* or *pointe.* Can be prepared with a *petit développé* or a *battement glissé* action *en fondu* and performed en *avant, en arrière,* and *de côté* into different positions, both *à terre* and *en l'air.* See *posé en avant.* Variations: *coupé posé, posé assemblé soutenu, posé coupé, posé coupé dessous posé (galop), posé grand jeté, posé passé, posé rotation, posé temps levé, posé pirouette.*

posé assemblé soutenu en dedans See *posé assemblé soutenu en tournant en dedans.*

posé assemblé soutenu en tournant en dedans [poze asɑ̃ble sutny ɑ̃ tuʀnɑ̃ ɑ̃ dədɑ̃] poh-ZAY a-sah-BLAY soot-NU ah toor-NAH ah d(u)-DAH (Fr. placed step; gathered step; sustained; turning; inward.) A composite step consisting of a *posé* and an *assemblé soutenu en tournant en dedans.* Starting with a step outward ending *en fondu*, the freed foot performs a *demi-assemblé soutenu à terre en dedans* circling forward, and draws into *5th devant en pointes* leading into a turn toward the back foot to finish in *5th position* with the other foot *devant.*

posé coupé [poze kupe] poh-ZAY koo-PAY (Fr. placed step; cutting step.) A composite step consisting of a travelled step followed by a step or a *spring* under the body line. The first step is taken either on the whole foot or *en pointe* with the free leg extended *en l'air* or drawn to *retiré devant* or *derrière*. The second action is taken *en fondu* with the free foot anticipating the step which is to come. May be performed *en avant* with a *coupé dessous*, *en arrière* with a *coupé dessus*, or *de côté* with a *coupé dessus* or *dessous*. When taken with a step on the whole foot and a spring, this step is similar to a *galop*.

posé coupé de côté [poze kupe də kote] poh-ZAY koo-PAY d(u) koh-TAY (Fr. placed step; cutting step; sideways.) A *posé coupé* in which the dancer steps sideways, then transfers the weight onto the other leg *en fondu* cutting in front of or behind and replacing the *supporting foot.* The first step may be taken on the whole foot, or *en pointe* extending the *working leg en l'air to 2nd* or bringing it to *retiré devant* or *derrière*. The second action may be taken *dessus* or *dessous*, and performed *terre à terre* or jumped. See *posé coupé dessous, posé de côté*. This step is similar to a *galop*.

posé coupé dessous posé [poze kupe d(ə)su poze] poh-ZAY koo-PAY d(u)-SOO poh-ZAY (Fr. placed step; cutting step; under; placed step.) A *posé coupé de côté* in which the dancer steps sideways on the whole foot *en fondu*, then *springs* onto the other foot which cuts behind and replaces the push-off foot. Used as a preparation into jumps such as *saut de basque*. May be performed *en avant*. This step is similar to a *galop*.

posé coupé en arrière [poze kupe ɑ̃ naʀjɛʀ] poh-ZAY koo-PAY ah-nar-YER (Fr. placed step; cutting step; backward.) A *posé coupé* in which the dancer steps backward, then transfers the weight onto the other leg *en fondu* cutting in front and replacing the *supporting foot.* The first step may be taken on the whole foot, or *en pointe* extending the *working leg en l'air devant* or bringing it to *retiré devant*. The second action is performed *dessus*, either *terre à terre* or jumped. See *posé en arrière.*

posé coupé en avant [poze kupe ɑ̃ navɑ̃] poh-ZAY koo-PAY ah na-VAH (Fr. placed step; cutting step; forward.) A *posé coupé* in which the dancer steps forward, then transfers the weight onto the other leg *en fondu* cutting behind and replacing the *supporting foot.* The first step may be taken on the whole foot, or *en pointe* extending the *working leg en l'air derrière* or bringing it to *retiré derrière*. The second action is performed *dessous*, either *terre à terre* or jumped. See *posé en avant*.

posé coupé pirouette en dedans See *posé pirouette en dedans*.

posé de côté [poze də kote] poh-ZAY d(u) koh-TAY (Fr. placed; to the side.) A *posé* to the side. From *5th position devant* or *derrière,* the stretched *working leg* extends *derrière* to *glissé height en fondu.* The pressure through the *supporting leg* propels the weight sideways onto the extended leg on the whole foot, *en demi-pointe, or en pointe.* Can also be prepared with a *petit développé* action of the leading foot. May be completed with a *coupé dessus* or *dessous,* and performed in series.

posé écarté [poze ekaʀte] poh-ZAY ay-kar-TAY (Fr. placed step; wide.) A step taken sideways in relation to the dancer's body and toward an *upstage* or *downstage* corner of the dancer's square. See *écarté*.

posé en arrière [poze ɑ̃ naʀjɛʀ] poh-ZAY ah-nar-YER (Fr. placed; backward.) A *posé* backward. From *5th derrière,* the stretched back leg extends *derrière* to *glissé height en fondu.* The pressure through the *supporting leg* propels the weight backward onto the back leg on the whole foot, *en demi-pointe, or en pointe.* Can also be prepared with a *petit développé* action of the leading foot. May be completed with a *coupé dessus* and performed in series.

posé en avant [poze ɑ̃ navɑ̃] poh-ZAY ah na-VAH (Fr. placed; forward.) A *posé* forward. From *5th devant,* the stretched front leg extends *devant* to *glissé height en fondu.* The pressure through the *supporting leg* propels the weight forward onto the front leg on the whole foot, *en demi-pointe, or en pointe.* Can also be prepared with a *petit développé* action of the leading foot. May be completed with a *coupé dessous* and performed in series.

posé en demi-pointe sur place [poze ɑ̃ d(ə)mipwɛ̃t syʀ plas] poh-ZAY ah d(u)-MEE-pwet sur plas (Fr. placed; on half tiptoe; in place.) A step onto the ball of the foot, taken under the body line.

posé en pointe sur place [poze ɑ̃ pwɛ̃t syʀ plas] poh-ZAY ah pwet sur plas (Fr. placed; on tiptoe; in place.) A step onto the tip of the foot in *pointe shoes*, taken under the body line.

posé grand jeté en avant [poze gʀɑ̃ ʒ(ə)te ɑ̃ navɑ̃] poh-ZAY grah zh(u)-TAY ah na-VAH (Fr. placed; big; thrown; forward.) A *grand jeté en avant* initiated by a step onto the whole foot.

posé passé [poze pɑse] poh-ZAY pah-SAY (Fr. placed step; passing action.) 1. A step in which the foot passes from back to front or from front to back before receiving the body weight. May be performed *en avant* or *en arrière*. 2. A step in which the *working leg* unfolds forward or backward as the *supporting leg* bends *en fondu*. May be performed *devant* or *derrière*, and with the *supporting leg* remaining straight *en pointe*.

posé passé devant [poze pɑse d(ə)vɑ̃] poh-ZAY pah-SAY d(u)-VAH (Fr. placed step; passing action; front.) A step in which the *working leg* passes to the front. The dancer steps forward *en pointe*, and brings the tip of the *working foot* to *retiré* and continues unfolding the *working leg 4th devant* 45 degrees, as the *supporting leg* bends *en fondu*. Often performed in series. May be performed with the *supporting leg* remaining straight *en pointe* as the *working leg* unfolds *devant*.

posé passé en avant [poze pɑse ɑ̃ navɑ̃] poh-ZAY pah-SAY ah na-VAH (Fr. placed step; passing action; forward.) A step in which the foot passes from back to front before receiving the body weight. Using the leg which begins behind the body, the dancer steps forward *en pointe*.

posé pirouette [poze piʀwɛt] poh-ZAY peer-WET (Fr. placed step; turned.) A turn initiated by a step *en pointe*. May be performed *en dehors* or *en dedans*, and with the free foot *retiré devant* or *derrière*. Often performed in series. Also called *pirouette by posé.*

posé pirouette en dedans [poze piʀwɛt ɑ̃ dədɑ̃] poh-ZAY peer-WET ah d(u)-DAH (Fr. placed step; turn; inward.) A *pirouette* turning toward the leg onto which the dancer steps. Usually taken in series *en diagonale* with each *posé* stepping along the *line of dance*. With a *fondu* on the *supporting leg,* the extended leg is released just off the ground to make a small *rond de jambe en dehors* into a *posé* turning *en dedans en pointe* with the back foot placed in *retiré derrière.* The turn finishes with a *coupé dessous* facing the original direction, with the front foot extended *devant* just off the floor. The arms begin and end in *3rd position,* with the arm corresponding to the front foot placed forward: the leading arm opens to correspond with the action of the *rond de jambe,* and at the moment of *posé* it is immediately joined by the other arm to form the *pirouette position.* Also called *posé coupé pirouette en dedans.* Variation: *double posé pirouette en dedans.*

posé pirouette en dedans, double [poze piʀwɛt ɑ̃ dədɑ̃, -] poh-ZAY peer-WET ah d(u)-DAH, – (Fr. placed step; turn; inward; double.) A *posé pirouette en dedans* performed with two complete revolutions.

posé pirouette en dehors [poze piʀwɛt ɑ̃ dəɔʀ] poh-ZAY peer-WET ah d(u)-OR (Fr. placed step; turn; outward.) A *pirouette* turning away from the leg onto which the dancer steps *en pointe.* Usually taken in series *en diagonale,* with each *posé* stepping along the *line of dance.* The first step is taken forward into the *line of dance* onto a *fondu en ouvert*, with the back foot then opened *to 2nd;* and the second step is a very small *posé* forward *en pointe* bringing the free foot to *retiré devant*, turning away from the *supporting leg* to complete the turn. The leading arm usually opens from *3rd position* toward *2nd position* before the *posé*, and at the moment of *posé* it is immediately joined by the other arm to form the *pirouette position.* Variation: *double posé pirouette en dehors.*

posé rotation with développé en tournant [poze ʀɔtɑsjɔ̃ - devlɔpe ɑ̃ tuʀnɑ̃] poh-ZAY ro-ta-SYO

– dayv-loh-PAY ah toor-NAH (Fr. placed step; rotation; with unfolding action; turning.) An action in which the dancer steps *en pointe* along the *line of dance*, then turns toward the *working leg* which passes through *retiré* and unfolds along the *line of dance to 2nd* at or above 90 degrees, with the body tilted slightly away from the *working leg* and the arms in *4th position*. May be prepared and/or finished with a *tombé*.

posé temps levé [poze tɑ̃ l(ə)ve] poh-ZAY tah l(u)-VAY (Fr. placed step; time; lifted.) A step into a jump on the same foot, usually performed *en avant*. The dancer steps forward onto the whole foot, pushes off bringing the free leg to *retiré derrière* or *arabesque*, and lands in place on the foot that pushed off. May be used as a preparation into a series of runs.

posé temps levé in 1st arabesque [poze tɑ̃ l(ə)ve - aʀabɛsk] poh-ZAY tah l(u)-VAY – a-ra-BESK (Fr. placed step; time; lifted; in 1st arabesque.) A strong jump in *1st arabesque,* prepared by a transference of weight using a *posé* action. From *classical pose,* the movement commences with a *petit développé passé devant en fondu* and, stepping into *1st arabesque en fondu,* continues into the *temps levé,* retaining the line of the *arabesque* both in the air and on landing.

posé temps levé in retiré [poze tɑ̃ l(ə)ve - ʀ(ə)tiʀe] poh-ZAY tah l(u)-VAY – r(u)-tee-RAY (Fr. placed step; time; lifted; withdrawn.) An action in which the dancer steps onto the whole foot, immediately pushes off bringing the free foot to *retiré,* then lands on the same foot. Usually performed with a step forward bringing the free foot to *retiré position derrière.*

posé to 2nd [poze -] poh-ZAY – (Fr. placed step; to 2nd.) 1. A step sideways. See *posé de côté.* 2. Contracted form of *posé to 2nd en l'air,* a step sideways on the whole foot, on *demi-pointe,* or *en pointe,* with the freed leg raised to *2nd en l'air.*

posé to 5th [poze -] poh-ZAY – (Fr. placed step; to 5th.) A *posé* taken *en avant, de côté,* or *en arrière,* with the freed foot closing immediately to *5th en pointes.* To complete the action, the heels are lowered with a slight adjustment, allowing the feet to return and settle into *5th position.* Also called *temps lié to 5th en pointes.*

posé turns [poze -] poh-ZAY – (Fr. placed step; turns.) Turns performed in series often *en diagonale*, initiated by stepping *en pointe* and spinning on the foot which stepped. The step is taken either sideways or forward along the *line of dance*. See *posé pirouette*.

posé with battement glissé [poze - batmɑ̃ glise] poh-ZAY – bat-MAH glee-SAY (Fr. placed step; with; beating; sliding.) A *posé* in which the foot slides outward along the floor before receiving the body weight.

posé with petit développé [poze - p(ə)ti devlɔpe] poh-ZAY – p(u)-TEE dayv-loh-PAY (Fr. placed step; with small; unfolding action.) A *posé* in which the foot passes through *petit retiré devant* or *derrière* before extending to receive the body weight.

poses of the body (9) The nine basic *poses of the body* are: *en face devant, en face derrière, croisé devant, croisé derrière, effacé devant, effacé derrière, écarté devant, écarté derrière,* and *classical pose.* All are taken in a body *alignment* related to the audience.

position [pozisjɔ̃] poh-zees-YO (Fr. nf position.) See *petit retiré position, pirouette position, position of the arms, position of the feet, position of the supporting foot and leg, preparatory position, retiré position*.

position of the arms There are seven basic positions of the arms, *bras bas, 1st, demi-seconde, 2nd, 3rd, 4th, and 5th,* and one supplementary position, *demi-bras.* In all positions, the hands follow the line of the arms and the fingers are softly grouped. The centre finger continues the curve of the inner arm and the thumb is in line with the index and middle fingers. In *bras bas, 1st position,* and *5th position,* the arms are held slightly apart so that the centre fingers do not touch.

position of the arms, 1st A basic position in which both arms curve to form an oval in front of the body so that the little fingers are slightly above the level of the waist.

position of the arms, 1st with wrists crossed A *1st position* in which both arms curve to form an oval in front of the body, with the wrists crossing at waist height. The palms may face down.

position of the arms, 2nd A basic position in which the arms are held to the side and are just in front of the body. They are slightly curved and slope gently downward from the shoulders to the tips of the fingers. Variation: *demi-seconde.*

position of the arms, 3rd A basic position in which one arm is in *1st position* and the other arm is in *2nd position.* The arm corresponding to the *working foot* (when supported on one foot) or the front foot (when the weight is equally supported on two feet) is ordinarily in *1st position.* Sometimes referred to as *3rd ordinaire.* Variation: *3rd opposition.*

position of the arms, 3rd opposition A *3rd position of the arms* taken with the arm corresponding to the *working foot* (when supported on one foot) or the front foot (when the weight is equally supported on two feet) placed in *2nd position,* with the arm opposite to that foot placed in *1st position.* Also *3rd in opposition.*

position of the arms, 4th A basic position in which one arm is in *5th position* and the other arm is in *2nd position.* The arm corresponding to the *working foot* (when supported on one foot) or the front foot (when the weight is equally supported on two feet) is ordinarily in *5th position.* Sometimes referred to as *attitude* arms. Variations: *4th crossed, 4th opposition, 4th éffacé, open 4th.*

position of the arms, 4th crossed A position in which one arm is in *5th position* and the other arm is in *1st position.* The arm corresponding to the *working foot* (when supported on one foot) or the front foot (when the weight is equally supported on two feet) is in *5th.*

position of the arms, 4th crossed in opposition A *4th crossed* position in which the arm corresponding to the *working foot* (when supported on one foot) or the front foot (when the weight is equally supported on two feet) is in *1st position,* with the arm opposite to that foot in *5th position.*

position of the arms, 4th effacé [- efase] – ay-fa-SAY A *4th position* taken *en ouvert*, i.e., the *downstage* arm is overhead and slightly wider than *5th position* and the *upstage* arm is to the side in *2nd position.*

position of the arms, 4th opposition A *4th position of the arms* taken with the arm corresponding to the *working foot* (when supported on one foot) or the front foot (when the weight is equally supported on two feet) placed in *2nd position,* with the arm opposite to that foot placed in *5th position.* Also *4th in opposition.*

position of the arms, 5th A basic position in which both arms curve overhead to form an oval, and are held slightly in front of the body with the hands just within vision. The arm position incorporated in *attitude à deux bras.* Variations: *open 5th, wide 5th.*

position of the arms, arabesque See *arabesque; arabesque line; arabesque, 1st; arabesque, 2nd; arabesque, 3rd.*

position of the arms, attitude See *attitude, attitude à deux bras, attitude grecque, attitude opposition, attitude ordinaire.*

position of the arms, bras bas [-, bʀa ba] –, bra ba (Fr. arms; low.) A basic low position in which both arms curve down to form an oval in front of, and slightly away from, the body.

position of the arms, demi-bras [-, d(ə)mibʀa] –, d(u)-MEE-bra (Fr. half-arm position.) A supplementary position in which both arms are held in front of the body, wider and lower than *1st position,* with the palms slightly upward.

position of the arms, demi-seconde [-, d(ə)mis(ə)gɔ̃d] –, d(u)-MEE-s(u)g̲od (Fr. half-second position.) A basic position in which the arms are slightly curved halfway between *bras bas* and *2nd position* with the palms facing each other.

position of the arms, low 1st A variation of *1st position* in which the little fingers are just below the waist.

position of the arms, open 4th An elongated *4th position of the arms* in which one arm is in *open 5th* and the other arm is in *demi-seconde.* Sometimes referred to as *arabesque line.* See *entrechat six de volée de côté.*

position of the arms, open 5th An arm position corresponding to *demi-seconde*, but high. Both arms curve halfway between *5th position* and *2nd position,* so that the arms lengthen and the palms face outward.

position of the arms, pirouette See *pirouette position of the arms.*

position of the arms, wide 5th A variation of *5th position* taken with the forearms reaching outward, so that the elbows and wrists are extended with the hands and fingers lengthened.

position of the body See *body alignment, poses of the body.*

position of the feet The five basic *positions of the feet* are formed with the legs turned equally outward from the hip joints and the body weight equally distributed over the two feet. They may be taken with the feet flat on the floor, *en demi-pointe*, or *en pointes*.

position of the feet, 1st A closed position where the dancer stands with the feet together, so that the heels are touching. Also *en première*.

position of the feet, 1st natural A *1st position* in which the legs are naturally turned out, i.e., somewhere between parallel and turned out. Also *natural 1st*.

position of the feet, 2nd An open position where the dancer stands with the feet approximately shoulder width apart, i.e., about 1-1/2 times the length of the foot. A movement *to 2nd position* may be referred to as *à la seconde*, e.g., *chassé à la seconde*. The phrase *to 2nd* refers to a position or movement in which the dancer stands on one foot with the *working leg* extended or extending to the side *à terre* or *en l'air*, e.g., *dégagé to 2nd*.

position of the feet, 3rd A closed position where the dancer stands with the feet together with one foot in front of the other, so that the heel of the front foot is placed at the middle of the back foot. Used to prepare the dancer for *5th position*. *Exercises* performed in *5th position* may be practised in *3rd position*.

position of the feet, 4th An open position where the dancer stands with one foot placed in front of *5th position* and the other behind. The space between the feet is approximately the length of the dancer's foot. Sometimes referred to as *4th crossed*. The phrase *4th devant* refers to a position in which the dancer stands on one foot with the *working leg* extended to the front. The phrase *4th derrière* refers to a position in which the dancer stands on one foot with the *working leg* extended to the back. A *grand 4th en fondu* or *lunge* is taken in a wide *4th position*.

position of the feet, 4th crossed See *position of the feet, 4th*.

position of the feet, 4th en fondu [- ɑ̃ fɔ̃dy, -] – ah fo-DU, – (Fr. position of the feet; 4th; melted.) A *4th position of the feet* with the weight well forward over the front leg which is bent *en fondu*. May be used as a *preparatory position* for turning actions such as *pirouettes* and *adage pivots*. See *lunge*.

position of the feet, 4th opposite 1st A variation of *4th position* in which one foot is placed in front of *1st position* and the other behind. Sometimes referred to as *4th open* or *open 4th*.

position of the feet, 5th A closed position where the dancer stands with the feet together, with one foot in front of the other, so that the heel of the front foot is placed in line with the big toe joint of the back foot. The phrase *5th devant* refers to a *5th position* in which the *working foot* is in front. The phrase *5th derrière* refers to a *5th position* in which the *working foot* is behind.

position of the foot, flexed A position of the *working foot* in which the ankle is dorsi-flexed as much as possible, maintaining the shape of the foot, i.e., neither sickled in nor out, with toes aligned.

position of the head See *head; pirouette head*.

position of the supporting foot and leg The dancer's weight may be borne on the whole foot with the leg straight or bent, on the ball of the foot, or on the tip of the foot in *pointe shoes*. See *en demi-pointe*, *en fondu*, *en pointe*.

position, preparatory See *preparatory position*.

positions des bras See *position of the arms*.

positions des pieds See *position of the feet*.

première [pʀəmjɛʀ] pr(u)m-YER (Fr. adj nf first.) See *en première; pas de bourrée en première; position of the arms, 1st; position of the feet, 1st*.

preparatory position A position in which the arms are placed in *demi-seconde* as the dancer stands on one leg with the other leg bent so that the tops of the calves touch and the *working foot* is placed *à terre derrière*, fully pointed. May be used as a starting position for *enchaînements*. Performed with the ball of the *working foot* contacting the floor in Grade 3 *Balancés*.

promenade [pʀɔm(ə)nad] prom(u)-NAD (Fr. nf a walk.) 1. Stylised walks, introduced in the Character section of the Grade 3 syllabus. Term not used in current RAD Majors syllabus. 2. In the Cecchetti method, *pivots* in a held position are described as *promenade en dehors* or *en dedans*. See *pivot*.

prompt corner See *stage left.*

quarter plié [- plije] – plee-YAY (Fr. quarter bent.) A bending of the knees over the toes, halfway between straight legs and *demi-plié,* with the legs turned out and the heels remaining on the floor. May be performed in any of the five *positions of the feet,* as a preparation for *demi-* and *grand plié.*

quarter pointe See *pointe/s, 1/4.*

quatre [katʀə] KA-tr(u) (Fr. adj nm four.) See *entrechat quatre, pas de bourrée à quatre pas.*

quatrième [katʀijɛm] ka-tree-YEM (Fr. nmf fourth.) See *position of the arms, 4th; position of the feet, 4th.*

raccourci [ʀakuʀsi] ra-koor-SEE (Fr. pp of v raccourcir, to cut, shorten, or curtail; adj shortened; nm a shortened action.) See *coupé fouetté raccourci.*

relevé [ʀəlve, ʀləve] r(u)l-VAY, rl(u)-VAY (Fr. pp of v relever, to pull up, raise, lift, or push up; adj pulled up; nm a lifted or lifting action.) 1. A leg action which begins *en demi-plié* or *en fondu,* arrives *en demi-pointes* or *en pointes* with a strong and speedy stretch of the legs, and finishes again *en demi-plié* or *en fondu.* Taken in *1st, 2nd, 4th* or *5th position of the feet.* See *relevé en demi-pointe/s, relevé en pointe/s.* May also be performed from two feet to one or from one foot to one. See *relevé 1 to 1, relevé 2 to 1, relevé derrière, relevé devant, relevé passé.* 2. Term referring to a step performed with a *relevé* action as opposed to, for example, a jump. See *échappé relevé, renversé relevé, rotation relevé, sissonne relevée.*

relevé 1 to 1 [ʀəlve -] r(u)l-VAY – (Fr. pulled up; one foot to one foot.) A *relevé* which begins *en fondu,* arrives *en pointe* with a strong and speedy stretch of the leg, and ends again *en fondu.* The position of the *working foot* may be sustained throughout or extended at the height of the *relevé* and replaced *en fondu.* See *relevé 1 to 1 to open positions, relevé* in *pirouette position* or *arabesque.*

relevé 1 to 1 4th devant [ʀəlve - d(ə)vɑ̃] r(u)l-VAY – d(u)-VAH (Fr. pulled up; one foot to one foot; 4th front.) A *relevé 1 to 1* which begins in *cou-de-pied devant en fondu,* arrives *en pointe* with a strong and speedy stretch of the *supporting leg* and an extension of the *working leg* to *4th position devant en l'air,* and finishes again in *cou-de-pied devant en fondu.* When this step is taken in a series, it may travel *en avant.*

relevé 1 to 1 en avant See *relevé 1 to 1 4th devant.*

relevé 1 to 1 to open positions [ʀəlve -] r(u)l-VAY – (Fr. pulled up; one foot to one foot; open positions.) A *relevé 1 to 1* in which the *working leg* begins in *cou-de-pied,* extends to *4th* or to *2nd en l'air,* and finishes again in *cou-de-pied.*

relevé 2 to 1 [ʀəlve -] r(u)l-VAY – (Fr. pulled up; two feet to one foot.) A *relevé* which begins *en demi-plié,* arrives *en pointe* with a strong and speedy stretch of the leg, and ends *en demi-plié* or *en fondu.* The *working foot* may be lifted or extended to a variety of positions *en pointe.*

relevé derrière [ʀəlve dɛʀjɛʀ] r(u)l-VAY der-YER (Fr. pulled up; behind.) A *relevé* from *5th derrière en demi-plié* to *retiré derrière en pointe* and finishing in *5th derrière en demi-plié.*

relevé devant [ʀəlve d(ə)vɑ̃] r(u)l-VAY d(u)-VAH (Fr. pulled up; front.) A *relevé* from *5th devant en demi-plié* to *retiré devant en pointe* and finishing in *5th devant en demi-plié.*

relevé en demi-pointe/s [ʀəlve ɑ̃ d(ə)mipwɛ̃t] r(u)l-VAY ah d(u)-MEE-pwet (Fr. pulled up; on half tiptoe.) A strong and speedy pulled-up action of the leg or legs to *demi-pointe* or to *demi-pointes* commencing and ending *en demi-plié* or *en fondu.* The toes remain in contact with the floor throughout the movement. Taken in *1st, 2nd, 4th,* and *5th position of the feet;* from *2 to 1;* or from *1 to 1.* In *4th:* in order to maintain *4th position opposite 5th position en demi-pointes,* it is necessary to make minimal adjustment of the toes on the *relevé* action. The body weight is lifted in the *relevé* action and sustained during the direct return to *demi-plié.* In *5th:* the legs and feet are drawn firmly together with the *relevé* action into a *tight 5th position en demi-pointes.* The body weight is lifted in the relevé action and sustained during the direct return to *demi-plié.*

relevé en pointe/s [ʀəlve ɑ̃ pwɛ̃t] r(u)l-VAY ah pwet (Fr. pulled up; on tiptoe.) A strong rising action onto the tips of the toes, beginning and ending *en demi-plié* or *en fondu.* Taken in *1st, 2nd, 4th, and 5th position of the feet;* from *2 to 1;* or from *1 to 1.* Commencing from a *demi-plié,* the *relevé* is taken directly on to *pointes,* with a minimal adjustment of the toes, retracting them by a distance equivalent to the length of the toes to establish the extended line on *pointe.* In *relevé in 5th,* where the retraction of the toes is greater, the feet are drawn tightly together *en pointes,* one in front of the other. In all these *relevés,* when returning to *demi-plié,* there is an extra lift in the body which releases the weight off the feet, allowing the replacement of the toes. The lowering of the heels to the floor must be controlled.

relevé in 4th devant See *relevé 1 to 1 4th devant.*

relevé in arabesque [ʀəlve - aʀabɛsk] r(u)l-VAY – a-ra-BESK (Fr. pulled up; in arabesque.) A *relevé 1 to 1* usually executed in *1st arabesque.* When this step is taken in a series, it may travel slightly *en arrière.*

relevé in arabesque en arrière See *relevé in arabesque.*

relevé passé [ʀəlve pɑse] r(u)l-VAY pah-SAY (Fr. pulled up; passed.) A *relevé* in which the *working foot* begins *5th devant* or *derrière,* lifts to *retiré devant,* then passes as it lowers to *5th derrière* or *devant.* Taken *passé devant* or *passé derrière.* Variation: *relevé passé with half turn.*

relevé passé derrière [ʀəlve pɑse dɛʀjɛʀ] r(u)l-VAY pah-SAY der-YER (Fr. pulled up; passed; behind.) A *relevé passé* in which the *working foot* begins *5th devant,* lifts to *retiré devant,* then passes as it lowers to *5th derrière.*

relevé passé devant [ʀəlve pɑse d(ə)vɑ̃] r(u)l-VAY pah-SAY d(u)-VAH (Fr. pulled up; passed; front.) A *relevé passé* in which the *working foot* begins *5th derrière,* lifts directly to *retiré devant,* then passes as it lowers to *5th devant.*

relevé passé with half turn [ʀəlve pɑse -] r(u)l-VAY pah-SAY – (Fr. pulled up; passed; with half turn.) A *relevé passé* in which the dancer performs a 1/2-turn during the upward *relevé* action. *Relevé passé devant* with a 1/2-turn toward the *barre* may be used to change direction during a *barre exercise.* See *emboîté relevé en tournant.* When performed in series *en diagonale*, the dancer begins *en croisé*, performs a *relevé passé devant* with a 1/2-turn *en dedans*, then a *relevé passé devant* with a 1/2-turn *en dehors*, and ends *en croisé* ready to begin the next *relevé.*

relevé, échappé See *échappé relevé.*

renversé [ʀɑ̃vɛʀse] rah-ver-SAY (Fr. pp of v renverser, to upset or overturn; adj upset; nm an overturned action.) Term used to describe the bending of the body during a turn. In a *renversé* action, the body forces the leg to move. See *renversé relevé, renversé sauté.*

renversé relevé [ʀɑ̃vɛʀse ʀəlve] rah-ver-SAY r(u)l-VAY (Fr. overturned action; pulled up.) A strong action of the body which initiates a turn *en pointe,* either *en dehors* or *en dedans.* Usually taken *en dehors,* incorporating an outward circling of the *working leg* leading into a turn away from the *supporting leg.* The *working leg* is extended *devant en fondu;* then, with a *relevé* on the *supporting leg,* the *working leg* lifts forward and circles upward through *2nd,* and continues to *attitude derrière en fondu* with the torso arched slightly backward over the *supporting leg.* The action is completed with a *pas de bourrée dessous en tournant.* The *grand rond de jambe* action of the *working leg* ends *en fondu en croisé,* sustained by a counterbalancing action of the arched torso and arms (e.g., *4th crossed),* until the dancer's equilibrium appears to be momentarily lost. This leads into the quick *pas de bourrée en tournant,* with the arching sustained until the second step. The *relevé* action may be initiated by a *coupé dessous.*

renversé sauté [ʀɑ̃vɛʀse sote] rah-ver-SAY soh-TAY (Fr. overturned action; jumped.) A strong action of the body which initiates a turn in the air, either *en dehors* or *en dedans.* Usually taken *en dehors,* incorporating an outward circling of the *working leg* leading into a turn away from the *supporting leg.* The *working leg* is extended *devant en fondu;* then, with a *temps levé*, it lifts forward and circles upward through *2nd,* continuing the action to land *en attitude derrière* with the torso arched slightly backward over the *supporting leg.* The action is completed with a *pas de bourrée dessous en tournant.* The *grand rond de jambe* action of the *working leg* ends *en fondu en croisé,* sustained by a counterbalancing action of the arched torso and arms (e.g., *4th* with the arm corresponding to the *working leg* raised to *5th),* until the dancer's equilibrium appears to be momentarily lost. This leads into the quick *pas de bourrée en tournant,* with the arching sustained until the second step. The *temps levé* may be preceded by a *pas de bourrée dessus en tournant.*

retiré [ʀ(ə)tiʀe] r(u)-tee-RAY (Fr. pp of v retirer, to take away or remove; adj withdrawn; nm a withdrawn position or action.) A drawing up action of the *working foot* to *retiré position,* a position just below knee height. Can be executed with different qualities, performed with varying *ports* *de bras,* and set on different rhythms. See *retiré devant, retiré derrière, retiré passé, retiré position.* Variations: *petit retiré, retiré changement, retiré sauté.*

retiré changement [ʀ(ə)tiʀe ʃɑ̃ʒmɑ̃] r(u)-tee-RAY shahzh-MAH (Fr. withdrawn; change.) A *changement* in which the feet are drawn toward the hips so that the knees bend and the toes skim past each other at the height of the jump.

retiré derrière [ʀ(ə)tiʀe dɛʀjɛʀ] r(u)-tee-RAY der-YER (Fr. withdrawn; behind.) A drawing up action of the *working foot* to *retiré position derrière.* From *5th derrière,* the foot peels off the floor as in *petit retiré derrière,* and is drawn up the back of the *supporting leg* until the big toe joint contacts the leg at the same height as *retiré devant.* To return to *5th position,* the *working foot* tracks down the back of the *supporting leg* and through the foot to close *derrière.*

retiré devant [ʀ(ə)tiʀe d(ə)vɑ̃] r(u)-tee-RAY d(u)-VAH (Fr. withdrawn; front.) A drawing up action of the *working foot* to *retiré position devant.* Starting from *5th devant:,* the foot peels off the floor as in *petit retiré devant,* and is drawn up so that the little toe contacts the hollow under the knee. To return to *5th position,* the *working foot* tracks down the front of the *supporting leg* and through the foot to close *devant.*

retiré passé [ʀ(ə)tiʀe pɑse] r(u)-tee-RAY pah-SAY (Fr. withdrawn; passed.) A variation of *retiré* in which the *working foot* begins in *5th devant,* lifts to *retiré position,* and ends in *5th derrière,* or the reverse. Also referred to as *grand retiré passé.* See *retiré pasé derrière, retiré pasé devant.* Variation: *petit retiré passé.*

retiré passé derrière [ʀ(ə)tiʀe pɑse dɛʀjɛʀ] r(u)-tee-RAY pah-SAY der-YER (Fr. withdrawn; passed; behind.) A *retiré passé* in which the *working foot* begins in *5th devant* and ends *5th derrière.* After the front foot peels off the floor, it tracks directly through the *retiré position,* and closes behind.

retiré passé devant [ʀ(ə)tiʀe pɑse d(ə)vɑ̃] r(u)-tee-RAY pah-SAY d(u)-VAH (Fr. withdrawn; passed; front.) A *retiré passé* in which the *working foot* begins in *5th derrière* and ends *5th devant.* After the front foot peels off the floor, it tracks directly through the *retiré position,* and closes in front.

retiré position A position in which the toes of the fully pointed *working foot* are in contact with the side of the *supporting knee* (the tip of the big toe contacts the knee). Variation: *retiré position derrière, retiré position devant.*

retiré position derrière [ʀ(ə)tiʀe - dɛʀjɛʀ] r(u)-tee-RAY – der-YER (Fr. withdrawn; position; behind.) A *retiré position* in which the *working foot* touches the back of the *supporting knee* (the big toe joint contacts the back of the *supporting leg* at the same height as *retiré devant).*

retiré position devant [ʀ(ə)tiʀe - d(ə)vɑ̃] r(u)-tee-RAY – d(u)-VAH (Fr. withdrawn; position; front.) A *retiré position* in which the *working foot* touches the front of the *supporting knee* (the little toe contacts the hollow under the knee). Also called *pirouette position.*

retiré sauté passé [ʀ(ə)tiʀe sote pɑse] r(u)-tee-RAY soh-TAY pah-SAY (Fr. withdrawn; jumped; passed.) A withdrawn jumping action. Starting *5th position,* the push-off is from two feet, the *working foot* is drawn to *retiré position* as the other leg stretches fully in the air, and the landing is in *5th position* with a *change of feet.* May be performed *devant* or *derrière.* Often performed in series alternating legs. Variation: *petit retiré sauté.*

retiré sauté passé derrière [ʀ(ə)tiʀe sote pɑse dɛʀjɛʀ] r(u)-tee-RAY soh-TAY pah-SAY der-YER (Fr. withdrawn; jumped; passed; behind.) A *retiré sauté passé* with the *working foot* beginning *5th devant* and ending *5th derrière.*

retiré sauté passé devant [ʀ(ə)tiʀe sote pɑse d(ə)vɑ̃] r(u)-tee-RAY soh-TAY pah-SAY d(u)-VAH (Fr. withdrawn; jumped; passed; front.) A *retiré sauté passé* with the *working foot* beginning *5th derrière* and ending *5th devant.*

retiré, petit See *petit retiré.*

révérence [ʀeveʀɑ̃s] ray-vay-RAHS (Fr. nf bow or curtsey.) 1. Movement performed at the end of a class or examination to acknowledge and thank the pianist, then the teacher or examiner. Embellished form of a Girl's *curtsey* or a Boy's *bow.* 2. Girl's *curtsey* performed by placing the tip of the *working foot* on the floor just behind the *supporting foot* while bending both knees. Often preceded by steps and *port de bras* and enhanced by the use of *eye line.* 3. Boy's bow performed by standing with natural *turn-out,* while inclining the head forward. Often preceded by steps and *port de bras* and enhanced by the use of *eye line.*

reverse 1. Term used to indicate a change in direction, i.e., to indicate that *devant* positions are taken *derrière* or that *derrière* positions are taken *devant*. Also refers to movements such as *en avant/en arrière, dessus/dessous, en dehors/en dedans*. 2. Term used to describe a *port de bras* which changes in direction and intermediary positions. See *port de bras, reverse; reverse (simple) port de bras; reverse petit développé.*

reverse (simple) port de bras [- pɔʀ də bʀa] – por d(u) bra (Fr. reverse (simple) carriage of the arm or arms.) A movement of the arms beginning in *2nd position*, passing through *1st position* and *bras bas* to end as it began.

reverse petit développé [- p(ə)ti devlɔpe] – p(u)-TEE dayv-loh-PAY (Fr. reverse small; unfolding action.) An action of an extended leg in which the fully stretched foot passes through *cou-de-pied* before closing *5th position.*

reverse port de bras See *port de bras, reverse.*

rise An action of the *supporting foot* or feet. See *rising en demi-pointe/s, rising en pointe/s.*

rising en demi-pointe/s [- ɑ̃ d(ə)mipwɛ̃t] – ah d(u)-MEE-pwet (Fr. rising; on half tiptoe.) An ankle action in which the legs are straight and the heels are released gradually from the floor until the ankle is fully stretched. Rising strengthens the ankles in preparation for *relevés, pointe work,* and *allegro.* Taken in all *positions of the feet* and in positions on one leg, e.g., in *retiré position devant.*

rising en pointe/s [- ɑ̃ pwɛ̃t] – ah pwet (Fr. rising; on tiptoe.) An ankle and foot action in which the legs are straight and the heels are released gradually from the floor until the ankle is fully stretched, with the movement continuing onto the tips of the toes. The action lowers with control through the feet. Taken in all *positions of the feet* and in positions on one leg, e.g., in *retiré position devant.* In *2nd position,* before the rise occurs, the distance between the two heels should not be more than the length of the dancer's foot.

rond [ʀɔ̃] ro (Fr. nm circle.) See *demi-grand rond de jambe, demi-rond de jambe, rond de jambe.*

rond de jambe [ʀɔ̃ də ʒɑ̃b] ro d(u) zhahb (Fr. circle of the leg.) A circling action of the *working leg*. May be performed *à terre* or *en l'air*, *en dehors* or *en dedans*. Variations: *double rond de jambe, grand rond de jambe, demi-grand rond de jambe, demi-rond de jambe en dedans, jeté rond de jambe sauté, rond de jambe at glissé height, rond de jambe in attitude en l'air, rond de jambe jeté, rond de jambe sauté.*

rond de jambe à terre [ʀɔ̃ də ʒɑ̃b a tɛʀ] ro d(u) zhahb a ter (Fr. circle of the leg; on the ground.) A circling action of the *working leg* along the floor *either en dehors* or *en dedans.* An essential movement to develop and maintain the maximum turnout and control of both the *supporting* and *working legs.* The movement is continuous, both legs are fully stretched, and the toes of the *working foot* maintain contact with the floor throughout.

rond de jambe à terre en dedans [ʀɔ̃ də ʒɑ̃b a tɛʀ ɑ̃ dədɑ̃] ro d(u) zhahb a ter ah d(u)-DAH (Fr. circle of the leg; on the ground; inward.) An inward circling action of the *working leg* along the floor. Commencing and ending in *dégagé devant* opposite *1st:* the *working leg* passes through *1st position,* with the heel lowered, to *dégagé derrière,* and makes a 180-degree arc passing through *2nd position* to *4th devant.*

rond de jambe à terre en dehors [ʀɔ̃ də ʒɑ̃b a tɛʀ ɑ̃ dəɔʀ] ro d(u) zhahb a ter ah d(u)-OR (Fr. circle of the leg; on the ground; outward.) An inward circling action of the *working leg* along the floor. Commencing and ending in *dégagé derrière* opposite *1st:* the working leg passes through *1st position,* with the heel lowered, to *dégagé devant*, and makes a 180-degree arc passing through *2nd position* to *4th derrière.*

rond de jambe at glissé height [ʀɔ̃ də ʒɑ̃b - glise -] ro d(u) zhahb – glee-SAY – (Fr. circle of the leg; at sliding action height.) A circling action similar to a *rond de jambe à terre* but with the *working leg* extended *en l'air* with the toes just off the floor while tracing the 180-degree arc. May be performed *en dehors* or *en dedans.*

rond de jambe en dehors, demi-grand See *demi-grand rond de jambe.*

rond de jambe en dehors, low See *rond de jambe at glissé height.*

rond de jambe en l'air [ʀɔ̃ də ʒɑ̃b ɑ̃ lɛʀ] ro d(u) zhahb ah ler (Fr. circle of the leg; in the air.) A circling action of the lower leg in which the foot begins and ends in *2nd position* at 45 degrees. Taken either *en dehors* or *en dedans.*

rond de jambe en l'air en dedans [ʀɔ̃ də ʒɑ̃b ɑ̃ lɛʀ ɑ̃ dədɑ̃] ro d(u) zhahb ah ler ah d(u)-DAH (Fr. circle of the leg; in the air; inward.) An inward circling action of the lower leg. Commencing with the *working leg* in *2nd* at 45 degrees, the toes of the *working foot* trace an inward circular path forward of the *supporting leg,* lightly touch the calf, and continue outward in a straight line, with a sustained feeling of pushing the air away as the leg extends to *2nd.*

rond de jambe en l'air en dedans, double See *double rond de jambe en l'air en dedans.*

rond de jambe en l'air en dehors [ʀɔ̃ də ʒɑ̃b ɑ̃ lɛʀ ɑ̃ dəɔʀ] ro d(u) zhahb ah ler ah d(u)-OR (Fr. circle of the leg; in the air; outward.) An outward circling action of the lower leg. Commencing with the *working leg* in *2nd* at 45 degrees, the toes of the *working foot* trace a straight line into the *supporting leg* to lightly touch the calf and, leading with the heel, the foot continues with an outward circular action and a sustained feeling of pushing the air away as the leg extends to *2nd.*

rond de jambe en l'air en dehors, double See *double rond de jambe en l'air en dehors.*

rond de jambe en l'air, double See *double rond de jambe en l'air.*

rond de jambe jeté [ʀɔ̃ də ʒɑ̃b ʒ(ə)te] ro d(u) zhahb zh(u)-TAY (Fr. circle of the leg; thrown.) A thrown *rond de jambe* action in which the *working leg* traces a circular path from front to back *(en dehors)* or from back to front *(en dedans)* with the apex reached as the leg passes through *2nd en l'air.* Beginning in *dégagé to 4th,* the movement is initiated by the use of the floor as in a *battement tendu,* passing through *1st position* and a low *attitude,* followed by a light flight of the leg along an arc outward through *2nd* above 90 degrees and continuing the arc onward to finish in *dégagé to 4th.* The thrown action through *2nd* corresponds to the musical accent. In *rond de jambe jeté* the foot lifts upward and outward, passing through its apex in *2nd en l'air,* whereas in *grand battement en rond,* the foot traces a horizontal path between *4th* and *2nd en l'air.*

rond de jambe jeté en dedans [ʀɔ̃ də ʒɑ̃b ʒ(ə)te ɑ̃ dədɑ̃] ro d(u) zhahb zh(u)-TAY ah d(u)-DAH (Fr. circle of the leg; thrown; inward.) A *rond de jambe* action in which the *working leg* traces a circular path inward from back to front. Beginning in *dégagé devant,* the movement is initiated by the use of the floor as in a *battement tendu,* passing through *1st position* and a low *attitude derrière,* followed by a light flight of the leg along an arc outward through *2nd* above 90 degrees and continuing the arc onward to finish in *dégagé devant.*

rond de jambe jeté en dehors [ʀɔ̃ də ʒɑ̃b ʒ(ə)te ɑ̃ dəɔʀ] ro d(u) zhahb zh(u)-TAY ah d(u)-OR (Fr. circle of the leg; thrown; outward.) A *rond de jambe* action in which the *working leg* traces a circular path outward from front to back. Beginning in *dégagé derrière,* the movement is initiated by the use of the floor as in a *battement tendu,* passing through *1st position* and a low *attitude devant,* followed by a light flight of the leg along an arc outward through *2nd* above 90 degrees and continuing the arc onward to finish *dégagé derrière.*

rond de jambe sauté [ʀɔ̃ də ʒɑ̃b sote] ro d(u) zhahb soh-TAY (Fr. circle of the leg; jumped.) An *allegro* step consisting of a *rond de jambe en l'air* with the *working leg* and a simultaneous *temps levé* with the *supporting leg.* May be performed *en dehors* or *en dedans.* Variations: *double rond de jambe sauté.*

rond de jambe sauté en dehors, double See *double rond de jambe sauté en dehors.*

rond de jambe, grand See *grand rond de jambe en l'air.*

rotation [ʀɔtɑsjɔ̃] ro-tah-SYO (Fr. nm rotation.) A turn of the body toward the extended leg which often maintains its position in space. May be performed with the *working leg à terre* or *en l'air,* with the *supporting leg* pivoting flat or *en demi-pointe,* or performing a *rise, relevé,* or *sauté.* The opposite action is called *fouetté.*

rotation à terre [ʀɔtɑsjɔ̃ a tɛʀ] ro-tah-SYO a ter (Fr. rotation; on the ground.) One of the basic steps of *centre practice.* A fully coordinated movement where the body turns toward the extended leg with a pivoting action of the *supporting leg.* Can be executed with varying use of arms and *alignments,* and with a 1/4-turn or a 1/2-turn. 1. Basic *rotation à terre* with a 1/4-turn. From *1st arabesque à terre* standing on the *upstage* leg and facing 2 *(stage right)* or 4 *(stage left),* there is a pivoting action of the *supporting leg en dehors,* while the body makes a 1/4-turn toward the extended leg which rotates in its hip socket gradually adjusting to *2nd en face.* The arms move gradually from *1st arabesque* to *2nd position.* 2. Basic *rotation à terre* with a 1/2-turn. The movement of the first 1/4-turn is the same as that of a *rotation* with a 1/4-turn. From *2nd position,* the pivoting movement continues, making a further 1/4-turn toward the extended leg which rotates in its hip socket to finish *4th devant* facing the opposite side. The arms move gradually from *1st arabesque,* arriving in *2nd position* by the first 1/4-turn and continuing into *1st position* by the completion of the *rotation.*

rotation en l'air [ʀɔtɑsjɔ̃ ɑ̃ lɛʀ] ro-tah-SYO ah ler (Fr. rotation; in the air.) A turn of the body toward the extended leg which often maintains its position *en l'air* in space. The opposite action is called *fouetté en l'air.*

rotation relevé [ʀɔtɑsjɔ̃ ʀəlve] ro-tah-SYO r(u)l-VAY (Fr. rotation; pulled up.) A *rotation en l'air* with the *supporting leg* performing a *relevé* action.

rotation relevé with développé [ʀɔtɑsjɔ̃ ʀəlve - devlɔpe] ro-tah-SYO r(u)l-VAY – dayv-loh-PAY (Fr. rotation; pulled up; with unfolding action.) A *rotation en l'air* with the *supporting leg* performing a *relevé* action, preceded by a *développé derrière* to the *en l'air* position. The dancer begins in *5th position*, lifts the *working leg* to *retiré*, opens it *derrière* to 90 degrees *en fondu*, performs a *relevé* and simultaneous turn toward the extended leg which maintains its position *en l'air* to end *devant* 90 degrees, then finishes *en fondu.* May be initiated with a *ballotté dessus.*

run en avant [- ɑ̃ navɑ̃] – ah na-VAH (Fr. run; forward.) A series of runs forward, used to generate momentum for actions like *grand jeté en avant* and *posé en avant.* See *classical run.*

running pas de bourrée [- pɑ də buʀe] – pah d(u) boo-RAY (Fr. running; bourrée step.) A step used to generate momentum before a large *allegro* jump. The dancer steps forward or sideways along the *line of dance*, then runs forward along the *line of dance*, before stepping forward to push off into the jump. Used as a preparation into steps such as *grand jeté en tournant* or *fouetté relevé en tournant.*

saut [so] soh (Fr. nm a jump.) A jumping action. See *saut de basque.*

saut de basque [so də bask] soh d(u) bask (Fr. jump of the Basque.) A turning jump from one foot to the other. The dancer steps along the *line of dance*, turns *en dedans* and brushes the *working foot* forward along the *line of dance* opening it *to 2nd* 90 degrees as the body continues to turn in the air, then completes the turn to land in place on the foot that brushed, with the other foot placed mid-shin. In the Boys Intermediate syllabus, *saut de basque* is performed with great elevation, the legs widening in *2nd position* at the height of the jump. May be initiated by *posé coupé dessous posé (galop).* The arms usually pass from *2nd position* to just below *1st position* on the step forward, and move through *1st* to *5th position* on the brush. Variation: *double saut de basque.*

saut de basque, double See *double saut de basque.*

sauté [sote] soh-TAY (Fr. pp of v sauter, to jump; adj jumped; nm a jump.) 1. A basic jump from two feet to two feet, taken in *1st, 2nd, or 4th position.* Jumps always begin and end *en demi-plié,* with the knees and feet fully stretched at the height of the jump. See *changement, échappé sauté, sauté en première, sauté in 2nd, sauté in 4th, soubresaut.* Variation: *sauté en pointe/s.* 2. Term used to describe a jumped action. See *ballotté sauté, coupé fouetté raccourci sauté, coupé sauté, échappé sauté, emboîté sauté, fouetté sauté, jeté rond de jambe sauté, pas de basque sauté, petit retiré sauté, renversé sauté, retiré sauté passé, sauté pirouette.*

sauté en pointe/s [sote ɑ̃ pwɛ̃t] soh-TAY ah pwet (Fr. jump; on tiptoe.) A small, low jump performed on the tip/s of the foot/feet in *pointe shoes*, with the foot positioned vertically and the ankle and knee slightly relaxed on the landing.

sauté en première [sote ɑ̃ pʀəmjɛʀ] soh-TAY ah pr(u)m-YER (Fr. jump; in 1st.) A jumped action performed in *1st position.* The dancer begins in *1st position*, performs a *demi-plié*, springs into the air stretching both legs, then lands in *1st position en demi-plié.* Often performed in series to warm up the legs and feet.

sauté in 2nd [sote -] soh-TAY – (Fr. jump; in 2nd.) A jump *sur place* beginning and ending in *2nd position.*

sauté in 4th [sote -] soh-TAY – (Fr. jump; in 4th.) A jump *sur place* beginning and ending in *4th position.*

sauté pirouette en tournant en dedans [sote piʀwet ɑ̃ tuʀnɑ̃ ɑ̃ dədɑ̃] soh-TAY peer-WET ah toor-NAH ah d(u)-DAH (Fr. jump; turn; turning; inward.) A male *grand allegro* step consisting of a *temps levé* (with the *working leg* closing to *retiré devant)* with a simultaneous revolution in the air in the direction of the push-off leg, and a landing *en arabesque*.

sauté pirouette in 2nd [sote piʀwɛt -] soh-TAY peer-WET – (Fr. jump; turn; in 2nd.) A male *grand allegro* step consisting of a *temps levé* in *2nd* with the *working leg en l'air* and a simultaneous revolution in the air in the direction of the push-off leg. Variation: *pirouettes in 2nd with petits sautés.*

sauté pirouette in arabesque [sote piʀwɛt - aʀabɛsk] soh-TAY peer-WET – a-ra-BESK (Fr. jump; turn; in arabesque.) A male *grand allegro* step consisting of a *temps levé en arabesque* with a simultaneous revolution in the air in the direction of the push-off leg.

sauté, échappé See *échappé sauté*.

second See *arabesque, 2nd; position of the arms, 2nd; position of the feet, 2nd.*

seconde [s(ə)gɔ̃d] s(u)-GOD (Fr. adj nf second.) See *à la seconde; position of the arms, demi-seconde*.

seconde, à la See *to 2nd.*

seconde, demi- See *position of the arms, demi-seconde*.

serré [seʀe] say-RAY (Fr. pp of v serrer, to grip or hold tight; adj tight.) See *petits battements serrés*.

set exercise A specific sequence of movements. *Set exercises* are performed in a formal executant examination setting.

side bend A lifted movement of the torso curving to the side from above the waist.

sideways port de bras See *port de bras with side bend*.

simple [sɛ̃pl(ə)] sepl(u) (Fr. adj simple.) As *ballonné simple.*

single pirouette See *pirouette en dedans, single; pirouette en dehors, single*.

sissonne [sisɔn] see-SON (Fr. nf term not found in Fr. dictionaries but thought to originate from ciseau, scissors, or to be named after the step's creator.) A jump from two feet to one foot, often with a scissor-like action. See *petite sissonne, sissonne battue, sissonne changée, sissonne développée, sissonne doublée, sissonne fermée, sissonne ordinaire, sissonne ordinaire passée, sissonne ouverte*. May also be performed with a *relevé* action. See *sissonne relevée.* Note that the masculine form is also seen, e.g., *petit sissonne, sissonne relevé.*

sissonne battue [sisɔn baty] see-SON ba-TU (Fr. sissonne; beaten.) A *sissonne* in which the legs push off opening slightly, then beat with or without a *change of feet* before the scissors-like action. May be taken *fermée* or *ouverte*; travelled *en avant, de côté,* or *en arrière;* and done *changée.*

sissonne changée [sisɔn ʃɑ̃ʒe] see-SON shah-ZHAY (Fr. sissonne; changed.) A *sissonne* which incorporates a *change of feet.* When travelled *en avant,* the *working foot* begins *5th devant* and passes back to end *derrière.* When travelled *en arrière,* the *working foot* begins *5th derrière* and passes forward to end *devant.*

sissonne changée battue [sisɔn ʃɑ̃ʒe baty] see-SON shah-ZHAY ba-TU (Fr. sissonne; changed; beaten.) A *sissonne* incorporating the beat of a *changement battu* and landing with a *change of feet*, i.e., the legs push off, beat, then change. When travelled *en avant,* the *working foot* begins *5th devant,* beats *devant,* and passes back to end *derrière.* When travelled *en arrière,* the *working foot* begins *5th derrière,* beats *derrière,* and passes forward to end *devant.*

sissonne derrière See *sissonne ordinaire derrière*.

sissonne derrière, petite See *petite sissonne derrière*.

sissonne devant See *sissonne ordinaire devant*.

sissonne devant, petite See *petite sissonne devant*.

sissonne développée [sisɔn devlɔpe] see-SON dayv-loh-PAY (Fr. sissonne; unfolding.) A jump from two feet to one foot in which the *working leg* performs a *développé* to finish *en l'air* at the height of the jump. Usually taken *de côté* with the *working leg* unfolding *to 2nd.* Also taken *en avant* or *en arrière,* and *passée derrière* or *passée devant*. See *sissonne doublée with développé.*

sissonne doublée [sisɔn duble] see-SON doo-BLAY (Fr. sissonne; doubled.) A composite step consisting of a *sissonne ouverte*, a *coupé*, and an *assemblé;* because of the momentum generated in the *sissonne*, the *assemblé dessus* or *dessous* may travel slightly. Taken *en avant*, *en arrière*, *dessus*, or *dessous*. May be embellished with a beat. Variation: *sissonne doublée with développé*.

sissonne doublée dessous [sisɔn duble d(ə)su] see-SON doo-BLAY d(u)-SOO (Fr. sissonne; doubled; under.) A composite step consisting of a *sissonne ouverte de côté devant*, a *coupé dessous*, and an *assemblé dessous*. The momentum generated by the *sissonne* may cause slight travel on the *assemblé dessous*.

sissonne doublée dessous with développé [sisɔn duble d(ə)su - devlɔpe] see-SON doo-BLAY d(u)-SOO – dayv-loh-PAY (Fr. sissonne; doubled; under; with unfolding action.) A *sissonne doublée dessous* in which the *sissonne ouverte de côté devant* is performed with the *working leg* passing through *retiré* before extending *to 2nd en l'air*.

sissonne doublée dessus [sisɔn duble d(ə)sy] see-SON doo-BLAY d(u)-SU (Fr. sissonne; doubled; over.) A composite step consisting of a *sissonne ouverte de côté derrière*, a *coupé dessus*, and an *assemblé dessus*. The momentum generated by the *sissonne* may cause slight travel on the *assemblé dessus*.

sissonne doublée dessus with développé [sisɔn duble d(ə)sy - devlɔpe] see-SON doo-BLAY d(u)-SU – dayv-loh-PAY (Fr. sissonne; doubled; over; with unfolding action.) A *sissonne doublée dessus* in which the *sissonne ouverte* is performed with the *working leg* passing through *retiré* before extending *en l'air*. Usually taken *dessus* or *dessous* but also taken *en avant* or *en arrière*.

sissonne doublée en arrière [sisɔn duble ɑ̃ naʀjɛʀ] see-SON doo-BLAY ah-nar-YER (Fr. sissonne; doubled; backward.) A composite step consisting of a *sissonne ouverte en arrière*, a *coupé dessus*, and an *assemblé en arrière*.

sissonne doublée en avant [sisɔn duble ɑ̃ navɑ̃] see-SON doo-BLAY ah na-VAH (Fr. sissonne; doubled; forward.) A composite step consisting of a *sissonne ouverte en avant*, a *coupé dessous*, and an *assemblé en avant*.

sissonne doublée with développé [sisɔn duble - devlɔpe] see-SON doo-BLAY – dayv-loh-PAY (Fr. sissonne; doubled; with unfolding action.) A *sissonne doublée* in which the *sissonne ouverte* is performed with the *working leg* passing through *retiré* before extending *en l'air*. Usually taken *dessous* or *dessus*, but also taken *en avant* or *en arrière*.

sissonne fermée [sisɔn fɛʀme] see-SON fer-MAY (Fr. sissonne; closed.) A jump with a scissors-like action, taken from two feet, travelling, and landing on one foot before closing. The scissors-like action is performed by one leg (designated as the *working leg)* with the other leg stretched below the body in the air. *Sissonne fermée* lands on one leg with the *working leg* immediately closing *en demi-plié,* whereas *sissonne ouverte* ends with the *working leg* sustaining its open position *en fondu.* Taken *de côté (dessus, dessous, devant,* and *derrière), en avant,* or *en arrière.* Variations: *sissonne fermée battue, sissonne fermée changée.*

sissonne fermée battue [sisɔn fɛʀme baty] see-SON fer-MAY ba-TU (Fr. sissonne; closed; beaten.) A *sissonne fermée* done with a beat at the beginning of the jump. May be performed *en avant*, *en arrière*, or *de côté;* and *changée*.

sissonne fermée battue de côté [sisɔn fɛʀme baty də kote] see-SON fer-MAY ba-TU d(u) koh-TAY (Fr. sissonne; closed; beaten; to the side.) A *sissonne* in which the dancer begins in *5th position*, jumps into the air, opens the feet slightly before beating in *5th position* with or without a *change of feet*, travels sideways away from the leg which opens *to 2nd*, lands on the other foot, and closes the extended foot immediately into *5th position en demi-plié*. May be performed *dessus* and *dessous* (without a *change of feet* on the *beat);* or *devant* and *derrière* (with a *change of feet* on the *beat)*.

sissonne fermée battue de côté dessous [sisɔn fɛʀme baty də kote d(ə)su] see-SON fer-MAY ba-TU d(u) koh-TAY d(u)-SOO (Fr. sissonne; closed; beaten; to the side; under.) A *sissonne* in which the dancer begins in *5th position* with the *working leg* front, jumps into the air, opens the feet slightly before beating in *5th position* without a *change of feet*, travels sideways in the direction of the back foot as the front foot opens *to 2nd*, lands on the back foot, and closes the other immediately into *5th position derrière en demi-plié*.

sissonne fermée battue de côté dessus [sisɔn fɛʀme baty də kote d(ə)sy] see-SON fer-MAY ba-

TU d(u) koh-TAY d(u)-SU (Fr. sissonne; closed; beaten; to the side; over.) A *sissonne* in which the dancer begins in *5th position* with the *working leg* behind, jumps into the air, opens the feet slightly before beating in *5th position* without a *change of feet*, travels sideways in the direction of the front foot as the back foot opens *to 2nd*, lands on the front foot, and closes the other immediately into *5th position devant en demi-plié*.

sissonne fermée battue dessus See *sissonne fermée battue de côté dessus*.

sissonne fermée changée battue [sisɔn fɛʀme ʃɑ̃ʒe baty] see-SON fer-MAY shah-ZHAY ba-TU (Fr. sissonne; closed; changed; beaten.) A *sissonne fermée* incorporating the beat of a *changement battu* and ending with a *change of feet*. May be performed *en avant* or *en arrière*. Variation: *sissonne fermée changée battue devant*, *sissonne fermée changée battue en tournant*.

sissonne fermée changée battue devant [sisɔn fɛʀme ʃɑ̃ʒe baty d(ə)vɑ̃] see-SON fer-MAY shah-ZHAY ba-TU d(u)-VAH (Fr. sissonne; closed; changed; beaten; front.) A *sissonne fermée changée battue* performed *devant* and *sur place*. The dancer begins in *5th position*, jumps into the air beating in *5th position* without a *change of feet*, lands on the foot which began in front with the other leg extended *devant en l'air*, and immediately closes *5th position en demi-plié*. Variation: *sissonne fermée changée battue en tournant*.

sissonne fermée changée battue devant en tournant See *sissonne fermée changée battue en tournant*.

sissonne fermée changée battue en arrière [sisɔn fɛʀme ʃɑ̃ʒe baty ɑ̃ naʀjɛʀ] see-SON fer-MAY shah-ZHAY ba-TU ah-nar-YER (Fr. sissonne; closed; changed; beaten; backward.) A *sissonne* in which the dancer begins in *5th position* with the *working leg* behind, jumps into the air, beats in *5th position* without a *change of feet*, travels backward as the back foot opens to *4th devant*, and lands on the foot which began in front, closing the other immediately into *5th position en demi-plié*.

sissonne fermée changée battue en avant [sisɔn fɛʀme ʃɑ̃ʒe baty ɑ̃ navɑ̃] see-SON fer-MAY shah-ZHAY ba-TU ah na-VAH (Fr. sissonne; closed; changed; beaten; forward.) A *sissonne* in which the dancer begins in *5th position* with the *working leg* in front, jumps into the air, beats in *5th position* without a *change of feet*, travels forward as the front foot opens to *4th derrière*, and lands on the foot which began behind, closing the other immediately into *5th position en demi-plié*.

sissonne fermée changée battue en tournant [sisɔn fɛʀme ʃɑ̃ʒe baty ɑ̃ tuʀnɑ̃] see-SON fer-MAY shah-ZHAY ba-TU ah toor-NAH (Fr. sissonne; closed; changed; beaten; turning.) A *sissonne fermée changée battue devant* performed with a change in *alignment*. Two *sissonnes* may be performed in series to complete a turn, with the first landing *en croisé* and the second continuing in the same direction to land *en croisé*.

sissonne fermée de côté [sisɔn fɛʀme də kote] see-SON fer-MAY d(u) koh-TAY (Fr. sissonne; closed; sideways.) A *sissonne fermée* travelling sideways away from the *working leg* which begins in *5th position,* opens outward, and closes with or without a *change of feet.* From *5th position en demi-plié:* the jump travels sideways with one leg fully stretching under the body as the other leg opens *to 2nd position* at 45 degrees; and it lands on one foot with the open foot immediately closing *5th position en demi-plié.* May be taken without a *change of feet (derrière* or *devant),* or with a *change of feet (dessous* or *dessus).* Also taken *battue.*

sissonne fermée de côté derrière [sisɔn fɛʀme də kote dɛʀjɛʀ] see-SON fer-MAY d(u) koh-TAY der-YER (Fr. sissonne; closed; sideways; behind.) A *sissonne fermée de côté* in which the *working leg* begins and ends behind. From *5th derrière en demi-plié,* the jump travels sideways toward the foot which began in front, with that leg fully stretching under the body as the other leg opens *to 2nd position* at 45 degrees; and it lands on one foot with the open foot immediately closing *5th derrière en demi-plié.*

sissonne fermée de côté dessous [sisɔn fɛʀme də kote d(ə)su] see-SON fer-MAY d(u) koh-TAY d(u)-SOO (Fr. sissonne; closed; sideways; under.) A *sissonne fermée de côté* in which the *working leg* begins in front and ends behind. From *5th devant en demi-plié,* the jump travels sideways toward the foot which began behind, with that leg fully stretching under the body as the other leg opens *to 2nd position* at 45 degrees; and it lands on one foot with the open foot immediately closing *5th derrière en demi-plié.*

sissonne fermée de côté dessus [sisɔn fɛʀme də kote d(ə)sy] see-SON fer-MAY d(u) koh-TAY d(u)-SU (Fr. sissonne; closed; sideways; over.)

A *sissonne fermée de côté* in which the *working leg* begins behind and ends in front. From *5th derrière en demi-plié,* the jump travels sideways toward the foot which began in front, with that leg fully stretching under the body as the other leg opens *to 2nd position* at 45 degrees; and it lands on one foot with the open foot immediately closing *5th devant en demi-plié.*

sissonne fermée de côté devant [sisɔn fɛʀme də kote d(ə)vɑ̃] see-SON fer-MAY d(u) koh-TAY d(u)-VAH (Fr. sissonne; closed; sideways; front.) A *sissonne fermée de côté* in which the *working leg* begins and ends in front. From *5th devant en demi-plié,* the jump travels sideways toward the foot which began behind, with that leg fully stretching under the body as the other leg opens *to 2nd position* at 45 degrees; and it lands on one foot with the open foot immediately closing *5th devant en demi-plié.*

sissonne fermée en arrière [sisɔn fɛʀme ɑ̃ naʀjɛʀ] see-SON fer-MAY ah-nar-YER (Fr. sissonne; closed; backward.) A *sissonne fermée* which travels backward. From *5th position en demi-plié,* the jump travels straight backward with the front leg fully stretching under the body as the other leg opens *to 4th devant* at 45 degrees; and it lands on one foot with the open foot immediately closing *5th devant en demi-plié.*

sissonne fermée en avant [sisɔn fɛʀme ɑ̃ navɑ̃] see-SON fer-MAY ah na-VAH (Fr. sissonne; closed; forward.) A *sissonne fermée* which travels forward. From *5th position en demi-plié,* the jump travels straight forward with the front leg fully stretching under the body as the other leg opens *to 4th derrière* at 45 degrees; and it lands on one foot with the open foot immediately closing *5th derrière en demi-plié.*

sissonne fermée relevée [sisɔn fɛʀme ʀəlve] see-SON fer-MAY r(u)l-VAY (Fr. sissonne; closed; pulled up.) A *sissonne relevée* ending in *5th position en demi-plié.* May be performed *en avant*, *en arrière*, or *de côté devant, derrière, dessus,* or *dessous*. Also *sissonne relevée fermée*.

sissonne fermée relevée de côté derrière [sisɔn fɛʀme ʀəlve də kote dɛʀjɛʀ] see-SON fer-MAY r(u)l-VAY d(u) koh-TAY der-YER (Fr. sissonne; closed; pulled up; sideways; behind.) A *sissonne relevée* travelling sideways away from the back foot and ending in *5th position* without a *change of feet*. The dancer begins in *5th position en demi-plié*, performs a *relevé* from 2 to 1 travelling sideways away from the back leg as it opens *to 2nd*, then closes the extended foot *5th derrière en demi-plié*.

sissonne fermée relevée de côté dessous [sisɔn fɛʀme ʀəlve də kote d(ə)su] see-SON fer-MAY r(u)l-VAY d(u) koh-TAY d(u)-SOO (Fr. sissonne; closed; pulled up; sideways; under.) A *sissonne relevée* travelling sideways away from the front foot and ending in *5th position* with a *change of feet*. The dancer begins in *5th position en demi-plié*, performs a *relevé* from 2 to 1 travelling sideways away from the front leg as it opens *to 2nd*, then closes the extended foot *5th derrière en demi-plié*.

sissonne fermée relevée de côté dessus [sisɔn fɛʀme ʀəlve də kote d(ə)sy] see-SON fer-MAY r(u)l-VAY d(u) koh-TAY d(u)-SU (Fr. sissonne; closed; pulled up; sideways; over.) A *sissonne relevée* travelling sideways away from the back foot and ending in *5th position* with a *change of feet*. The dancer begins in *5th position en demi-plié*, performs a *relevé* from 2 to 1 travelling sideways away from the back leg as it opens *to 2nd*, then closes the extended foot *5th devant en demi-plié*.

sissonne fermée relevée de côté devant [sisɔn fɛʀme ʀəlve də kote d(ə)vɑ̃] see-SON fer-MAY r(u)l-VAY d(u) koh-TAY d(u)-VAH (Fr. sissonne; closed; pulled up; sideways; front.) A *sissonne relevée* travelling sideways away from the front foot and ending in *5th position* without a *change of feet*. The dancer begins in *5th position en demi-plié*, performs a *relevé* from 2 to 1 travelling sideways away from the front leg as it opens *to 2nd*, then closes the extended foot *5th devant en demi-plié*.

sissonne fermée relevée en arrière [sisɔn fɛʀme ʀəlve ɑ̃ naʀjɛʀ] see-SON fer-MAY r(u)l-VAY ah-nar-YER (Fr. sissonne; closed; pulled up; backward.) A *sissonne relevée* travelling backward away from the front foot and ending in *5th position*. The dancer begins in *5th position en demi-plié*, performs a *relevé* from 2 to 1 travelling backward away from the front leg as it opens *devant*, then closes the extended foot *5th position en demi-plié*.

sissonne fermée relevée en avant [sisɔn fɛʀme ʀəlve ɑ̃ navɑ̃] see-SON fer-MAY r(u)l-VAY ah na-VAH (Fr. sissonne; closed; pulled up; forward.) A *sissonne relevée* travelling forward away from the back foot and ending in *5th position*. The dancer begins in *5th position en demi-plié*, performs a *relevé* from 2 to 1 travelling forward away from the back leg as it opens *derrière*, then closes the extended foot *5th position en demi-plié*.

sissonne ordinaire [sisɔn ɔʀdinɛʀ] see-SON or-dee-NER (Fr. sissonne; ordinary.) A jump *sur place* from two feet landing on one foot with the *working foot* placed *sur le cou-de-pied.* From *5th position en demi-plie,* the jump commences with a strong push-off drawing the legs together, fully stretched, and lands on one foot *en fondu,* with the other foot *sur le cou-de-pied.* Taken *devant* or *derrière, passée,* and *en tournant.* Also called *petite sissonne.* Variation: *sissonne ordinaire en pointe.*

sissonne ordinaire derrière [sisɔn ɔʀdinɛʀ dɛʀjɛʀ] see-SON or-dee-NER der-YER (Fr. sissonne; ordinary; behind.) A *sissonne ordinaire* which commences in *5th position* and lands on the front foot with the back foot *sur le cou-de-pied derrière.* Also *sissonne derrière.*

sissonne ordinaire derrière en pointe [sisɔn ɔʀdinɛʀ dɛʀjɛʀ ɑ̃ pwɛ̃t] see-SON or-dee-NER der-YER ah pwet (Fr. sissonne; ordinary; behind; on tiptoe.) A *sissonne ordinaire derrière* performed with the jump on the tips of the feet.

sissonne ordinaire devant [sisɔn ɔʀdinɛʀ d(ə)vɑ̃] see-SON or-dee-NER d(u)-VAH (Fr. sissonne; ordinary; front.) A *sissonne ordinaire* which commences in *5th position* and lands on the back foot with the front foot *sur le cou-de-pied devant.* Also *sissonne devant.*

sissonne ordinaire devant en pointe [sisɔn ɔʀdinɛʀ d(ə)vɑ̃ ɑ̃ pwɛ̃t] see-SON or-dee-NER d(u)-VAH ah pwet (Fr. sissonne; ordinary; front; on tiptoe.) A *sissonne ordinaire devant* performed with the jump on the tips of the feet.

sissonne ordinaire passée [sisɔn ɔʀdinɛʀ pɑse] see-SON or-dee-NER pah-SAY (Fr. sissonne; ordinary; passed.) A *sissonne ordinaire* in which the foot which begins behind passes to end in front, or the reverse. May be performed *devant* or *derrière.* Also *sissonne passée.*

sissonne ordinaire passée derrière [sisɔn ɔʀdinɛʀ pɑse dɛʀjɛʀ] see-SON or-dee-NER pah-SAY der-YER (Fr. sissonne; ordinary; passed; behind.) A *sissonne ordinaire* in which the foot which begins in front passes to end behind. The jump commences with a strong push-off from a *demi-plié* drawing the legs together fully stretched, and lands having passed the front foot *sur le cou-de-pied derrière.* Also *sissonne passée derrière.*

sissonne ordinaire passée derrière en tournant finished in 4th lunge [sisɔn ɔʀdinɛʀ pɑse dɛʀjɛʀ ɑ̃ tuʀnɑ̃-] see-SON or-dee-NER pah-SAY der-YER ah toor-NAH – (Fr. sissonne; ordinary; passed; front; turning; finished in 4th lunge.) A variation of a *tour en l'air,* finishing in an open position. The dancer begins in *5th position* with the arms *3rd ordinaire;* he then springs into the air bringing the arms to *1st* and making a full turn in the direction of the original front foot while moving that foot to or slightly above *cou-de-pied derrière,* and lands on the original back foot with the other leg extending back to finish in *4th en fondu,* often *en croisé.* May be performed with one or more revolutions.

sissonne ordinaire passée devant [sisɔn ɔʀdinɛʀ pɑse d(ə)vɑ̃] see-SON or-dee-NER pah-SAY d(u)-VAH (Fr. sissonne; ordinary; passed; front.) A *sissonne ordinaire* in which the foot which begins behind passes to end in front. The jump commences with a strong push-off from a *demi-plié* drawing the legs together fully stretched, and lands having passed the back foot *sur le cou-de-pied devant.* Also *sissonne passée devant.*

sissonne ordinaire passée devant by 1/2 turn [sisɔn ɔʀdinɛʀ pɑse d(ə)vɑ̃ -] see-SON or-dee-NER pah-SAY d(u)-VAH – (Fr. sissonne; ordinary; passed; front; by half turn.) A *sissonne ordinaire passée devant* in which the dancer makes a 1/2-turn *en dedans* while in the air. Often used to initiate a series of *petits jetés en tournant.*

sissonne ordinaire passée devant en tournant [sisɔn ɔʀdinɛʀ pɑse d(ə)vɑ̃ ɑ̃ tuʀnɑ̃] see-SON or-dee-NER pah-SAY d(u)-VAH ah toor-NAH (Fr. sissonne; ordinary; passed; front; turning.) A *sissonne ordinaire passée devant* in which the dancer turns *en dedans* while in the air to change *alignment.*

sissonne ouverte [sisɔn uvɛʀt] see-SON oo-VERT (Fr. sissonne; open.) A jump with a scissors-like action, taken from two feet, travelling, and landing on one foot. The scissors-like action is performed by one leg (designated as the *working leg)* with the other leg stretched below the body in the air. *Sissonne ouverte* ends with the *working leg* sustaining its open position *en fondu,* whereas *sissonne fermée* lands on one leg with the *working leg* immediately closing *en demi-plié.*

Taken *en avant, de côté,* or *en arrière.* Variations: *sissonne ouverte battue, sissonne ouverte changée, sissonne ouverte to arabesque.*

sissonne ouverte battue [sisɔn uvɛʀt baty] see-SON oo-VERT ba-TU (Fr. sissonne; open; beaten.) A *sissonne ouverte* incorporating the beat of an *entrechat quatre.* The dancer begins in *5th position,* jumps into the air, opens the feet slightly before beating in *5th position* with a *change of feet,* travels forward or backward as one leg opens to *4th,* and lands *en fondu.* May be performed *en avant* or *en arrière.*

sissonne ouverte battue en arrière [sisɔn uvɛʀt baty ɑ̃ naʀjɛʀ] see-SON oo-VERT ba-TU ah-nar-YER (Fr. sissonne; open; beaten; backward.) A *sissonne* in which the dancer begins in *5th position,* pushes off, beats in *5th* with a *change of feet,* passes the front foot backward as the body travels backward, and lands *en fondu* en *4th devant en l'air.*

sissonne ouverte battue en avant [sisɔn uvɛʀt baty ɑ̃ navɑ̃] see-SON oo-VERT ba-TU ah na-VAH (Fr. sissonne; open; beaten; forward.) A *sissonne* in which the dancer begins in *5th position,* pushes off, beats in *5th* with a *change of feet,* passes the back foot forward as the body travels forward, and lands *en fondu en arabesque.*

sissonne ouverte changée [sisɔn uvɛʀt ʃɑ̃ʒe] see-SON oo-VERT shah-ZHAY (Fr. sissonne; open; changed.) A *sissonne ouverte* with a *change of feet* before the landing. May be performed *en avant* or *en arrière.* Variations: *sissonne ouverte changée en tournant, sissonne ouverte changée to attitude.*

sissonne ouverte changée en tournant [sisɔn uvɛʀt ʃɑ̃ʒe ɑ̃ tuʀnɑ̃] see-SON oo-VERT shah-ZHAY ah toor-NAH (Fr. sissonne; open; changed; turning.) A *grand allegro* jump in which the dancer jumps from *5th position,* turns toward the back foot and travels forward opening the front leg *en l'air derrière,* and lands *en fondu,* often *en attitude.*

sissonne ouverte changée en tournant in attitude See *sissonne ouverte changée en tournant.*

sissonne ouverte changée to attitude [sisɔn uvɛʀt ʃɑ̃ʒe - atityd] see-SON oo-VERT shah-ZHAY – a-tee-TUD (Fr. sissonne; open; changed; to attitude.) A *grand allegro* jump in which the dancer jumps from *5th position,* travels forward opening the front leg to *attitude derrière,* and lands *en fondu.*

sissonne ouverte de côté derrière [sisɔn uvɛʀt də kote dɛʀjɛʀ] see-SON oo-VERT d(u) koh-TAY der-YER (Fr. sissonne; open; to the side; behind.) A *sissonne* in which the dancer begins in *5th position* with the *working leg* behind, jumps from two feet travelling sideways away from the back leg which extends *to 2nd en l'air,* and lands *en fondu.*

sissonne ouverte de côté devant [sisɔn uvɛʀt də kote d(ə)vɑ̃] see-SON oo-VERT d(u) koh-TAY d(u)-VAH (Fr. sissonne; open to the side; in front.) A *sissonne* in which the dancer begins in *5th position* with the *working leg* front, jumps from two feet travelling sideways away from the front leg which extends *to 2nd en l'air,* and lands *en fondu.*

sissonne ouverte en arrière [sisɔn uvɛʀt ɑ̃ naʀjɛʀ] see-SON oo-VERT ah-nar-YER (Fr. sissonne; open; backward.) A *sissonne ouverte* travelling backward and ending *en fondu* with the other leg extended *devant en l'air.*

sissonne ouverte en avant [sisɔn uvɛʀt ɑ̃ navɑ̃] see-SON oo-VERT ah na-VAH (Fr. sissonne; open; forward.) A *sissonne ouverte* travelling forward and ending *en fondu* with the other leg extended *derrière en l'air.*

sissonne ouverte to arabesque [sisɔn uvɛʀt - aʀabɛsk] see-SON oo-VERT – a-ra-BESK (Fr. sissonne; open; to arabesque.) An *allegro* jump in which the dancer jumps from *5th position,* travels forward opening the back leg *en arabesque,* and lands *en fondu.* May be performed with greater elevation as a *grand allegro* step.

sissonne passée See *sissonne ordinaire passée.*

sissonne passée derrière See *sissonne ordinaire passée derrière.*

sissonne passée devant See *sissonne ordinaire passée devant.*

sissonne relevée [sisɔn ʀəlve] see-SON r(u)l-VAY (Fr. sissonne; pulled up.) A *relevé* from two feet to one foot, travelling on the upward action, with the *working leg* extended parallel to the *line of dance.* May finish *en demi-plié,* i.e., *fermée,* or *en fondu,* i.e., *ouverte.* May travel *en avant, de côté,* or *en arrière.*

sissonne relevée fermée [sisɔn ʀəlve fɛʀme] see-SON r(u)l-VAY fer-MAY (Fr. sissonne; pulled up; closed.) A *sissonne relevée* which ends *en demi-plié*. May travel *en avant*, *de côté*, or *en arrière*. Also *sissonne fermée relevée*.

sissonne relevée fermée en arrière See *sissonne fermée relevée en arrière*.

sissonne relevée fermée en avant See *sissonne fermée relevée en avant*.

sissonne relevée ouverte [sisɔn ʀəlve uvɛʀt] see-SON r(u)l-VAY oo-VERT (Fr. sissonne; pulled up; open.) A *sissonne relevée* which ends *en fondu*. May travel *en avant*, *de côté*, or *en arrière*.

sissonne relevée ouverte de côté [sisɔn ʀəlve uvɛʀt də kote] see-SON r(u)l-VAY oo-VERT d(u) koh-TAY (Fr. sissonne; pulled up; open; sideways.) A *relevé* from two feet to one foot, travelling sideways on the upward action with the *working leg* extended *to 2nd en l'air*, and finishing *en fondu*.

sissonne relevée ouverte en arrière [sisɔn ʀəlve uvɛʀt ɑ̃ naʀjɛʀ] see-SON r(u)l-VAY oo-VERT ah-nar-YER (Fr. sissonne; pulled up; open; backward.) A *relevé* from two feet to one foot, travelling backward on the upward action with the *working leg* extended *devant en l'air*, and finishing *en fondu*.

sissonne relevée ouverte en avant [sisɔn ʀəlve uvɛʀt ɑ̃ navɑ̃] see-SON r(u)l-VAY oo-VERT ah na-VAH (Fr. sissonne; pulled up; open; forward.) A *relevé* from two feet to one foot, travelling forward on the upward action with the *working leg* extended *en arabesque*, and finishing *en fondu*.

sissonne tombé en avant [sisɔn tɔ̃be ɑ̃ navɑ] see-SON to-BAY ah na-VAH (Fr. sissonne; fallen step; forward.) A composite step consisting of a *sissonne ordinaire devant* and a *tombé en avant to 4th en fondu*. May be done with *extended chassé pas de bourrée* as a preparation for *pirouettes*.

six [sis] sees (Fr. adj nm six.) See *entrechat six*, *entrechat six de volée de côté*.

skip en avant en pointe [- ɑ̃ navɑ̃ ɑ̃ pwɛ̃t] – ah na-VAH ah pwet (Fr. skip; forward; on tiptoe.) Skip travelling forward on the tips of the feet. A composite step consisting of a *temps levé en pointe* with a *petit développé devant* followed by a *posé en avant en pointe*. Often performed in series alternating feet.

soubresaut [subʀəso] soo-br(u)-SOH (Fr. nm a start, jolt, or convulsive movement.) A jump from *5th position* which lands in *5th position* with the same foot in front. At the height of the jump, the legs are strongly drawn together with the feet fully stretched in *5th position*. May be taken *sur place* or travelling *en avant* or *en arrière*, and executed *en pointes*.

soubresaut en pointes [subʀəso tɑ̃ pwɛ̃t] soo-br(u)-SOH tah pwet (Fr. jolt; on tiptoe.) A small, low jump performed on the tips of the feet in *5th position* in *pointe shoes*, without a *change of feet*, with the feet positioned vertically and the ankles and knees slightly relaxed on the landing.

soubresaut sur place [subʀəso syʀ plas] soo-br(u)-SOH sur plas (Fr. jolt; on the spot.) A *soubresaut* performed in place.

soutenu [sutny] soot-NU (Fr. pp of v soutenir, to support, hold up, sustain; adj sustained; nm a sustained action.) See *pas soutenu*, *assemblé*, *demi-assemblé soutenu*, *petit soutenu*.

soutenu to 2nd [sutny -] soot-NU – (Fr. sustained action; to 2nd.) A *demi-assemblé soutenu* action of the *working leg*, beginning in *dégagé devant* or *derrière* and ending *to 2nd*.

soutenu to 4th derrière [sutny - dɛʀjɛʀ] soot-NU – der-YER (Fr. sustained action; to 4th; behind.) A *demi-assemblé soutenu* action of the *working leg*, beginning in *2nd* and ending *dégagé derrière*.

soutenu to 4th devant [sutny - d(ə)vɑ̃] soot-NU – d(u)-VAH (Fr. sustained action; to 4th; front.) A *demi-assemblé soutenu* action of the *working leg*, beginning in *2nd* and ending *dégagé devant*.

soutenu, demi-assemblé See *demi-assemblé soutenu*.

soutenu, pas See *pas soutenu*.

spotting The technique of directing the *eye line* toward a fixed point in space (for turns *sur place*) or along the *line of dance* (for turns which travel), in order to maintain equilibrium, prevent dizziness, and add brilliance to turning actions. See *pirouette head*.

spring A jump from one foot to the other. See *jeté*.

spring points A series of *springs* from one foot to the other, performed *sur place* with the *working foot devant à terre*. May also be performed with *hops* instead of *springs*. This term is not found in the current Majors syllabus but may be used for *free work*.

stage left 1. Term used to describe the location of the dancer on the left centre portion of the stage, or anywhere on the left half of the stage. Also: prompt side or *prompt corner*, since this is where the stage manager is traditionally located. 2. Term used to describe a direction faced in relation to the dancer's body: when a dancer faces *stage left,* s/he is facing 4. See *direction numbering.*

stage locations These terms were coined to describe the location of the dancer on the stage at a time when stages were raked or slanted. The raised or *upstage* portion of the stage was farthest from the audience and the lowered or *downstage* portion was closest to the audience. Although most stages built today are flat with the audience seating area raked, the reference to *downstage* and *upstage* has persisted. The terms *stage right* and *stage left* are taken from the dancer's perspective looking out into the audience. See *direction numbering.*

stage right 1. Term used to describe the location of the dancer on the right centre portion of the stage, or anywhere on the right half of the stage. Also *opposite prompt side*. 2. Term used to describe a direction faced in relation to the dancer's body: when a dancer faces *stage right,* s/he is facing 2. See *direction numbering.*

step 1. A defined dance action or composite action. See *pas*. 2. A transfer of weight. See *posé.*

step en arrière [- ɑ̃ naʀjɛʀ] – ah-nar-YER (Fr. step; backward.) A step backward. Also *posé en arrière.*

stretching at barre [- ba(ɑ)ʀ] – bar Sequence used to lengthen the muscles of the torso and legs by bending the upper body toward or away from the *working leg* while it is supported on the *barre devant*, *to 2nd*, or *derrière*. May be performed at the end of the *Barre* section of a class.

supporting leg/foot The leg or foot bearing all or most of the dancer's weight. May be either *en fondu* or straight with the foot flat, *1/4 pointe, en demi-pointe, 3/4 pointe,* or *en pointe*.

sur [syʀ] sur (Fr. prep on, on top of, or upon.) See *sur la demi-pointe*, *sur la pointe*, *sur le cou-de-pied*, *sur place*.

sur la demi-pointe [syʀ la d(ə)mipwɛ̃t] sur la d(u)-MEE-pwet (Fr. on; the half tiptoe.) Phrase used to describe steps which are performed with the ball of the *supporting foot* or *feet* contacting the floor.

sur la pointe [syʀ la pwɛ̃t] sur la pwet (Fr. on; the tiptoe.) Phrase used to describe steps which are performed with the tip of the *supporting foot* or *feet* contacting the floor. Such steps require the use of specially designed shoes known as *"pointe"* shoes. See *battement glissé sur la pointe*.

sur le cou-de-pied [syʀ l(ə) kudpje] sur l(u) koo-d(u)-pyay (Fr. on the neck of the foot.) Phrase used to describe the placement of the *working foot* on the *cou-de-pied* of the *supporting leg.* In this *Dictionary* when the term *sur le cou-de-pied* is used it indicates that the foot is fully pointed unless otherwise indicated. See *battement frappé, cou-de-pied*, *petit battement sur le cou-de-pied.*

sur place [syʀ plas] sur plas (Fr. on; place.) Phrase referring to an action performed without travelling. See *courus sur place, posé en demi-pointe sur place, posé en pointe sur place, soubresaut sur place.*

temps [tɑ̃] tah (Fr. nm time or beat; in gymnastics and fencing, "temps" is each simple movement of a certain duration, which occurs in the execution of a movement or combination of movements.) See *temps de cuisse*, *temps de flêche*, *temps de poisson, temps levé*, *temps lié*.

***temps de cuisse* (French)** [tɑ̃ də kɥis -] tah d(u) kuwees – (Fr. time; of the thigh.) A composite step consisting of a quick *petit retiré* with a straight *supporting leg*, and a *sissonne fermée de coté* closing on the beat. May be performed *dessus* and *dessous* (with a *petit retiré passé), devant* and *derrière* (with a *petit retiré),* or *en avant* and *en arrière.* Similar to *temps de cuisse* (Italian).

***temps de cuisse* (Italian)** [tɑ̃ də kɥis -] tah d(u) kuwees – (Fr. time; of the thigh.) A composite step consisting of a quick *battement glissé to 2nd* closing *en demi-plié* with or without a *change of feet,* and a *sissonne fermée de coté* closing on the beat. May be performed *dessus* and *dessous* (closing the *glissé* with a *change of feet),* or *devant* and *derrière* (closing the *glissé* without a *change of feet).* Not included in current RAD Majors syllabus.

***temps de cuisse dessous* (French)** [tɑ̃ də kɥis d(ə)su -] tah d(u) kuwees d(u)-SOO – (Fr. time; of the thigh; under.) A *temps de cuisse* consisting of a *petit retiré passé derrière* and a *sissonne fermée de côté derrière*. The dancer starts *5th position en demi-plié* with the *working leg devant*, lifts the tip of the foot to *petit retiré*, and closes *5th derrière en demi-plié;* s/he then jumps from two feet travelling sideways away from the back leg which extends *to 2nd*, lands on the other, and immediately closes *5th derrière en demi-plié*.

***temps de cuisse dessous* (Italian)** [tɑ̃ də kɥis d(ə)su -] tah d(u) kuwees d(u)-SOO – (Fr. time; of the thigh; under.) A *temps de cuisse* consisting of a *battement glissé to 2nd* closing with a *change of feet,* and a *sissonne fermée de côté derrière*. The dancer starts *5th position* with the *working leg devant*, performs a *battement glissé to 2nd* opening with straight legs and closing *5th derrière en demi-plié;* s/he then jumps from two feet travelling sideways away from the back leg which extends *to 2nd*, lands on the other, and immediately closes *5th derrière en demi-plié*. Not included in current RAD Majors syllabus.

***temps de cuisse dessus* (French)** [tɑ̃ də kɥis d(ə)sy -] tah d(u) kuwees d(u)-SU – (Fr. time; of the thigh; over.) A *temps de cuisse* consisting of a *petit retiré passé devant* and a *sissonne fermée de côté devant*. The dancer starts *5th position en demi-plié* with the *working leg derrière*, lifts the tip of the foot to *petit retiré*, and closes *5th devant en demi-plié;* s/he then jumps from two feet travelling sideways away from the front leg which extends *to 2nd*, lands on the other, and immediately closes *5th devant en demi-plié*.

***temps de cuisse dessus* (Italian)** [tɑ̃ də kɥis d(ə)sy -] tah d(u) kuwees d(u)-SU – (Fr. time; of the thigh; over.) A *temps de cuisse* consisting of a *battement glissé to 2nd* closing with a *change of feet,* and a *sissonne fermée de côté devant*. The dancer starts *5th position* with the *working leg derrière*, performs a *battement glissé to 2nd* stretching both legs on the opening with straight legs and closing *5th devant en demi-plié;* s/he then jumps from two feet travelling sideways away from the front leg which extends *to 2nd*, lands on the other, and immediately closes *5th devant en demi-plié*. Not included in current RAD Majors syllabus.

temps de flêche, temps de flèche [tɑ̃ də flɛʃ] tah d(u) flesh (Fr. time; of the arrow.) A jump performed with an arrow-like quality. A composite *grand allegro* step consisting of a *temps levé en arabesque*, a *battement en cloche* to *attitude devant*, a jump onto the other leg with the *working leg* performing a *développé devant* and immediately closing *5th position en demi-plié*. The arms may pass from *2nd position* to *1st* on the *battement* and through *5th to 2nd position* on the jump. Although the jump is performed in place, the *battement* action generates some forward momentum so that, when performed in series, the sequence travels slightly *en avant*.

temps de poisson [tɑ̃ də pwasɔ̃] tah d(u) pwa-SO (Fr. movement or movements of the fish.) A jump of high elevation, in which the dancer springs up into the air, with the feet held in a tight *5th position* and thrown backward and upward while arching the upper back so that the body line resembles a flying fish, and lands on the foot which began in front with the other leg released *to 4th derrière* just off the floor. Usually taken with the piked position *en ouvert.* The arms may begin in *bras bas*, then sweep through *1st* to *5th*, complementing the curve of the body, with the head turn and raised to project the *eye line* toward the audience.

temps levé [tɑ̃ l(ə)ve] tah l(u)-VAY (Fr. time or beat; lifted.) A jump off one foot landing on the same foot. Commencing with a *fondu,* there is a vertical spring into the air off the *supporting leg* which remains exactly in line under the body with the foot fully stretched. The *working foot* is sustained *sur le cou-de-pied* in a basic *temps levé*. See *temps levé sur le cou-de-pied.* Also taken in a variety of positions. See *posé temps levé in retiré*, *temps levé chassé*. Variation: *temps levé* with *petit développé passé*.

temps levé chassé [tɑ̃ l(ə)ve ʃase] tah l(u)-VAY sha-SAY (Fr. time; lifted; chased.) A composite step in which the dancer begins with the *working leg* in *dégagé*, usually *derrière;* s/he performs a *temps levé* with the *working leg* moving forward, then slides forward through the foot to end *en fondu* in anticipation of the following movement. At the Intermediate and Advanced levels, this may be performed as an *extended chassé*. See *extended chassé*.

temps levé chassé pas de bourrée [tɑ̃ l(ə)ve ʃase

pɑ də buʀe] tah l(u)-VAY sha-SAY pah d(u) boo-RAY (Fr. time; lifted; chased; bourrée step.) A composite step often used as a preparation for *pirouettes*. The dancer begins in *dégagé derrière*, performs a *petit développé passé devant* and a simultaneous *temps levé*, slides the free foot forward taking the weight onto it, then performs a *pas de bourrée dessous* finishing in *4th* or *5th position en demi-plié*. The arms usually begin *demi-bras*, pass below *1st* to *1st position* during the *temps levé*, open *to 2nd* during the *pas de bourrée*, and finish in *3rd position* in preparation for a subsequent *pirouette*.

temps levé posé en arrière [tɑ̃ l(ə)ve poze ɑ̃ naʀjɛʀ] tah l(u)-VAY poh-ZAY ah-nar-YER (Fr. time; lifted; placed; backward.) The dancer begins *dégagé derrière*, pushes off lifting the leg *en arabesque*, lands on the same foot, and steps backward *en fondu*. May be used as a preparation into steps such as *relevé*.

temps levé sur le cou-de-pied [tɑ̃ l(ə)ve syʀ l(ə) kudpje] tah l(u)-VAY sur l(u) koo-d(u)-pyay (Fr. time; lifted; on the neck of the foot.) A jump off one foot landing on the same foot with the *working foot* sustained *sur le cou-de-pied*. A basic *temps levé*. Commencing with a *fondu*, there is a vertical spring into the air off the *supporting leg* which remains exactly in line under the body with the foot fully stretched. Executed with the working foot held either *sur le cou-de-pied devant* or *sur le cou-de-pied derrière* throughout the movement.

temps lié [tɑ̃ lje] tah lyay (Fr. time; linked.) One of the basic steps of *centre practice*. A linking movement incorporating a transference of weight, with coordinated use of arms, legs, head, and body, which may be executed in different *alignments* and into different poses both *à terre* and *en l'air*. Develops the ability to move smoothly and harmoniously from one position to another. Taken *en avant, to 2nd,* and *en arrière*. Variation: *temps lié to 5th*.

temps lié à la seconde See *temps lié to 2nd*.

temps lié à terre [tɑ̃ lje a tɛʀ] tah lyay a ter (Fr. time; linked; on the ground.) A *temps lié* performed with the tip of the *working foot* contacting the floor after the transfer of weight. Usually prepared with an extension *en fondu à terre*. A basic *temps lié en avant, to 2nd,* or *en arrière*.

temps lié at 90 degrees [tɑ̃ lje -] tah lyay – (Fr. time; linked; at 90 degrees.) A *temps lié* performed with the *working leg* extended *en l'air* parallel to the floor after the transfer of weight.

temps lié en arrière [tɑ̃ lje ɑ̃ naʀjɛʀ] tah lyay ah-nar-YER (Fr. time; linked; backward.) Linked step involving a transference of weight backward. A basic *temps lié en arrière* starts *5th derrière, bras bas.* Commencing with a *demi-plié,* the back foot is extended to *dégagé derrière en fondu* as the arms are raised to *1st position.* The heel of the *working foot* lowers to the floor, transferring the weight backward in a continuous movement through the *demi-plié,* then straightening onto the back leg and stretching the front leg to *dégagé devant.* The arms arrive in *2nd position* with the completion of the transfer. The extended leg then closes to *5th devant* with the arms lowering to *bras bas.* The head and *eye line* are the same as in the basic *port de bras.*

temps lié en avant [tɑ̃ lje ɑ̃ navɑ̃] tah lyay ah na-VAH (Fr. time; linked; forward.) Linked step involving a transference of weight forward. A basic *temps lié en avant* starts *5th devant, bras bas.* Commencing with a *demi-plié,* the front foot is extended to *dégagé devant en fondu* as the arms are raised to *1st position.* The heel of the *working foot* lowers to the floor, transferring the weight forward in a continuous movement through the *demi-plié,* then straightening onto the front leg and stretching the back leg to *dégagé derrière.* The arms arrive in *2nd position* with the completion of the transfer. The extended leg then closes to *5th derrière* with the arms lowering to *bras bas.* The head and *eye line* are the same as in the basic *port de bras.*

temps lié to 2nd [tɑ̃ lje -] tah lyay – (Fr. time; linked; to 2nd.) Linked step involving a transference of weight to the side. A basic *temps lié to 2nd* starts *5th position, bras bas.* Commencing with a *demi-plié* and raising the arms to *1st,* the front foot is extended to *dégagé in 2nd en fondu* with the arms opening to *2nd position.* The weight is then transferred sideways in a continuous movement through the *demi-plié,* straightening onto the leading leg and stretching the other leg to *dégagé in 2nd.* As the extended leg closes to *5th devant* the arms lower to *bras bas.* May also be executed commencing with the back foot and closing in *5th derrière.*

temps lié to 5th [tɑ̃ lje -] tah lyay – (Fr. time; linked; to 5th.) A *temps lié* commencing with a *dégagé en fondu* just off the floor or a *petit développé en fondu,* leading into a step outward *en pointe* past the extended foot, and closing the freed foot immediately to *5th position en pointes.* Taken *en avant, de coté,* or *en arrière.*

temps lié with petit développé [tɑ̃ lje - p(ə)ti devlɔpe] tah lyay – p(u)-TEE dayv-loh-PAY (Fr. time; linked; with; small unfolding action.) A *temps lié* in which the *working leg* is initially extended through *petit retiré devant* or *derrière* before receiving the body weight.

temps lié with petit développé derrière [tɑ̃ lje - p(ə)ti devlɔpe dɛʀjɛʀ] tah lyay – p(u)-TEE dayv-loh-PAY der-YER (Fr. time; linked; with; small unfolding action; behind.) A *temps lié* in which the *working leg* is initially extended to the back through *petit retiré derrière* before receiving the body weight.

temps lié with petit développé devant [tɑ̃ lje - p(ə)ti devlɔpe d(ə)vɑ̃] tah lyay –p(u)-TEE dayv-loh-PAY d(u)-VAH (Fr. time; linked; with; small unfolding action; front.) A *temps lié* in which the *working leg* is initially extended to the front through *petit retiré devant* before receiving the body weight.

temps lié with petit développé to 2nd [tɑ̃ lje - p(ə)ti devlɔpe -] tah lyay – p(u)-TEE dayv-loh-PAY – (Fr. time; linked; with; small unfolding action; to 2nd.) A *temps lié* in which the *working leg* is initially extended to the side through *petit retiré devant* or *derrière* before receiving the body weight.

tendu [tɑ̃dy] tah-DU (Fr. pp of v tendre, to stretch; adj tight, taut; nm an outstretched position or action.) See *battement tendu, pointe tendu.*

terre [tɛʀ] ter (Fr. nf ground, land.) See *à terre, terre à terre, tombé à terre.*

terre à terre [tɛʀ a tɛʀ] ter a ter (Fr. ground; to; ground.) Phrase describing a sub-category of *petit allegro* executed rapidly with the toes staying close to the ground, and requiring a sensitive use of the forefoot and toes, as *petits changements terre à terre.* Taken *sur place* or travelling in all directions. *Terre à terre* movements include *jeté battement, glissade,* and *pas de bourrée.*

terre, à See *à terre.*

third See *arabesque, 3rd; position of the arms, 3rd; position of the feet, 3rd.*

three-quarter pointe See *pointe/s, 3/4.*

to 2nd 1. Position in which the *working leg* is extended to the side of the body, either *à terre* or *en l'air.* See *dégagé to 2nd.* 2. Term used to describe the direction of an action which occurs to the side of the body, e.g., *ballotté dessous to 2nd; battement fondu to 2nd; battement jeté to 2nd; battement tendu to 2nd; battement glissé to 2nd; battement frappé to 2nd; chassé to 2nd; demi-assemblé soutenu en dehors to 2nd; développé to 2nd; échappé relevé to 2nd; double battement frappé to 2nd; échappé sauté to 2nd; grand battement relevé to 2nd; grand battement retiré to 2nd; grand battement to 2nd; pas soutenu to 2nd; petit développé to 2nd; port de bras, simple; port de bras to 2nd, reverse; posé to 2nd; soutenu to 2nd; temps lié to 2nd; tombé to 2nd; transfer of weight to 2nd.*

toe chassé See *extended chassé.*

toe shoes See *pointe shoes.*

tombé [tɔ̃be] to-BAY (Fr. pp of v tomber, to fall, adj fallen, nm a falling step.) An off-balance action resulting in a transfer of weight from one foot to the other. The dancer begins on one foot, usually *en demi-pointe* with the *working leg* extended *en l'air;* s/he shifts the weight momentarily off balance in the direction of the outstretched leg, then gradually lowers it to receive the body weight, often ending *en fondu* with the free foot *à terre* or *en l'air.*

tombé à terre [tɔ̃be a tɛʀ] to-BAY a ter (Fr. falling step; on the ground.) A *tombé* which finishes with the tip of the free foot on the floor.

tombé en arrière [tɔ̃be ɑ̃ naʀjɛʀ] to-BAY ah nar-YER (Fr. falling step; backward.) A *tombé* in which the weight shifts backward.

tombé en avant [tɔ̃be ɑ̃ navɑ̃] to-BAY ah na-VAH (Fr. fallen step; forward.) A *tombé* in which the weight shifts forward.

tombé to 2nd [tɔ̃be -] to-BAY – (Fr. falling step; to 2nd.) A *tombé* in which the weight shifts sideways.

tour [tuʀ] toor (Fr. nm a turn or revolution.) See *tour en l'air, double tour.*

tour en l'air [tuʀ ɑ̃ lɛʀ] toor ah ler (Fr. turn; in the air.) A *changement en tournant* as practised by male dancers. Taken from *5th devant,* arms *3rd position* with the front arm corresponding to the front foot. Commencing with a *demi-plié,* the front arm starts to move toward *2nd.* The force of the turn in that direction is achieved by a combination of a strong push-off from both feet to jump in the air, with the side arm joining the front arm in *1st position.* As for *pirouette en dehors,* the head and eye focus remain by the first quarter of the turn. The revolution is completed by a swift turning action of the head, with the eyes refocusing as soon as possible *(spotting).* The arms are held in *1st* on landing in *5th.* May be performed with one revolution *(single tour)* or more (e.g., *double tour).*

tour, double See *double tour.*

tournant [tuʀnɑ̃] toor-NAH (Fr. adj turning or revolving.) See *en tournant.*

tournant, en See *en tournant.*

training exercise A suggested sequence of movements to be practised in the classroom as preparation for more difficult steps, but not to be performed in a formal executant examination setting.

transfer of weight 1. An action in which the dancer's weight is shifted horizontally from two feet to one, one foot to the other, or one foot to two, with minimal visible disruption of the body *alignment.* 2. A basic *exercise* beginning in *1st* or *5th position,* consisting of a *dégagé to 2nd* or *4th position,* a lowering of the heel with or without *demi-plié,* a continuous shift of weight onto the same or the other foot stretching both legs to reach *dégagé à terre,* and a closing in *1st* or *5th position.* May be performed *en avant* or *en arrière,* or *to 2nd* with or without a *change of feet.* Used as a preparatory *exercise* for *chassé* and *temps lié.* 3. At the Intermediate level, *transfer of weight* is performed with the *working leg* extending *en l'air,* then lowering to receive the body weight through the *demi-pointe* with the free leg extending *en l'air.*

transfer of weight, basic An exercise in which the *working foot* moves from a closed *position of the feet* to an open *position of the feet* by means of a *dégagé action,* then returns by the reverse action. Taken from *1st position* to *2nd position* and returning to *1st,* and also starting and ending in *5th position;* and *en avant* or *en arrière* from *5th position* and returning to *5th position.* 1. From *1st position* to *2nd position* and returning to *1st:* the leg is extended to a *dégagé in 2nd.* The heel is then lowered through the foot into *2nd position* and the weight is centralised over the feet. To return to *dégagé,* the transfer of weight onto the *supporting leg* occurs as the foot stretches; then the leg closes to *1st.* May also start and end in *5th position.* 2. *En avant* from *5th position* and returning to *5th position:* the front foot is extended to a *dégagé devant.* The foot adjusts slightly to lower into *4th position* centralising the weight over the feet. To return to *dégagé devant,* the transfer of weight onto the *supporting leg* occurs as the foot stretches; then the leg closes to *5th.* 3. *En arrière* from *5th position* and returning to *5th position:* the back foot is extended to a *dégagé derrière.* The foot adjusts slightly to lower into *4th position* centralising the weight over the feet. To return to *dégagé derrière,* the transfer of weight onto the *supporting leg* occurs as the foot stretches; then the leg closes to *5th.*

transfer of weight, full An exercise in which the *working foot* moves from a closed *position of the feet* to an *open position en demi-plié* by means of a *dégagé* action, then the other foot returns to a closed position by the reverse action. Taken from *1st* or *5th position* through *2nd;* and *en avant* and *en arrière* through *4th.* 1. From *1st position* through *2nd:* the working leg is extended to a *dégagé in 2nd,* then the weight is transferred through the foot into *2nd position en demi-plié* and onto that leg to finish with the other leg in a *dégagé in 2nd.* The extended leg then closes to *1st.* Can also be taken commencing and ending in *5th position.* 2. *En avant* through *4th:* commencing *5th devant,* the front leg is extended to a *dégagé in 4th devant,* then the weight is transferred through the foot into *4th position en demi-plié* and onto that leg to finish with the other leg in a *dégagé in 4th derrière.* The extended leg then closes to *5th derrière.* 3. *En arrière* through *4th:* commencing *5th derrière,* the back leg is extended to a *dégagé in 4th derrière,* then the weight is transferred through the foot into *4th position en demi-plié* and onto that leg to finish with the other leg in a *dégagé in 4th devant.* The extended leg then closes to *5th devant.*

transference of weight An action in which the weight is transferred from one foot to two feet by lowering the heel from a *dégagé* into an open position simultaneously centralising the weight over two feet, or from two feet to one foot by returning from the open position to a *dégagé.*

triple pirouette [- piʀwɛt] – peer-WET (Fr. triple; turn.) A *pirouette* in which the dancer's body turns through three revolutions. May be done with just less than or just over three revolutions to start and end in various alignments.

trois [tʀwɑ] trwa (Fr. adj nm three.) See *entrechat trois.*

troisième [tʀwɑzjɛm] trwa-ZYEM (Fr. adj nmf third.)

turn-out Maximum outward rotation of the leg at its hip joint.

turning movements A category of rotary actions which build from the smoothly controlled pivoting actions introduced in *centre practice.* The most basic form is the *détourné,* a swivel performed on both feet *en demi-pointes* or *en pointes.* Turns on one foot, known as *pirouettes,* are uniquely characterized by the quality of spinning or whirling, and may be taken outward away from the *supporting leg (en dehors),* or inward towards it *(en dedans).* Turning movements may be performed on the ground *(à terre)* or in the air *(en l'air).*

un [œ̃] uh (Fr. adj nm one.)

undersweep 1. Term used to describe the curved path of an arm or arms passing just below a position en route to it, e.g., *port de bras* with a slight *undersweep.* 2. The action of moving the arm or arms along a curved path passing just below a position en route to it, e.g., arms *undersweep* from *2nd* to *1st position*: the arm moves from *2nd* to just below *1st position* before lifting to *1st.*

upper back bend See *back bend.*

upstage 1. Term used to describe the location of the dancer on the centre back portion of the stage, or anywhere on the back of the stage. 2. Term used to describe a direction faced in relation to the dancer's body: when a dancer faces *upstage,* s/he is facing 3. See *direction numbering.*

upstage left 1. Term used to describe the location of the dancer on the left back portion of the stage, or near the back left corner. 2. Term used to describe a direction faced in relation to the dancer's body: when a dancer faces *upstage left,* s/he is facing 8. See *direction numbering.*

upstage right 1. Term used to describe the location of the dancer on the right back portion of the stage, or near the back right corner. 2. Term used to describe a direction faced in relation to the dancer's body: when a dancer faces *upstage right,* s/he is facing 7. See *direction numbering.*

valse [vals] vals(u) (Fr. short for G. waltzer, < walzen, to roll, to waltz ; akin to welter; nf a ballroom dance in which the couples glide in a revolving motion around the floor to music in three-quarter time; the music for such a dance; waltz.) See *pas de valse.*

volé [vɔle] vo-LAY (Fr. pp of v voler, to fly; adj flying; nm a flown action.) See *brisé volé, entrechat six de volée de côté.*

walks en arrière [- ɑ̃ naʀjɛʀ] – ah-nar-YER (Fr. walks; backward.) A series of steps travelling backward. See *classical walk.*

walks en avant [- ɑ̃ navɑ̃] – ah na-VAH (Fr. walks; forward.) A series of steps travelling forward. See *classical walk.*

walks, classical See *classical walk.*

waltz 1. A musical form in 3/4 rhythm. 2. Dance study performed to waltz music.

warm up exercise A simple sequence of dance movements, such as rises, *relevés,* or *sautés,* used at the beginning of a category of *exercises* to enhance circulation in a particular part of the body, usually the feet and legs, and to prepare the dancer for more demanding movements. Also *warm-up exercise.*

wide pas de bourrée dessous en tournant [- pɑ də buʀe d(ə)su ɑ̃ tuʀnɑ̃] – pah d(u) boo-RAY d(u)-SOO ah toor-NAH (Fr. wide; bourrée step; under; turning.) A *pas de bourrée dessous en tournant* performed with each step taken along a curved *line of dance* to finish facing *croisé* having completed 1/2 to 3/4 of a turn, as opposed to in place.

working leg/foot The leg or foot designated to perform an action, usually a non-weightbearing action. May be placed either *à terre* or *en l'air,* or may begin from one of the five *positions of the feet.* There are three basic placements of the *working leg* with the knee flexed and the foot placed at the front, side, or back of the supporting leg. Front: *cou-de-pied devant* or *petit retiré position devant;* mid-shin height; and *retiré position devant* or *pirouette position.* Side: *cou-de-pied* or *petit retiré position;* mid-calf height; and *retiré position.* Back: *cou-de-pied derrière* or *petit retiré position derrière;* mid-calf height; and *retiré position derrière.* The *working leg* may also be extended to the front or the back at four basic heights: *dégagé* height; *glissé* height; at 45 degrees; at 90 degrees.

About the Author

Rhonda Ryman MA AI Chor FI Chor is currently an Associate Professor at the University of Waterloo, Ontario, Canada, where she has taught courses including Dance Notation and Reconstruction as well as Principles of Dance Technique for over thirty years. Since 1995 she has been an Adjunct Professor in the Graduate Program in Dance, York University, Toronto. She is a Fellow of the International Council of Kinetography Laban and of The Benesh Institute, and has published reviews and articles in publications such as *Dance in Canada, Dance Notation Journal, Dance Research, Dance Research Journal*, and *The Choreologist*.

She has authored the two-volume *RAD Grades Examination Syllabus Recorded in Benesh Movement Notation* (London: The Benesh Institute, 1994), *Dictionary of Classical Ballet Terminology* (London: Royal Academy of Dancing, 1998), and *Ryman's Dictionary of Classical Ballet Terms: Cecchetti Method* (Toronto: Dance Collection Danse, 1998). She served as editor and member of the Artistic Panel for the RAD publications, *The Foundations of Classical Ballet Technique* (1997) and *The Progressions of Classical Ballet Technique* (2002), and also wrote the introductory essays and Benesh Movement Notation. Her recent electronic publication, *Ballet Moves II* (http://www.charactermotion.com), uses DanceForms computer animation software to represent classical ballet movements and repertoire. Building on this work, she created DanceForms illustrations for Nadia Potts's book, *Betty Oliphant: The Artistry of Teaching: A Series of Ballet Classes* (Dance Collection Danse, 2007).

Designed and printed by aquatint | bsc